SIMLA MIST

LIZ HARRIS

HEYWOOD PRESS

PROLOGUE

N orth Calcutta, India
February 1908

THE HANDFUL of people in one of the high-ceilinged rooms
that led from the verandah encircling a three-storey house
set back from the oft-trodden road to Chitpore, stood
together in silent groups.

The only sounds inside the room were those from the
world outside, which seeped through the narrow slits in the
wooden shutters—the strains of high-pitched native voices
raised in conversation, the clip-clop of horses' hooves on the
hard dusty road, the ringing of bells from temples and
passing *tongas* and the creaking of the bullock-carts
trudging to and from the Burra Bazaar.

But inside the room, a heavy gloom weighted the air.

Gradually, people started to move across the polished
white-plaster floor that was covered with matting, and to
gather around the mandap erected in haste at the back of

the room for the wedding of Frederick Hunt to his adored Binita.

The pillars of the covered structure had been decorated according to custom with colourful pots filled with water, and garlands of mango, coconut and banana leaves.

But Frederick knew that this had been done by people whose hearts were heavy.

By people whose sorrow was so great that they could scarcely bring themselves to acknowledge him.

Undaunted, however, by the stony gaze and tangible antipathy of Binita's family and close friends, Frederick stood resolute, his head held high, his friend Wilfred Chatsworth at his side, as he waited to be united with the woman he deeply loved, and always would.

And then he heard her arrive.

When he felt the movement of air at her approach, he turned and looked at her.

A slender veiled figure in a gold-trimmed red sari, her hair scented and braided with flowers instead of rich jewels, she was being led by her visibly upset father to the mandap, around which her relatives stood, their eyes filled with sorrow and apprehension.

But all he could see was Binita. His beautiful Binita.

An overwhelming love for her welled up within him. His eyes filled with tears and he took an involuntary step towards her. He was about to embrace his destiny. Binita was his destiny. Marrying her was the right thing to do.

It was the *only* thing he could do.

He loved Binita with the same all-consuming passion that she felt for him. Theirs was a love that would never die.

Her family just didn't understood the depth of their love.

From the moment that her parents had learnt that he and Binita were serious about each other, they'd made their disapproval clear, and their anxiety, and they'd done their best to dissuade her from marrying him.

He understood their concerns.

They'd desired a hardworking Hindu husband for their daughter, not one of the people they saw as unwanted rulers who strode in arrogance across their land.

He'd cease to love her, they'd warned her. She'd become an embarrassment to him and he'd leave her. And he wouldn't respect her beliefs.

But all their entreaties had failed.

And in the face of the love that Binita professed for her Englishman, and her repeated insistence that there was no way she could live apart from him, they'd become fearful of what she might do if they attempted to force her into a more suitable marriage, and they'd yielded to her wishes.

Admittedly not gracefully, he thought, glancing fleetingly at their unsmiling faces.

But he'd known with absolute confidence that her family would come to see that he and Binita were perfect for each other, and to understand that without him, Binita's life would be empty.

As would his without her.

It was something the two of them had realised that moment a few months ago, when Binita, who'd been helping her uncle in his café in the heart of Calcutta, had approached his table, her tray in her hand, and their eyes had met.

He'd seen in the depths of the large dark-brown eyes that looked out from a beautiful face, his future.

From that moment on, he'd pursued her in every free moment, and before long, she was searching the area outside the café every time she went there, waiting for the glorious moment when she saw again the man she'd come to love.

A man of whose presence in her life her parents would never approve.

He was confident that when her parents finally stopped lamenting that he wasn't a Hindu suitor, and allowed themselves to see how much he loved their daughter, and that his was a love that would last forever, they'd welcome him into their lives.

But all the same, seeing the reaction of Binita's parents to their determination to marry, he'd been wise, he decided, not to write to his parents about Binita.

When he returned to England with his beautiful wife, and told them he was married, he was sure that they, too, would come to love her.

And Wilfred would come to see that as with Binita's parents, he, too, had been wrong.

His friendship with Wilfred went back to the day they'd started at the same preparatory school, and Wilfred had shared his supply of conkers with Frederick, who'd come without any. From that day on, they'd grown up together, so close in friendship that each was able to complete the sentence of the other.

When their school years had ended, they'd both sat the Indian Civil Service exams, had passed and had gone to India to work for the colonial government.

They'd always thought alike and had shared the same dreams.

At least they had until the day that Binita came into their lives.

He realised that Wilfred had meant well in his attempts at persuading him not to marry Binita, in saying repeatedly that to do so would be the biggest mistake that Frederick had made in the nineteen years of his life.

But quite simply, Wilfred had been wrong.

In marrying his beautiful Binita, he was doing the very best thing he could do—the only thing that anyone who felt as he did could possibly do: he was ensuring his happiness for the rest of his life.

And he knew that when Wilfred, too, fell in love, he would come to understand that nothing was as important as being with the person you love, and that you'd risk everything to make that happen.

Not that there *was* much risk involved in marrying Binita.

For years, the colonial administration had encouraged their officials to develop a closeness with an Indian woman, given the shortage of suitable English women.

It was true that there were signs of a decreasing enthusiasm for such arrangements, and indeed some voices were starting actively to advise against them. But those voices were faint, and they were outnumbered by those who continued to carry on living with their Indian woman just as they always had, which was evidenced by the growing number of Anglo-Indian children.

No, the only real risk to him in marrying Binita was that for a colonial official to marry at such a young age was greatly frowned upon. Indeed, it was far more reprehensible than marrying an Indian woman.

At nineteen, he would without doubt be considered too young to embark upon something that could be a distraction from his career, and had his superiors known of his plans, they would have instantly transferred him elsewhere to prevent the marriage from taking place.

But they didn't know.

And they weren't going to know.

He had every intention of rising high in the colonial government, and the fact that he'd fallen in love at an age they'd consider too young, certainly wasn't going to stop him.

No one but Wilfred would ever know what he'd done.

Or not for some years, at least.

Not until he'd reached an age when he could bring Binita openly into his life without fear of damaging his career. When that time came, he'd be able to give her the sort of house she deserved, and to shout from the rooftops how much he loved her.

Until then, though, their marriage would have to remain a secret.

But keeping it secret wouldn't be difficult.

None of the British ever went into the native area of Calcutta, so whenever his work allowed and he wasn't under an obligation to attend a social function, he'd be able to visit her in the two rooms set aside for them in her parents' house, and no one British would be likely to see him.

He looked down into Binita's lovely face, now unveiled, and was overwhelmed with happiness and confidence about their future.

He was a husband. Binita's husband.

She was his wife. Or about to become so.

His joy overflowing, his hands shaking, he applied the orange-red sindoor powder along the line of her hair parting as he'd been instructed to do, and then put a dot of the red powder in the centre of her forehead, signifying that she was a married woman.

Feeling Wilfred's eyes upon him as he gazed down at Binita in adoration, he glanced across at his friend, and smiled in delight.

Wilfred nodded in response.

Then he turned back to Binita.

'You must always wear this necklace,' he said, taking from his pocket a heavy gold chain from which hung a locket. His face solemn, he placed the chain around her slender neck.

'This is a symbol of my love for you, Binita. Your name and mine are entwined on the back of the locket. I love you with all my heart. And every day, when you put on the necklace, whether I'm at your side or not, you'll feel my love. My love is yours for ever more, and I promise you, I'll never let you down.'

She gazed shyly up at him, her dark brown eyes worshipping him.

'I know you won't, my husband. You're a good man, Frederick Hunt, and I know I'll never regret entrusting my heart to you.'

1

---

edars, Simla, the summer capital of the British Raj
24 years later: Friday, April 1932

LILIAN HUNT PAUSED HALFWAY up the narrow gravelled drive
and looked back at Cedars, the two-storey gabled house that
stood on a piece of flat ground just below the road that ran
along the ridge.

Her parents had rented this same house for the past two
years, but having left India to go to school in England eleven
years earlier, this was going to be the first time she'd stayed
in that particular house for their annual six months in
Simla.

What a view it had!

She stared beyond the house to the folds of dark-green
forested slopes and valleys, backed by the distant snow-
capped Himalayas. She'd certainly paint that scene before
the summer was over.

A gentle breeze stirred the air, and she sighed in pleasure. It was sheer bliss to have escaped the stifling heat of the dry dusty plains around Delhi.

And blissful, too, to be staying in a town that was one long social whirl from May to October! And to know that her best friend, Daisy, was spending the summer in Blue Pine Lodge, the house next to theirs, which Uncle Wilfred and Aunt Gladys had rented!

Although she and Daisy had been to Simla in the summers before they'd left India, they'd been much too young to join in all the activities. But now, they'd be able to attend the many dinners, parties and dances, and she just couldn't wait for the season to begin.

Lowering her gaze, she stared down the gravelled drive, which was flanked by rhododendron bushes, to the terrace that opened out at the foot of the drive.

It was just wide enough for their rickshaws to turn on, which it had to be as, like Uncle Wilfred, they had three rickshaws and three teams of four *jampanis* to pull them.

Her gaze rose to the grey stone wall that ran along the back of the terrace, buttressing the house from below, and ensuring that it didn't slip down the steep slope behind it were there to be a landslide caused by the violence of the annual monsoon that generally arrived in July.

A row of sturdy wooden railings had been dug into the top of the wall to prevent anyone from tumbling over the side. Seen from a distance, the tips of the railings resembled the teeth of a dragon.

She turned to look up at the house itself, her gaze travelling from the sloping roof of corrugated iron sheets, which gleamed bright red in the sun, down to the upper verandah that encircled the first storey of the house.

It was glassed-in at the back, and her parents had told her that they liked to sit there in the evenings and stare at the view.

Now that she'd finished her years of schooling, they'd added, she could sit up there with them after dinner, as she, too, was sure to be endlessly fascinated by the changing hues of the jagged crests as the sun sank slowly behind the peaks.

She'd smiled politely.

But inwardly, she'd hoped very much that she'd be doing something far more exciting in the evenings than sitting with her parents.

Her gaze settled on the lower front verandah. Deep pink bougainvillea, pink and white roses, white double dahlia and green leaves, were all tumbling wildly over the wooden balustrade.

And she remembered the headmistress's request to her just before she left the English school.

So many pupils had been sent there from India in the way that Lilian had, she'd told her, that she'd been thinking it might be pleasant for them to have a touch of the familiar while they were away from the country they considered home.

She'd wondered, therefore, if Lilian, who showed a marked talent for painting, would consider sending them a few watercolours of Simla and the surrounding area.

The idea had caught her imagination, and she'd readily agreed to do so.

And now that they were in Simla, she was even keener than she'd originally been.

Painting was seen as a worthwhile, ladylike activity, so their mothers or *ayah*, or whoever chaperoned them, might be more relaxed in their vigilance when they were painting, and it would give them a welcome feeling of freedom.

And that would help her and Daisy with a plan they'd formed.

She would definitely give the school a watercolour of the scene in front of her, she decided. She'd try to find an angle that allowed her to show the mountains in the background and the house and flowers in the foreground.

And the lower verandah was where she'd sit in the mornings after she'd breakfasted.

She'd enjoy looking across to the road, to the people going to or from the town that lay further along on the ridge, some in rickshaws, some on horseback, and possibly some on foot.

And her family would be able to get to town easily, too.

As her father was a member of the British Government in India, he needed to be in easy reach of the Secretariat, which they were because it was on this side of the town.

And she'd heard her father and Uncle Wilfred mention several times how pleasant they'd found it to be living in such easy reach of the Secretariat, the Mall, and also the Royal Club.

And the house itself, Cedars, was a much better house than the one her father used to rent in the years before she'd left for England.

Properties in Simla had benefited, her father had told her when he'd described the house to her, from the innovations introduced by Lord Dufferin when, as Viceroy, he was living at Viceregal Lodge. As a result, Simla was now streaks ahead of other Indian towns in having electricity, telephones and a functioning water supply, all of which they had in Cedars.

And whereas the old house had a thunder-box in the

bathroom, which had to be emptied twice a day by a sweeper, Cedars had a flush toilet.

Indeed, a growing number of properties in Simla now had a flush toilet, her father had told her. And so, too, did a number of public latrines.

Despite what her father said about proximity to the town, she knew how much he'd loved the earlier house they'd rented, which had stunning views, it was thanks to her mother that they were now living in a better location, in a house that had a lovely view, but one that wasn't quite so striking.

Her mother had told her that a couple of years earlier, knowing that Lilian's schooling was drawing towards a close, and that she'd be returning to India eager to meet young people of her age, she'd encouraged Lilian's father to find somewhere for the following summer that was closer to the town and club.

Before they had left Simla to return to Delhi for the winter months, they had been shown Cedars, and as soon as her father had seen the house, he had taken it for the following summer.

To his pleasure and relief, the house servants and *jampanis* whom he'd been employing every summer, had agreed to transfer with him to Cedars.

And Uncle Wilfred, Daisy's father, had done the same thing, too.

Her family's house and the Chatsworths' accounted for two of the three houses in their section of the road that ran along the ridge between the town and Viceregal Lodge.

Daisy's house, Blue Pine Lodge, was on the town side of their house. And on the other side, beyond a small cluster of dark green deodar trees, there was a third house.

They called that the Gillespie house, but apparently

Harold Gillespie, who'd lived there for years with his wife, Vera, had died at the end of the previous summer, and they didn't yet know who was living in the house.

They'd soon find out, however, as when they'd got over the effects of the journey from Delhi, her father would leave his calling card with the new people.

Both they and the Chatsworths had reached their houses late the night before. As the only cars allowed in the town were those of the Viceroy and the Commander-in-Chief, they had left their cars in a couple of garages below the Hotel Cecil in Simla, and had been taken to their houses by rickshaws.

Their *abdar*, Sunil, had been there for their arrival. His feet bare as always, he was clad in his uniform of a long white shirt over loose white trousers, with his cummerbund and the band on his turban in the same colour as the livery worn by Frederick's *jampanis*.

He had organised a light refreshment of egg and mango chutney sandwiches, and also egg, fillet of anchovy and watercress sandwiches. As soon as they'd finished eating, they'd gone to their rooms, too tired to do anything other than go to bed.

That morning, when she'd come downstairs for breakfast, and had been told by Sunil that her father was in his office, she'd knocked on his office door, and asked if he would be joining her for breakfast. He'd promptly got up, and had followed her into the dining room. Her mother had joined them moments later.

Immediately after breakfast, during which her father had seemed somewhat preoccupied, she and her parents had left one of the maids and her former *ayah*, who had remained with them to look after her mother's clothes, to unpack their cases, and had gone first into the kitchen to greet their cook, and then to the stables, where her father had given the *syce* instructions about grooming his horse.

Finally, they'd gone to the servants' compound, which straggled along the curve of the hill between their house and the Chatsworths' Blue Pine Lodge.

The compound was screened from their sight by a gated latticework fence that ran from the ridge road down to the wall behind their house, its wooden slats half-hidden beneath the prolific white flowers of the potato-creeper.

While her parents had been inspecting the servants' quarters, she'd been gazing longingly towards Daisy's house, which was on the other side of the servants' compound.

But much as she'd wanted to get together with Daisy to discuss the course of action they had worked out between them to unite Daisy with Eric Stanford, the man who'd caught her eye, and who appeared to be equally interested in Daisy, she knew that Uncle Wilfred and Aunt Gladys would have been displeased had she called upon them so early in the day, so she'd forced herself to rein in her impatience.

After her mother and father had inspected their rickshaws, and exchanged a few words with their teams of *jampanis*, they'd all gone back indoors.

Sunil had immediately stepped forward and proffered a silver salver to her father, who'd hesitated a moment, but had then taken from it a message that had been left for him.

He'd glanced at it, had seemed relieved, and had promptly asked Sunil to see that a rickshaw was readied for him as he needed to go to the Secretariat.

How strangely her father was behaving that morning, she'd thought. He'd looked almost nervous as he took the message. But what was there to be nervous about?

It was about work, her father had told her mother, who'd

been about to go into the sitting room, which led off the teak-panelled hall, and he had headed to the room next to it, which he used as his office.

Minutes later, he had returned with his briefcase. After a promise to come back as soon as he could, he'd left the house, and soon after that, they'd heard the creaking of the rickshaw wheels.

Her mother had sat down in the sitting room and rung for the butler.

Lilian had sat opposite her, but when her mother had asked for their cook to bring her the day's menu, she felt she'd had enough. Stifling a yawn of boredom, she had jumped up, excused herself, and had gone outside to have a good look at the house in the daylight.

Turning away from the house, she strolled to the top of the drive, glancing to her left as she went at the small patch of grass between the house and the road with a single flowerbed in its centre.

Their *mali* wasn't going to be overworked, she thought wryly, with hardly any grass to cut and such a limited space for flowers and plants.

Crossing the road, she went up to the protective wooden railings, put a hand on the railing on either side of her, and for a few minutes peered over the side at the steep slope on which grew a tangle of tree roots, interspersed with wild violets.

Well, she'd certainly never be short of subject matter for a picture, she thought, turning to go back to the house.

And Daisy was going to be doing some painting, too.

Daisy was the first to admit that she wasn't as talented, but she wanted to get better, and she had said that whenever Lilian went painting, she would join her. And she'd be grateful, she'd added, if Lilian could help her to improve.

She'd told Daisy quite honestly that she wouldn't have a clue how to set about teaching her in a way that was different from the futile attempts of the art teacher at their school, but she might be able to demonstrate at times by taking over Daisy's brush and showing her an alternative way of building the scene.

Daisy had been delighted with that idea, and hoped to be much better by the time they returned to Delhi, or New Delhi, as she really ought to call it, since New Delhi had been the new name for the capital city for the past three or four years.

Reaching the terrace at the foot of the drive, she paused and drew in a deep breath of air scented with wild balsam and lily-of-the valley.

'What are you doing out there, Lilian?'

Glancing towards the front door, she saw her mother standing in the open doorway.

'I'm breathing, Mama,' she called.

'Well, that's a relief,' Constance said with a smile, and she went across to her.

Lilian laughed. 'You know what I mean.'

She raised her face to the cerulean sky, and inhaled deeply again.

'D'you think you could now come and breathe inside?' Constance asked. 'Sunil's arranging for coffee to be brought to the sitting room. When Papa returns, which should be soon, we must go through the pile of invitations we've received, and this, of course, now involves you, too.'

'So it does,' Lilian said happily. She tucked her arm into her mother's and they walked back to the house. 'I feel as though something exciting is about to happen.'

'Well, I hope it lives up to your expectations, whatever it is, darling,' Constance said in amusement.

'Oh, it will, Mama. I'm sure of that.'

With a confident smile at her mother, she stepped into the house.

2

T*he Secretariat, Simla*

BENEATH THE RHYTHMIC hum of the electric ceiling fans rotating above them in the senior officers' lounge in the Secretariat, Cecil Stanford settled comfortably into his chair, picked up his glass and raised it to Frederick.

'Your health, Frederick,' he said, and he took a drink. 'I wouldn't normally have a Scotch so early in the day, but I asked them to be generous with the soda water and ice. It's not as if we're formally at work at the moment, so I think this is acceptable. Wouldn't you agree?'

'Of course, sir,' Frederick said, and he took a sip of his drink and replaced the glass on the wooden table between them.

'On an informal occasion such as this,' Cecil said, swirling his whisky around the glass, 'I think we can drop the formality.'

'Thank you, Cecil.'

Cecil cleared his throat. 'You must be wondering why I asked you to join me here this morning, given you've only just arrived,' he began. 'I'm grateful to you for coming. I'm sure there're things you'd rather be doing. Or at least, that Constance would rather you were doing. You might not have been quite so keen on doing them,' he added with a smile.

Frederick laughed. 'I'm sure I wouldn't have been. No, Constance understands, as do I, that work comes first.'

'Strictly speaking, this isn't about work,' Cecil said, and he cleared his throat again.

Frederick raised his eyebrows. 'That sounds intriguing, Cecil.'

'It's about my son, Eric.'

Frederick swallowed his surprise. 'A very pleasant young man, if I may say so,' he ventured. 'In what way can I be of help? If you need my help, that is.'

Cecil gave him a wry smile. 'I hope your expression of liking was genuinely felt, and not just to please me. Especially as he's now a neighbour of yours. Vera Gillespie decided to stay on after Harold's death, and she's opened her house as a guest house. Rose Bank Guest House it's called. Eric's lodging with her for the summer, as is someone else from our ranks, I believe.'

'I'm delighted to hear it, sir,' Frederick said warmly. 'I hope Eric's proximity means that we'll see a lot of him this summer. He has always been quite charming on the few occasions I've met him.'

Cecil nodded. 'He's a good lad, and he'll go far in the Service, if he doesn't make any mistakes along the way. And that's what I wanted to talk to you about. Unfortunately, he seems to have become attracted to Miss Chatsworth, and I fear she could be the mistake to which I referred.'

'To Daisy!' Frederick exclaimed in surprise. 'Wilfred's daughter? And that's a mistake, you say?'

Cecil stiffened. 'It most definitely is. Fortunately, he can hardly know the girl so he can't be committed to her at this early stage, and I'd like to ensure that he never is.'

'With respect, Cecil, I'm surprised that you feel so strongly against such a union. I've known Wilfred virtually all my life—we've been close friends since we met at the start of our school years. He's a fine man, and his family reflects his many good qualities. Gladys is an impeccable wife, and Daisy has a very sweet nature. She and Stephen are a credit to their parents. I've known both since they were born.'

'I don't disagree. But my problem with the family goes back a number of years, and as it's a very personal matter, I don't wish to go into it. Suffice it to say that something happened between the two families many years ago that makes me not want to see us united by marriage.'

'I see,' Frederick said slowly.

'But that's one reason only. There's another reason, too. If Eric wishes to aspire to one of the most senior positions in the Indian Civil Service, and I'm sure he does, he will have my full support. But he'd benefit, also, from having the right woman at his side.'

'Indeed,' Frederick murmured.

'Miss Chatsworth gives the appearance of being a very pleasant girl, but not a dynamic one, if that's the right word. Not a woman who could organise her husband's social life in such a way as to promote his interests to his seniors. She's too quiet, too reserved. And those two words also describe my son. Put bluntly, Eric needs a wife who can provide the characteristics he lacks.'

'I understand.' Frederick paused. 'I take it, you think I can help.'

Cecil coughed. 'Your daughter, Lilian,' he began, 'is a very beautiful girl, who's endowed with a delightful, lively personality and, from what I've seen, she's a good conversationalist, which Miss Chatsworth isn't. With a wife such as Lilian at his side, Eric would be helped in his career trajectory.' He paused. 'Am I correct in thinking that no marriage has been arranged for Lilian, and that her affections aren't attached to anyone?'

Frederick stifled his rising sense of excitement.

'That's so, Cecil. She's just completed her schooling, where contact with boys was kept to a minimum. And Constance and I have yet to give any thought to a suitable husband for her. But perhaps we should have done so. From overheard snatches of the conversation between her and Daisy recently, she seems ready to find a young man.'

Cecil nodded. 'I should be delighted if that young man were to be Eric. The projects you've undertaken on my behalf have been excellent in their standard, and show great ability. As a result, I intend to fully support your recent request for promotion.'

'I'm most grateful, sir.'

'Lilian, I'm sure, is a chip off the old block,' Cecil continued. 'And with her combination of brains and good looks, she would be a welcome addition to my family, and the perfect wife for Eric.' He paused. 'I'm hoping you'd feel the same way about Eric becoming a part of your family.'

'Most definitely, Cecil. As I say, I've always found him to be charming. I'd see it as an honour if my family were to be allied to yours through marriage. I'm most gratified by your comments about Lilian, and I can assure you that I'll do all I can to promote Eric's interests. She'd be fortunate indeed to have such a husband.'

Cecil smiled warmly. 'Thank you, Frederick.' He looked at his glass. 'Perhaps we should have another whisky to celebrate the hopes we share concerning our children and your request for promotion, and this time we'll have one that isn't quite so heavily diluted.'

3

———

 short time later

'SO YOU LIKE the house do you?' Constance asked as she relaxed in one of the floral upholstered armchairs that flanked each side of the hearth.

Lilian sat on a matching wood-framed sofa facing the open fireplace.

'Very much,' she said. 'And the location's perfect.'

'Have you any plans for the rest of the day?' Constance asked.

Lilian shook her head. 'Only to go to Daisy's. We've so much to talk about.'

'I'm not surprised,' Constance said drily. 'You haven't seen her since yesterday.'

'Very funny,' she said with a laugh. 'I'll go there after lunch.'

'You must wait till the siesta's over.'

'I don't need a rest. The air up here's so invigorating—it doesn't sap your energy like it does in Delhi. And Daisy won't want one, either. We got out of the habit in England, and we weren't in Delhi long enough to get used to it again.'

'That may be. But you're not to go next door till late in the afternoon,' Constance said firmly. 'Ah, I think I hear your father! That's good. I'm ready for coffee.'

A moment later, Frederick came into the sitting room. He crossed to the armchair on the other side of the fireplace, and sat down opposite Constance.

Constance rang the bell for the butler.

'You may bring our coffee in now,' she said when Sunil came into the room.

He bowed. 'Certainly, *memsahib*.' And he left the room.

'I was beginning to wonder if we'd be obliged to have coffee without you, Frederick,' Constance said with a smile. 'I've never known you begin work so soon after getting here. I hope you'll give yourself time to relax over the weekend. We've had a long journey, and unsurprisingly you've seemed a little strained this morning, if strained is the right word.'

He waved his hand dismissively. 'It's just I've a lot on my mind. The message was from Cecil. He wanted a quick word with me.' He smiled at them both. 'So what have you been up to in my absence?'

The door opened and Sunil came in, a metal stand in his hand. He was followed by the *khitmatgar*, who was carrying a large tray on which there was a pot of coffee, three bone china cups, saucers and plates, a matching milk jug and sugar bowl, and a platter of small scones.

Sunil opened out the stand. The *khitmatgar* rested the tray on it, and then filled the three cups with coffee, put a cup for each on the small polished-oak table next to their chair, and the plate of scones on the low centre table.

'Thank you,' Constance said, inclining her head to Sunil and the table steward. 'There's no need for either of you to stay.'

With a slight bow, the servants left.

'Don't forget to check daily that the milk has been boiled, Lilian,' Constance remarked, picking up her cup. 'And that includes the milk we put in our tea and coffee. This is something you must check that your servants are doing.'

Lilian giggled. 'Is there something you haven't told me? Am I soon to start running a home?'

Constance smiled at Lilian. 'Of course not, darling. But you've reached the age to learn how to do so.'

Frederick cleared his throat. 'Since you brought up the subject, Lilian, perhaps this is something we should discuss now.'

He sounded unmistakably nervous, and Constance glanced at Frederick in surprise.

Lilian's mouth went dry. 'What d'you mean, Papa?'

Frederick gave an awkward shrug. 'Just that I'd like to ask what you think of Eric Stanford?'

'Why?'

Frederick cleared his throat. 'Cecil believes that his son is interested in you. That's what he wanted to see me about just now. He thought I should be aware of it, and that I should also know that he'd favour a union between the two of you. I felt quite proud, I don't mind telling you.'

'I'm sorry to burst that bubble of pride, Papa, but although I've met Mr Stanford a few times only, that's more than enough to know he isn't for me.'

Frederick frowned. 'It's early days yet,' he said, a trifle coldly. 'I'd be most displeased if you closed your mind to the idea without giving it any thought.'

Her brow crinkled. 'If I do, why does it matter? No amount of thought is going to make him attractive to me.'

'Not to put too fine a point on it, because his father is my superior, and a marriage between you and Eric would be advantageous for the whole family. It would certainly advance my career, which Cecil made clear today, and it would increase your status here and in New Delhi.'

'I'm quite happy with my status as it is, thank you,' she said sharply. 'If Eric is interested in anyone, it's Daisy.'

Frederick coughed. 'On the subject of Daisy, her name came up in passing, and Cecil made it quite clear than an alliance with Daisy would be completely against his wishes.'

'But why?' Lilian exclaimed. 'Daisy and Eric are much better suited than I am to Eric.'

'That's irrelevant. Cecil thinks that you're the one who's caught Eric's eye, not Daisy. There's a saying to the effect that opposites attract, and maybe this is such an occasion.'

Lilian opened her mouth to reply.

'I'm sure Papa just wants you to keep an open mind about young Mr Stanford, darling,' Constance said quickly, and she frowned in warning at Frederick. 'From the fleeting occasions you've met him, you can't possibly know him yet. You might be surprised by how much you like him when you've spent a little more time with him.'

'I very much doubt it,' she said bluntly.

Constance took a sip of coffee. 'We'll see. All Papa is asking is that you give Eric a chance.'

'Your mother's right, Lilian,' Frederick said. 'We'll make sure that you have plenty of occasions to meet him throughout the summer. If a man of some standing, with such a potential for career advancement, shows an interest in you, that must surely be worth pursuing.'

If the older Mr Stanford was right, Lilian thought, he, Eric and her father were in for a great disappointment.

Since returning from school, she'd met Eric on several occasions in Delhi, and she'd known from the very first meeting that they had nothing in common.

He was very quiet, which she wasn't, and boringly studious, which she also wasn't. He was extremely keen on flowers and trees, and while she liked to look at them, and to paint them, there was a limit to how much she wanted to know about them.

There was nothing about him to dislike, but there was nothing at all about him that made her heart beat faster.

And that was just as well, since Daisy was looking longingly in Eric's direction.

Daisy had met Eric on the same few occasions as she had, and each time afterwards she'd confided to an amazed Lilian how much she liked him.

After the third occasion, she'd told Lilian that she thought that Eric seemed interested in her. So whatever his father's objections to Daisy, Eric obviously didn't know them, or if he did, he didn't share them.

But Daisy hadn't been certain that she was right about Eric being interested in her—it might just have been that she was hoping so much that he liked her that she was seeing what wasn't there. And she'd asked Lilian to watch them when they were together in Simla, and to tell her if there was any sign of Eric reciprocating her feelings.

She certainly intended to do that.

And she and Daisy had decided to try to create some occasions on which Daisy and Eric could meet. Obviously, one of her servants or Daisy's would have to chaperone them, or one of their mothers, but with a small amount of ingenuity, Daisy and Eric should be able to have a few minutes to themselves.

As she opened her mouth to tell her father that she knew for certain that Eric and Daisy had feelings for each other, a sudden thought hit her, and she swallowed her words.

If her father was set on her marrying Eric, which he seemed to be, and that wasn't surprising as he was an ambitious man and his career would benefit if that happened, he was sure to agree to anything that would enable her to meet with Eric—provided that he was ignorant of Eric's interest in Daisy.

And if she went further than just staying silent on the subject, but feigned an interest in Eric when they were in public, her father might actually arrange occasions for her to meet with Eric, and he might be relaxed about who she had as a chaperone.

Her *ayah* and Daisy's would be preferable to their mothers as the *ayahs* would be less vigilant. It would be helpful, therefore, if her father was content to let them be accompanied by their *ayahs*.

They would just have to make sure that Eric and Daisy's interest in each other wasn't apparent to their chaperones or to anyone else. If too many people knew, her parents or Eric's would be sure to find out.

Keeping her mouth firmly shut, she assumed a resigned expression.

'Cheer up, Lilian,' Frederick said, a hint of impatience colouring his words. 'This is a great opportunity for you. I've always thought Eric a most pleasant young man. Not a great talker, it must be said, but as that's not a charge that could ever be levelled at you, I'm sure you'd make up for any such deficiency on his part. And you'd have married a good listener, which I imagine would please you.'

'Very funny,' Lilian said sullenly. 'You're making it sound as if it's a decided thing, but it isn't. I suppose I could make an effort to get to know him, but I won't say more than that.'

'Thank you, Lilian,' Frederick said, a note of relief in his voice.

'Well, I think we've exhausted that subject for the moment, don't you?' Constance said. She glanced pointedly at the pile of cards on the dark wood mantlepiece. 'We really ought to go through our invitations. That's a most flattering number, Frederick. And very nicely presented, too, some of them are.'

Constance reached up and took the card closest to her. 'Take this card, for example. It has a most attractive water-colour design in the corner. You could make us some cards like this, Lilian. After all, you have a way with watercolour. In fact, I was going to suggest that you join the Simla Fine Arts Society and exhibit in their annual show.'

'Maybe I will,' Lilian said with a shrug. 'If I can stop gazing lovingly at Eric for long enough to contact them.'

With an exclamation of annoyance, Frederick angled himself in his armchair so that he was facing the fireplace and Constance, rather than Lilian.

'I agree, that's an impressive pile, Constance,' he said. 'And the season's not even begun. It's helped that we're in the same house as last year, so our friends knew where to find us. And of course, senior officers are expected to go everywhere, and to call on everyone of status in the area. And play tennis, attend dances, and go on picnics. The list of obligations is endless, and it seems to get longer every year.'

'It all sounds lovely,' Constance said with a smile. 'And I know you think so, too, darling, whatever you say.'

He gave a theatrical sigh. 'You know me too well, Constance. Sadly, I've lost the ability to surprise you.'

'I'm sure you haven't, if you put your mind to it,' she said, laughing. 'But I'd rather you didn't—I've never been the sort of person who likes surprises.'

'I realise that,' he said. 'So I promise to remain tediously boring and predictable.'

They smiled at each other.

'Have you had a chance to glance at the invitations,' Constance asked, 'to see if there's anything of interest?'

'I had a quick look through them. As for anything inter-esting, there was one from Viceregal Lodge. We're all invited to an afternoon tea.'

Lilian groaned. 'That sounds stuffy.'

'Don't dismiss it out of hand, Lilian,' Constance said in mild rebuke. 'You can be sure that Eric will be there.'

Lilian pulled a face.

Constance sent her a cautionary look.

'And there's also an invitation from Cecil,' Frederick continued. 'He told me this morning that we'd find a couple of invitations from him and Margaret. We're invited to luncheon a week on Sunday. And also to join their picnic party on the first day of the Annandale Races.'

'Good gracious! Are we thinking as far as June already?'

'So it seems. It's very kind of Cecil to include us. I imagine that one of the reasons for the invitations is to give Lilian and Eric an opportunity to get to know each other.'

Constance smiled. 'Possibly. But you're one of his best private secretaries, darling. Of course he'd invite you to social occasions that he and Margaret are hosting. Are they in their usual house?'

He nodded. 'That's right. Just down from Viceregal Lodge.'

'Fancy wanting to live that far out of Simla,' Lilian said with disdain.

Frederick moved back in his chair and glanced at Lilian. 'Work doesn't stop for the summer, Lilian. Cecil needs to be close to Viceregal Lodge to facilitate contact with the Viceroy. But it seems that Eric will be very near us. He's going to be living at Vera Gillespie's. He'll be going into the Secretariat nearly every day, so it's better to be within easy reach of the place.'

Constance nodded. 'That makes good sense. Now, let's see what else there is.' And she rose to her feet, and gathered up the invitations on the mantelpiece. 'I've a feeling that this is going to be a very exciting summer,' she added as she sat down again.

Inwardly, Lilian smiled.

4

L*ater that day*

JACK LEIGHTON SETTLED himself comfortably in one of the two wooden-framed upholstered armchairs in the drawing room of the Rose Bank Guest House, and stared in satisfaction around the room.

A highly polished heavy oak cabinet stood against one of the walls which were covered with wallpaper patterned with violets. On top of the cabinet, a silver tray held a bone china teapot and tea set. And on the wall above the cabinet hung a painting of Simla as it had been some years earlier.

Around the room, in similarly gilded plaster frames, paintings of the landscape were interspersed with sepia photographs of people whom, Jack assumed, were ancestors of the owner.

Next to each of the armchairs, there was a small oak table on which stood a fringed violet-silk lampshade and a cluster of faded photographs, each in a silver frame. Facing the fireplace, an oak-framed sofa was upholstered with the same chintz as the armchairs.

Their landlady, Vera Gillespie, had rolled up the wooden Venetian blinds on the windows, and Jack could see the pine-clad hills that lay at the end of the narrow drive.

His gaze returned to the upholstered armchair opposite his, and to Eric Stanford, who was sitting in it.

'I wouldn't get too comfortable,' he told Eric. 'Stephen's got everything planned. We're going to be leaving for the Club fairly early this evening, and calling for him on the way. He's warned us that just about everyone who's got here in the past few days will be heading for the Club tonight, so we'll need to be early if we want any choice about where to station ourselves.'

Eric pulled a face. 'I hope it won't be too crowded. An evening with just a few pleasant people would be my preference.'

Jack grinned at him. 'I don't need to ask who you'd list among those few pleasant people, as there's one name you've managed to bring into nearly every conversation. And amazingly, her family's staying a couple of houses down from us. But I'm sure that's pure coincidence, and it isn't the reason you selected this particular guest house out of the many there are.'

Eric went pink. 'I don't know who you mean. Obviously I mention the people I work with, and their families, too, if I've met them. And as I'm not familiar with that many people, it may be that I repeat the same few names.'

'Quite,' Jack said.

'So, if I do, it doesn't mean anything,' Eric added.

'Of course it doesn't,' Jack said gravely. 'Anyway, I'm looking forward to seeing her for myself, and also to meeting Frederick Hunt's daughter. I've heard that Miss Hunt's extremely attractive.'

Eric nodded. 'I suppose she is. But I must admit she terrifies me. She's so lively that she makes me feel even more boring than usual.'

'You're not boring, Eric. On the contrary. You take more of an interest in what goes on around you than most people. For example, you can give a name to the flowers and trees that most of us walk past without ever noticing. And you know quite a bit about Simla, whereas to most people, it's just a place for the summer.'

'Unfortunately, none of that would really interest young ladies,' Eric said in despair. 'When I meet any, I struggle to think of things to say that *would* catch their attention. I'm afraid I've never really mastered the art of flirting or making small talk. I just wish I knew how it was done. If there were to be anyone agreeable in Simla for the summer,' he said, and he went pink again, 'I'd like her to notice me. But I'm not sure that she would.'

Jack grinned at him. 'She will. It isn't essential to be a great conversationalist in order to win a woman's heart. You're sincere and thoughtful, and—'

He stopped abruptly as he heard the door open.

'Excuse me interrupting you, gentlemen, but I wanted to check that you've everything in your rooms that you need,' Vera Gillespie said, coming into the room.

Both men rose to their feet.

'We have,' they said at once.

'Please, do sit.' She indicated that they should sit again.

'This feels much more than a guest house, Mrs Gillespie,' Jack said. 'It feels more like a home. We're very lucky to be staying here.'

Eric nodded. 'I agree.'

'Thank you, both of you. It *was* a home until last year when my dear husband, Harold, died very suddenly. He'd worked for the Railway Board so we were among the few British residents who lived here throughout the year. I couldn't bring myself to leave the place where we'd spent so many happy years, and go back to England, where I now know very few people. By turning my home into a guest house, I've been able to continue living here, where I can cherish the memories of my years with Harold.'

'I'm very sorry for your loss, Mrs Gillespie,' Eric said.

Jack nodded. 'I echo that. We'll try to be model guests so that you don't have any regrets about allowing us into your home.'

Vera smiled. 'I'm sure I won't. Men in the colonial service can be relied upon to act with decorum. And indeed, Mr Stanford,' she said, glancing at Eric, 'you come recommended, in effect. I've met your father a number of times over the years. So, since we've established that this is a home, I hope you'll both feel free to relax and be yourselves.'

'You're very kind,' Jack murmured. 'And your *syce* seems most competent, I might add. I'm very happy with the horse I've been given. I hope to ride before breakfast every morning, but if I can't do so for any reason, the *syce*'s going to take him out for me.'

'I'm delighted to hear that, Mr Leighton. Harold, too, thought very highly of him. As for mealtimes, I usually serve breakfast at half past seven, *tiffin* at half past one, and dinner at half past eight. Would that be satisfactory?'

The two men chorused that it would.

'If you have any favourite dishes, do please tell me and I'll ask Cook to make them. But now to dinner this evening,' she said. 'Will you be dining here?'

Jack shook his head. 'We won't, thank you. We're going to the Club, and we'll eat there.'

'I thought you might. I'll ask after breakfast every day if you'll be wanting lunch and dinner that day, and I'll pass that on to Cook. If you're to be in the Secretariat all day and want to take your lunch with you, rather than come back here or eat in their restaurant, Cook will prepare you something. It's whatever your preference is.'

'Thank you, Mrs Gillespie,' they said in unison.

'And one last thing, hot water. If each of you tells me in advance roughly what time you'd like to take your bath, I'll have my housekeeper ensure that there's sufficient hot water to fill the tub for the time you want it.'

'That's very thoughtful, Mrs Gillespie. Thank you,' Eric said.

'I'll be dropping in at the Secretariat this afternoon,' Jack told Vera. 'Perhaps you'd arrange for me to have some hot water when I get back, before I go to the Club.'

'Of course, Mr Leighton.' With a smile at them both, she went out.

'So, Eric,' Jack said. 'What are you planning to do this afternoon? Or rather, who are you planning to think about all afternoon?'

Eric went bright red, and laughed.

5

L*ater*

FREDERICK STOOD at his office window, his hands in his jacket pockets as he stared through the metal-netting at the cluster of rhododendron bushes and deodar trees that separated their house from the Rose Bank Guest House.

Two macaque monkeys, a mixture of coffee-brown and pale grey, swung down in front of the window, saw the wire-netting screening the windows, made a sound that could have been anger or frustration, and scampered back up the wall.

Infernal monkeys, he'd thought in irritation.

They'd been an increasing nuisance over the past few years, in the town itself and in the surrounding hills, forever chasing each other, and gathering everything they could in the markets, before swarming up the sides of the houses and making a din as they hurtled themselves across the corrugated tin roofs.

He'd hoped they'd be less of a nuisance that year, but so far the signs weren't good.

He thrust his right hand more deeply into his pocket, and tightened his grip on the small envelope he'd earlier secreted there.

He could hear Lilian upstairs, chatting with the *ayah*, and he knew that Constance was out in the kitchen, talking to their cook ahead of lunch being served.

As it didn't seem likely that anyone would interrupt him for a while, he could finally have a proper look at the strange card left for him in an envelope that morning.

When he'd come downstairs, he'd seen at once that there was a small white envelope on the silver salver on the hall table. He'd gone across to it, picked it up and seen his name printed in a simple ink script.

He'd rung for Sunil and asked him where it had come from. But all Sunil had been able to tell him was that it appeared to have been pushed under the door between late last night, after they'd all gone to bed, the servants included, and early that morning.

Holding the envelope, as yet unopened, he'd gone into his office, and while waiting for his morning tea to be brought to him, he'd opened the envelope and seen a small white card inside.

He'd pulled it out, checked that there was nothing else inside the envelope, and then looked at the card. It was blank. He'd turned it over, and had gasped aloud.

A hideous image stared up at him.

A shudder ran through him, and he'd taken a step back, still holding the card.

It was the unexpectedness of it, the ugliness of it, he told himself as he gazed at the picture in momentary fear of he knew not what.

Why would anyone send him such a thing?

He'd been about to look at the image more closely, to see if he could make sense of the picture, and work out why it had been sent to him, but before he could do so, he'd heard footsteps coming down the stairs.

Hastily, he pushed the card back into the envelope, thrust it into his pocket and composed himself as he heard a knock on his door.

There was no need to upset Lilian and Constance by telling them about the card, he'd decided as he followed Lilian to the breakfast table. Almost certainly, it had been delivered to him by mistake. And when he'd had time to study it, he might be able to guess to whom it should have been sent.

But being their first morning back in Simla, it had been a busy morning, and this was the first chance he'd had to take a good look at the picture.

He took the envelope out of his pocket, and paused, glancing nervously over his shoulder at the door. But there was no sound of anyone approaching. And there wouldn't be. They wouldn't disturb him as they'd assume he'd started on some work.

He pulled the card from the envelope.

Again he checked that there was nothing written on either side of the envelope, nor inside it. There wasn't anything at all to indicate who'd sent it, nor why.

Taking a deep breath, he turned it over to look at the image.

The figure depicted was female with four arms, dark

blue in colour, her hair dishevelled, her eyes crimson-red with rage. A large tongue lolled from her mouth, and small fangs protruded.

In one of the hands, she held a bloody sword, and in another the severed head of a demon, whose blood dripped into a bowl. Around her waist, she wore a belt from which hung severed heads.

It was Kali, he realised with a shock. The Hindu goddess believed to destroy evil in order to protect the innocent.

He'd seen different images of her before, but nothing as gruesome as this.

He gave an involuntary shiver.

Why had the card been sent to him, if, indeed, he was the intended recipient? And by whom?

It must be a mistake, he reassured himself. The sender must have confused him with someone else. That's all it was. He'd do well to forget about it, and he would.

He went across to his desk, threw the card and envelope into the bin by his chair, turned away and started to head for the door.

Halfway across the room, he paused.

Mistake or not, it wasn't really something he'd want Sunil and the other servants to see, and he certainly wouldn't want Constance or Lilian to come upon it. The ferocity on the face of the goddess would alarm them.

It would be safer to throw it away in the town, he decided, and he returned to the bin, removed the card and envelope, put the card back into the envelope and put it in his pocket.

When they went for their stroll along the Mall that evening, he'd throw it in one of the litter bins there. And that would be the end of the matter.

· · ·

AT LEAST HE was sharing a house in the part of Simla where Anglo-Indians, Indian clerks and others who worked for the colonial government tended to live, Kamesh thought in satisfaction, as he sat on his bed, his knees drawn up to his chin, in the cramped room in the small house which he rented with three of the *chaprassis* who worked alongside him in the Secretariat.

Office messengers like him played an important part in the running of the Secretariat, collecting countless documents each day from people who ignored them, and delivering them to others who also ignored them, not that they were ever given credit for the role they played by the arrogant officers of the ICS, who considered themselves the Heaven-born and better than everyone else.

But without messengers like him, the Secretariat wouldn't run as smoothly.

It was only right, therefore, that he and other *chaprassis* lived in one of the better parts of the town.

Their house was close to one of the several flights of steps that led down from the Mall to Lower Bazaar. It was just before the place where the road forked into two, with one of the lanes dropping sharply down through the Lower Bazaar.

Seen from above, the bazaar was a cascade of flat corrugated-iron tin roofs above flimsy wooden structures. The fact that he lived above Lower Bazaar showed that he had some status, even though he hadn't yet attained the status he should have—the status he deserved.

Those of lesser status lived further down the slope, among the narrow tiers of wooden houses that crisscrossed the slope, each tier separated from the tier above and below by a narrow airless alley lined with market stalls and shops.

All the houses in each tier opened out on to a verandah

that ran the length of the tier, and all the windows and open doorways were covered with a kind of curtain to allow the family some privacy.

That was where people such as shopkeepers, cloth merchants, cooks and bakers, charcoal burners, wood carriers, carpenters, coolies, labourers, maids, and the *dhobi*s who did the washing for other people, lived and plied their trade.

Down there, the stench of manure from the ponies stabled throughout the Bazaar was strong, and the stink of the sewage runoff from above was rank.

Not that the British would know about the ever-present acrid aroma and the over-crowded living conditions endured by so many, Kamesh thought bitterly.

The British who ventured into the warren of alleys and shops in the Lower Bazaar looked no further than the wares set out on the stalls. It was of no interest to them at all how the native people lived.

Well, it was time that it was. And indeed, their eyes would soon be opened.

For too long, the arrogant British had assumed that it was their right to enjoy the high degree of comfort made possible for them by the hard work of so many natives, and by the wealth they'd plundered from a country that wasn't theirs.

And increasingly, Indian voices were now being heard, urging the British to leave. Soon, the clamour they made would be so loud, so insistent, that the British would be shaken out of their complacency, and forced to leave India.

He'd actually thought about joining the terrorist wing of the Quit India Movement, but had decided against it, preferring to leave the fight against the British to others.

His fight was with one man—Frederick Hunt.

Frederick Hunt had more than most to answer for. Much more.

And answer for it he would.

6

B lue Pine Lodge
The same afternoon

WILFRED CHATSWORTH PUT his napkin down on the dining table and frowned at his daughter.

'You'll do as you're told, Daisy. You're not to go to Cedars this afternoon, and that's that. The Hunts need time to settle in before visitors descend, just as we do. You'll see Lilian this evening when we take a walk along the Mall, and you're not to speak to her till then.'

'What happens if Lilian comes here before this evening and asks for Daisy?' Stephen asked in amusement. 'Does Daisy have to ignore her, or instruct Mittu to tell her that she's out?'

Daisy laughed.

Wilfred smiled. 'Of course not. If Lilian comes here, it's different. But if she doesn't, and I'm sure she won't, and if you don't want an afternoon siesta, Daisy, I suggest you read your book or get on with your knitting until it's time for tea.'

Daisy turned to her mother, who was sitting at the opposite end of the table from her father. 'Is there anything you'd like me to help with, Mama?'

'Nothing at all, Daisy, thank you,' Gladys told her. 'I suggest you go up for a rest. We had a long journey yesterday, and you'll be more tired than you realise. I'm sure you want to feel fresh for this evening.'

Wilfred nodded. 'Well said, Gladys. Do as your mother has advised, Daisy. But not you, Stephen. I'd like a word with you before you go upstairs.'

Stephen raised his eyebrows. 'How intriguing, Father.'

Wilfred waited until Daisy and Gladys had left the dining room, then stood up, picked up his cup and moved across to the door leading to the lower back verandah. 'Come on, Stephen,' he said. 'We'll take our coffees outside and enjoy the wonderful view of the mountains.'

Stephen followed him. 'This is not about the birds and the bees, I hope,' he said with a grimace as he sat down next to his father, placing his cup on the small cane table between them. 'Given I'm twenty-two, you can assume that I've gathered a rough idea of what goes on.'

'It is, but not in the way I suspect you mean,' Wilfred said, smiling. 'And it's because you're the age you are that we're having this conversation. I'm only saying what any father would say in these circumstances, and indeed, what the paternal British Government used to tell the troops before they embarked on their journey to India. The troops were issued with a booklet telling them not to go down to the brothels, to wear a *topi* at all times during the day, and not to drink water that hadn't been boiled.'

'Now you've told me, can I go?' Stephen asked, getting up.

'In a minute. Just sit back down, will you, son?'

Stephen gave a theatrical groan, and sat down again.

'You've an excellent future ahead of you, Stephen, and I don't want to see you throw it away, which could be so easily done in a place like Simla. You did extremely well in the highly competitive examination for the Indian Civil Service, and the reports from the Institute during your probationary period in Oxford were most pleasing.'

'So you don't need to worry about me.'

'They confirm that you're a bright young man,' Wilfred continued, ignoring Stephen's interruption, 'who could go far. I hope you'll keep that thought in your mind throughout the summer. There are all sorts of temptations in Simla, and if you give in to them, you could seriously damage your career.'

'I'll obviously be careful what I do, Father. I want to go as far as I can in the ICS.' He paused. 'Is that it? Could I have got let off that lightly?'

Wilfred smiled. 'Not quite. There's just one more thing, I'm afraid. When the time is right, we want to see you make a good marriage.'

Stephen's eyes narrowed, and he sat upright, alarm on his face. 'You and Frederick are great friends. You're not going to suggest that Lilian and I bring the two families even closer, are you? Because if you are, you're hoping in vain. Lilian's like another sister.'

Wilfred laughed. 'Not at all. Both Frederick and I can see that the two of you have a different sort of closeness. Mind you, there was a time when you were both babies that we wondered. But that was long ago. And anyway, Frederick has great plans for Lilian.'

Stephen grinned at his father. 'You two are worse than women. You could have gone into business as matchmakers.'

'You can laugh, but that's the way things are often done in the ranks of the senior officials, my boy. Frederick phoned me this morning to say that Cecil Stanford's son, Eric, has taken a shine to Lilian. Frederick's an ambitious man. He's got his eye on a senior position in the Central Board of Revenue, and as a nomination from Stanford would certainly be acted upon, he's very much in favour of such a union.'

'Lilian marry that bore!' Stephen exclaimed. 'Never! I may not have been long in Delhi before we came here, but it was long enough to know that Stanford's an exceedingly dull fellow. He's no real conversation. He'd be a nightmare to sit next to at dinner. And from what I've seen of the adult Lilian, she's lively, intelligent and fun. She couldn't possibly be happy with such a quiet, colourless man.'

'That remains to be seen. Eric's staying at the Gillespie house, which is a guest house now. I took a walk up there this morning to leave my card with Harold and Vera, whom we've known for years, of course. I was shocked to learn that Harold had died.'

'That's sad to hear. Is Mrs Gillespie planning on staying here, then, at least for the summer?'

'I think she's staying throughout the year. Having a guest house will make that possible. Rose Bank Guest House it's called. All credit to the poor woman.'

'So that's where Jack Leighton will be. I know he's staying in the same guest house as Eric,' Stephen told him. 'I don't know if you met Jack in Delhi—he's a recent appointment to the Revenue Department.'

'I expect I've seen him there. Fortunately, Rose Bank is

only a little way up from Cedars, so Lilian and Eric will have plenty of opportunity to get to know each other. But to get back to you, young man.'

Stephen pulled a face. 'Must we? You know I'll work hard. I always do.'

'Yes, we must. But there's more to summer in Simla than just covering paper with words and distributing that paper to the various desks in the Secretariat, you know. It's also a non-stop round of picnics, garden fetes, balls, amateur theatricals, paper chases, cocktail parties, races, sporting tournaments, to name but a few of the entertainments on offer. And it's famous for the level of flirtation and debauchery.'

Stephen raised his hand. 'You can stop there. You've sold it to me.'

Wilfred gave him a wry smile. 'You'll find that you're not the only one to be drawn to such attractions. Any number of young British girls will have come here for the sole purpose of finding a husband. We call them the fishing fleet.'

'So I believe.'

'And there'll also be the ladies who've come to Simla while their husbands are detained in Delhi by reason of work. I believe that their experience, coupled with their lack of interest in marriage since they're already married, makes them extremely popular with the young men here, and in fact they're more sought after than the fishing fleet girls.'

'Why are you telling me this, Father? All this is common knowledge in the ICS, and you must know that. The idea of marrying a fishing fleet girl doesn't appeal to me. In my way of thinking, if they were worth having, they'd have been snapped up in England.'

'That may be true of some, but a number are actually quite pretty, and I'd be derelict in my duty as a father,

Stephen, if I didn't remind you of the harm that any attachment at this time could do to your career. You're far too young to marry, and to do so would be extremely detrimental to your future prospects. And equally, to attach yourself to the wrong person, such as to someone else's wife, would be greatly frowned upon by the people in a position to promote you, or to do the opposite.'

Stephen laughed. 'No one would be stupid enough to openly flaunt such an affair.'

'I'm afraid the evidence says otherwise. But even if you *were* discreet, it'd be found out, believe me. Nothing stays secret here for long. The favourite topic of conversation among women—and men, too, I think it's true to say—is who's involved with someone they shouldn't be.'

'I'll bear that in mind.' Stephen finished his coffee, and started to stand up. 'Now if you'll excuse me, I'll do what my mother and sister are doing, and that's have a rest.'

'And there's one other type of woman you need to avoid, Stephen,' Wilfred continued. He paused.

Stephen gave an audible sigh, and sat down again. 'Is that so?' he said with exaggerated weariness.

'There are a number of very beautiful Indian women working in Simla in different capacities. To attach yourself to one of them would be a huge mistake. Long gone are the days when officials were encouraged to liaise with an Indian woman, either as a mistress or a wife. These days, it's most definitely not the done thing, and you can be sure that if you were to be so unwise, all social invitations would instantly cease.'

Stephen stood up. 'I think you must have covered every possible pitfall by now, Father,' he said, 'and with an attention to detail that even Eric Stanford would struggle to surpass. You can relax. I plan to stop on my way to my room and have a word with Mother. I'm intending to ask her to teach me how to knit. It'll be a way of getting through the long solitary evenings ahead of me.'

He grinned at his father, turned and went back into the dining room and across to the hall.

GLADYS CHATSWORTH SAT on the edge of Daisy's bed, and watched her daughter hold up a white dress and study it in an effort to decide whether to wear it that evening.

'If you don't get a move on, Daisy, you won't have much of a sleep,' she said at last.

'If I don't know what I'm wearing, I won't be able to get any sleep at all. I'd never relax,' Daisy replied, and she went back into the dressing room and swapped the cap-sleeved white dress for a pale-blue cotton dress with short sleeves.

She returned to the full-length mirror in the corner of her bedroom, and held the blue dress in front of her. 'What do you think, Mama?' she asked. 'Which shall I wear?'

'I think all this fuss is quite unnecessary,' Gladys replied with a tinge of impatience. 'It's just an evening stroll on the Mall, after all.'

Daisy glanced at her mother in surprise. 'Surely it's important how we look tonight. It's our first evening here. Yesterday doesn't count as we arrived so late that we went to bed as soon as we'd eaten. Tonight will be the first time that Lilian and I have been in Simla as adults, and we must look our best. As Lilian said, we don't know who might see us. First impressions are very important. You're always telling me that.'

She turned sideways to try a different pose with the dress.

'While it's pleasing to know that you listen to me,'

Gladys said, 'I *do* think you're rather overdoing it for a walk. Save your effort for parties and dances, is my advice.'

'If I look too awful for words tonight, people will be so put off that no one will come near me when it comes to those parties and balls.'

'You couldn't look too awful for words, Daisy. You're a very pretty girl. When you're not looking so worried, that is.'

'Prettiness doesn't last. You get less pretty each year. And anyway, Lilian's prettier than I am. And she's got a gorgeous dress to wear this evening. It's ankle-length, in a sort of floaty pale-pink muslin, and she's got a matching wide-brimmed hat, shoes and gloves.'

'She isn't prettier than you, darling; it's a different pretti-ness, that's all. She's got wavy dark hair, dark eyes and the colouring that goes with it, and you have curly blonde hair and blue eyes, and the delicate colouring that goes with that. Both of you are very attractive.'

'You *would* say that as you're my mother. Also I'm supposed to look like Father,' Daisy said, 'and as you love him, some might say you were biased. I'll try my green dress, I think.' And she headed for her dressing room again.

A moment later, she returned carrying a sage-green dress, and held it up to herself.

Gladys patted the place on the bed next to her. 'Why don't you stop what you're doing, Daisy, and sit here for a minute?'

A look of exaggerated horror on her face, Daisy faced her mother's reflection in the full-length mirror.

'This isn't what I think it might be, is it?'

Gladys went red. 'I want to talk to you about the way in which you comport yourself when you're outside the house. I'm well aware that you and Lilian have made a list of things to do while we're here, and I'm very pleased that you feel confident of being able to amuse yourself in such a small place. But it *is* a small place, and you need to be aware of what that means.'

She patted the place next to her again.

Daisy didn't move. 'It means it's a small place. Can there be any doubt about the meaning of those words?' she said lightly.

'It's their significance, not their meaning, that's important.'

Daisy threw the green dress on to the bed, and went and sat facing her mother on the wooden-backed chair at the side of the door leading to the verandah. 'What are you hinting at, Mama?'

'That you and Lilian can obviously go backwards and forwards between each other's houses—we're next door to the Hunts, after all. But you must be accompanied at all times if you go any further than that. Either Constance or I will go with you, or one of the *ayahs*. Or even Stephen.'

Daisy stared at her mother in dismay. 'Even if we just go down to the Mall? After all, the *jampanis* will be pulling the rickshaw, so they'll sort of be with us.'

'Yes, even that short distance,' Gladys said firmly. 'The *jampanis* are not chaperones—they're servants. If you instructed them to leave you for a while, they'd have to obey you. But you'd be jeopardising their position with us, which would be grossly unfair.'

'I wouldn't do that.'

'I'm not prepared to take such a chance,' Gladys said firmly. '*You* might not do so, Daisy, but Lilian can be quite headstrong. A chaperone wouldn't have to obey you, and would ensure that you didn't become the subject of unpleasant gossip. Just as you wouldn't dream of going out

in New Delhi unchaperoned, you mustn't do so here. Not for
any distance. Do you understand?'

Daisy glared at her mother. 'I suppose so.'

'And if you think your father and I are being hard on
you, just think back to your school years, and to how swiftly
rumours travel—especially unpleasant rumours. It's
extremely easy to lose one's good reputation, and very hard
to get it back. You're a kind, sweet-natured girl, Daisy, and if
you're to get the sort of husband you deserve, you need to be
seen to be above reproach.'

'I'd never do anything that could stop me from marrying
the person I love,' Daisy said, her tone heartfelt.

Her mother gave an awkward laugh, and pulled her skirt
further over her knees.

'It almost sounds as if you've someone in mind, Daisy,
but you can't have. You've not been out of school for long.'
She laughed again, this time dismissively.

After an imperceptible pause, Daisy joined in with her
laughter.

7

E *arly evening*

'IT'S SHRUNK,' Lilian wailed in dismay to Daisy when they caught their first glimpse of the town above the shoulders of the two barefoot *jampanis* pulling the rickshaw along the dusty road, while two ran behind, ready to push when necessary.

Constance heard her, and smiled across from her rickshaw.

'Could it be that you've both got bigger, darling?'

Lilian and Daisy exchanged glances and sat back, staring at the buildings they were approaching.

Both families had been eager to get the feel again for the place they loved but hadn't seen for several months, and the two girls for considerably longer than that, and they'd instructed their *jampanis*—the Hunts' team in a yellow and red livery, and the Chatsworths' in blue and red—to take them all the way along the line of the ridge.

It meant that they would pass some of the main buildings in the town, and go past Scandal Point as far as Christ Church, which stood on the far eastern side of the town at the back of the only wide open space in Simla, which was called The Ridge.

They would then turn round, and go back to Scandal Point, the place where the road at the top of the ridge met Mall Road, which ran alongside the ridge road for some of the way, and they would do as did most visitors to the Mall, leave their rickshaws at Scandal Point and take a stroll down Mall Road before returning home.

If they set themselves the goal of doing a watercolour of the most important buildings along the top road, Lilian told Daisy, it would give them another enjoyable reason for going out, in addition to a lunch, party or dance.

And Eric might even see them when they were sitting outside painting, and come and speak to them.

What's more, she had a plan to make that more likely to happen, she told a beaming Daisy. If it worked, she and Eric would be able to spend time more together getting to know each other.

'What plan?' Daisy asked, her eyes hopeful.

When they were in a group with their parents, she'd show an interest in Eric, Lilian told her, and she would do all she could to attract his attention.

And then, as soon as her parents were engaged in conversation with friends, she'd step back and let Daisy and Eric talk to each other. As she and Daisy would have decided in advance which scene they'd next be painting, Daisy would be able to tell Eric, so he might be able to stop by at wherever that was.

Her idea was to make her father so confident that his wishes were going to come to fruition that he wouldn't be too concerned about who chaperoned them, she explained. It meant that although he'd know that the *ayahs* were less vigilant than their mothers, he'd be relaxed about it.

'Then you and Eric can talk together without any mothers hovering over you,' she added with a giggle.

Daisy bit her lip. 'D'you think that'll work?'

'I don't know, but as I can't think of how else to help you, it's worth a try. And that'll be one of the first places we'll paint,' she said as they approached Gorton Castle, which stood on the edge of the town.

The large four-storey building in which the Secretariat was housed stood back on the left of the road, surrounded by a line of dark green deodar trees.

'Eric works there so he could easily come out and talk to me,' Daisy said happily.

Lilian shook her head. 'I'm afraid that won't be one of the places he joins us. His father seems to want to see Eric with me for some reason, and although his father works somewhere else, someone's bound to tell him that you and Eric were talking.'

'So why are we painting Gorton Castle?'

'Because it would look strange if we painted the other buildings, but not the building that's second only to Viceregal Lodge. We'll do it very quickly, though.'

Daisy stared at the building as they were pulled past it, and frowned. 'It looks very difficult.'

'It won't be that hard. We'll need a lot of reds and greens —a variety of greens for the trees, but mainly dark green. And we'll need red for the pointed towers and the red galvanized iron roofing that you can see above the trees. And obviously we'll need grey for the stone walls.'

She glanced at Daisy and laughed. 'You don't look convinced.'

'I'm not,' Daisy said in a woeful tone. 'I'll give it a try though.'

Lilian smiled at her, and then looked back at the next building they were approaching, which was the Telegraph Office. It was home to one of the first automatic telephone exchanges, her father had told her on the way to the house their first night back.

But after the brilliance of Gorton Castle, with its red roofing bright in the sunlight, the Telegraph Office seemed no more than a functional brick building. They'd do that one quickly, too, she decided.

'Ah, that's better,' she said, pointing towards the half-timbered, red-coloured General Post Office. 'That's more interesting. It'll be fun to paint.'

Daisy pulled a face. 'That one also looks difficult to me. Look at the carved wooden verandah in front of each of the three storeys. It would be so hard to get that right.'

Lilian shrugged. 'If you make a mess of it, who'll know?' She glanced towards the red-painted rickshaws lined up at the side of the Post Office. 'We'll include the rickshaws as they're the ones that bring the mail from the railway station.'

And they'd have to do a picture of Scandal Point, she said, staring to her right as they passed the first of several short flights of steps leading down to the Mall, and drew close to Scandal Point.

Being the most notorious place in Simla, where lots of assignations were made and gossip exchanged, they could write out the story of how Scandal Point got its name, and illustrate it. That would be something different, she said in excitement.

It had been given its name after an affair between a British woman, believed to be the Viceroy's daughter, and an Indian Maharaja.

One day, while the Viceroy's daughter had been strolling through the area, she'd disappeared, and it was later discovered that she'd eloped with the Maharaja.

That had caused a great scandal, not only in Simla, people said, but throughout the British administration, and it was the sort of subject that might appeal to people who buy pictures, Lilian told Daisy.

She sat back and glanced towards the turreted Railway Board Building on her left.

She wasn't sure that she was a good enough painter to get the metallic colour right. There was a lot of visible metal—its skeleton was built of cast iron and steel, and held together with nuts and bolts. And the side rails, too, were made of cast iron, which had been beautifully decorated.

Capturing the many different tones in the iron and steel wouldn't be easy, nor of much interest to her, and she might decide against doing it.

As they neared a group of buildings on the right, which included the white-grey stone and timber building of the Gaiety Theatre, and next to it, the Town Hall, which contained the municipal offices, ball and supper room, the Freemasons' Hall, library and reading rooms, she sat up and exclaimed in surprise.

'Look at that, Daisy! I used to think the Town Hall so imposing, but it's nothing special. And as for the Gaiety Theatre, how on earth did they manage to hold so many shows and fit in so many people, when it looks so tiny?'

Daisy nodded. 'I know. It makes you wonder, doesn't it?' She raised her head, sniffed and smiled. 'We'll soon be at

The Ridge. The scent of spice is much stronger and the band's getting louder.'

In a matter of moments, they were passing the circular bandstand on their right. Beneath its conical slate roof, which rested on wooden posts, the Viceroy's band was sitting, playing.

At the far end of The Ridge stood Christ Church, striking with its yellow and white stone walls, and the bell clock tower that rose above a number of similar smaller spires that seemed to grow from the roof of the church.

'You forget how beautiful it is here,' Daisy murmured, glancing to her right at the forested hills that lay beyond the bandstand, and at the snow-white peaks of the Himalayas soaring up behind them, touching the deep blue sky.

A metallic creaking and sudden sharp swaying told them that the *jampanis*, at Frederick and Wilfred's request, were starting to turn the rickshaws in order to return to Scandal Point.

WHEN THEY REACHED SCANDAL POINT, they climbed down from their rickshaws, stretched themselves, and joined the throng of people on the Mall, some of whom were on foot, and some on horseback.

Fresh from being washed for the second time in the day by water-bearers with goat-hide bags strapped to their backs, the ground beneath their feet reflected the light beamed down from electricity poles, each one resembling a narrow black-painted sleeve, which stood at the height of a tall man.

'Where's Stephen tonight?' Lilian asked Daisy as they paused in front of the bootmaker's, one the Tudor-style structures that lined the street.

Daisy shrugged. 'I think he's going to the Club,' she said. 'Knowing him, he'll want to play billiards.'

Lilian pulled a face. 'Shopping is much more fun. Nowhere in England has better shops than here.' She gestured around her.

'Come on, girls!' she heard her mother call.

She groaned. 'I suppose we'll have to get a move on.'

'I heard what you were saying about the quality of the shops here, Lilian,' Frederick said when they caught up with their parents. 'You're right. The standard's steadily risen over the years as Simla's been forced to offer the sort of goods demanded by both Europeans and rich Indians. That's definitely a move in the right direction.'

'It certainly sounds it, Papa.'

'More debatable is the fact that since the end of the war,' Frederick continued, 'Indians have been allowed to own shops in Simla. On the understanding, of course, that they stock only quality goods.'

'How very interesting, Papa,' Lilian murmured.

Frederick smiled at her. 'You might try to sound as if you mean it.'

She giggled.

She glanced at Daisy, and then back at her father. 'Can we go to the Club this evening, Papa?' she asked sweetly. 'Daisy thinks Stephen will be there.'

He looked at her sharply. 'Why're you so interested in seeing Stephen?'

'Because he's like a brother. Since you haven't given me a brother, I'm having to share Stephen. Aren't I, Daisy?'

'Who's taking my name in vain?'

Stephen's voice reached them above the clip-clopping of horses' hooves.

Both families turned towards Stephen, smiling, and they

saw that Eric Stanford was riding alongside him. The two men brought their horses to a stop.

Lilian glanced quickly at Daisy, who was hastily pinching her cheeks to give them some colour.

Frederick smiled broadly. 'Why, Eric, how lovely to see you!' he exclaimed. 'And you, too, Stephen, of course.' He took a step towards them. 'We just mentioned you, in fact, Stephen.'

'I heard my name, but not what you were saying. It was something good, I hope. If it wasn't, I'm glad we arrived in time to stop you from saying more.'

'I don't think you've any reason to worry, Stephen,' Constance said in amusement. 'Have you just come from the guest house?'

'We spent about an hour in the Secretariat after leaving the house, and were on our way to the Club when we saw you walking down the Mall, and thought we'd make a slight detour to say hello.'

'And we're delighted you did,' Constance said. 'Why don't you dismount and walk with us?' she asked, her smile of encouragement centred on Eric.

'Yes, do,' Daisy urged, and she glanced shyly up at Eric.

Lilian clapped her hands in glee, and took a step towards Eric, putting herself a fraction in front of Daisy. 'That's an excellent idea! You *must* join us, Eric.'

'You're welcome to come back with us for dinner, if you want, Stephen,' Wilfred said. 'And Eric, too. Cook always makes considerably more than is necessary.'

'Alternatively, Uncle Wilfred, to avoid sending our cooks into a fluster,' Lilian said, 'Stephen could go with you and Aunt Gladys, and Mr Stanford could eat with us.'

Frederick nodded vigorously. 'You'd be most welcome, Eric.'

'It's a very kind invitation,' Stephen said before Eric could reply, 'but I'm afraid we can't accept it. We've arranged to meet Jack Leighton at the Club. We left him at the Secretariat, but he won't be far behind us. This is his first time in Simla. He's been assigned to the Revenue Department, so he'll be working in your area, Uncle Frederick.'

Frederick nodded. 'I've seen his name, but not yet met the man.'

'Why don't you all join us at the Club, then?' Stephen suggested.

'I'm afraid we can't,' Frederick said, his voice heavy with regret. 'We've arranged to dine at home, and our cooks will be preparing our meal as we speak.' He looked around the group. 'But I suggest we lunch at the Club tomorrow.'

Lilian dimpled. 'Perhaps Stephen and Mr Stanford would like to join us.' She smiled at Eric in a way that she thought might please her father, again stepping a little in front of Daisy.

Eric blushed.

Daisy moved to Lilian's side, glanced from Eric to Lilian, and then looked quickly away.

Frederick coughed. 'Excellent idea, Lilian.' He nodded towards Stephen and Eric. 'What about it? Would you both care to join us for lunch at the Club tomorrow?'

Stephen smiled. 'Thank you, Uncle. We would.'

Eric visibly hesitated. 'It's kind of you, sir, but it might seem a little unfriendly if I left Jack Leighton on his own. We're all boarding in the same guest house.'

Stephen nodded. 'Well said, Eric. I should have thought of old Jack.'

Frederick smiled at them both. 'You must pass the invitation on to him, too, of course. It'll be an opportunity to get to know him. Well, as that's decided, I expect you young fellows want to get off to your evening activities. I suggest the rest of us return to the rickshaws now, and go back home.'

Stephen and Eric took their leave of the two families, and rode back up to Scandal Point, where they turned right and headed for the Club which lay in the hills beyond Christ Church.

Lilian tucked her arm into Daisy's and, followed by their parents, they strolled back to the place where their *jampanis* were waiting with the rickshaws.

As they were almost at Scandal Point, Frederick caught sight of a litter bin at the side of the street.

He stopped abruptly.

He'd almost forgotten the card, he realised, berating himself.

He hurriedly took the envelope from his pocket, screwed it up as he went across to the bin, and dropped it in.

Overwhelmed by a sense of having escaped an irrational formless doom, he wiped his hand across his brow, and with relief coursing through him, hastened to catch up with the others.

L eaning forward in his saddle, Jack Leighton stroked the neck of his restless horse.

As he'd been riding along the ridge towards Christ Church, he'd seen Eric and Stephen make a detour to the Mall, and then stop and speak to a group of people they must have spotted as they were riding by. Rather than join them, he'd stopped where he was and had sat in his saddle, watching the group as they talked and laughed for several minutes.

Their conversation having come to an end, he saw his two friends ride up out of the Mall and turn in the direction of the Club, which Eric had earlier told him was reached by going as far as Christ Church, and then taking the road to its right.

Then he'd stared down the slope at the rest of the group, who were now walking back up the Mall, no doubt heading for the rickshaws clustered where the Mall met the ridge road.

They must be the two families Stephen had spoken

about, he decided—Stephen's own family and that of his father's friend, Frederick Hunt.

He'd seen Frederick Hunt several times in the distance in Delhi, but he hadn't been introduced to him. The whole of their section had been too busy preparing to move to Simla, which was to happen soon after his arrival in the capital.

He'd heard sufficient comments made by colleagues in the Secretariat, however, to know that Frederick Hunt's daughter was considered a very attractive brunette with wonderful eyes, and he he had been interested in seeing her for himself.

And as he was working with Stephen, and liked what he'd seen of him, he was curious also to meet Stephen's sister, Daisy.

Seeing the two girls thus, it had given him an excellent chance to observe them when they weren't aware that they were being watched. As a result, he'd gained a very good impression of the character of each.

The fair-haired girl would be Daisy Chatsworth, and the dark-haired girl next to her was obviously Frederick Hunt's daughter, whose name he knew to be Lilian.

He stared at Daisy, the girl with whom Eric was clearly besotted.

She looked a very pleasant, gentle girl, he thought, which wasn't a surprise. From what he'd seen of Eric, a somewhat quiet, reserved man, and from the things that Eric had said, he couldn't imagine him falling for anyone who was in any way loud or overbearing.

His gaze settled on Lilian Hunt.

His Secretariat colleagues were right—even from afar he could see that she was quite beautiful. It wasn't surprising that a number of people walking past the group glanced towards Miss Hunt as they went by. In the pink concoction she was wearing, she must have looked stunning when seen close up.

He frowned.

Beautiful, but rather too pushy, he thought.

Throughout the conversation, she'd seemed intent on securing Eric's attention. At least twice, she'd stepped in front of Daisy to respond to something Eric had said, when it had been clear that Eric had aimed the remark at Daisy or in general.

Well, Miss Hunt was likely to be disappointed, he thought wryly.

If she knew how Eric viewed her, she'd realise that she was going about things entirely in the wrong way, and that the effect she was having on Eric was probably the complete opposite of what she wanted.

And it was obvious what she wanted—she wanted Eric.

He looked back at Daisy. She came across as he'd imagined she would. She'd deferred to her friend, and had stood a little way back from her. Every so often, she'd glanced towards Eric, and despite her cloche, he could see enough of her face to know that each time she'd given him a little smile.

Daisy was clearly as keen on Eric as he was on her.

He was certain that he'd like Daisy.

And he was equally certain that he wouldn't like Lilian Hunt.

As he watched Eric and Stephen ride off towards the Club, and the two families start to trail back to their rickshaws, he stared down at them thoughtfully.

If, after the short amount of time he'd spent with Eric, he'd become aware of Eric's feelings for Daisy, Lilian, who spent so much time with Daisy, must surely know how Daisy felt about Eric.

Yet she hadn't missed a single opportunity to push herself forward and draw Eric's attention away from the girl she called her friend.

What's more, she must know that she was completely unsuited to Eric, and that he would never be happy with her, nor she with him, but have decided to ignore that.

It meant that she'd be making a beeline for Eric, not for himself, but because of his father.

With Eric's father being a highly placed official, marrying Eric would elevate Lilian's social status, both in Simla and back in Delhi. And she'd know that.

So, beautiful she might be, but that beauty was clearly on the outside only.

Self-interest obviously took precedence over everything else in her life, including her friendship with Daisy, and to advance herself she was prepared to lead a gentle man like Eric into a marriage that could bring him nothing but misery.

He despised women like that.

And he didn't think much of Frederick Hunt, either.

He must have known what his daughter was doing, and may have even encouraged it. He'd smiled throughout the conversation with Eric and Stephen, and on several occasions, when Lilian had pushed herself forward, he'd looked approvingly at her.

He focused his gaze on Frederick, who'd gone across to a nearby litter bin into which he was dropping what looked to be a piece of paper.

He'd wait until Frederick had re-joined the others and everyone had settled again in their rickshaws, and then he'd tug down the rim of his solar *topi* and ride past them.

Frederick Hunt had probably seen him from afar in Delhi, but they hadn't yet been introduced so he was unlikely to recognise him from what he'd be able to see beneath the *topi*. Neither of them, therefore, would be obliged to stop and say hello.

He tightened his hold on his reins, ready to squeeze the middle of his horse's ribcage to cue him to move forward, when out of the corner of his eye, he noticed a man standing in the middle of the Mall, staring up after Frederick.

He paused.

He couldn't tell if the man was Indian or British. He was wearing a white shirt and light-coloured trousers, clothes worn mainly by the British, but also increasingly by Indians.

What was running through the man's mind, he wondered, watching both the man and Frederick, who was hurrying to catch up with his family, his back to the man and the bin.

He saw the man go swiftly forward to the litter bin that Frederick had used, reach quickly in and then draw out his hand, holding something that he swiftly put into his pocket.

Given the interest he'd shown in Frederick, he'd most likely removed the item that Frederick had thrown away, he thought in surprise. But strangely, he hadn't looked to see what it was before pocketing it.

Frowning, he watched the man hurry back down the Mall, his head down, and disappear into one of the side alleys.

The whole thing seemed a little peculiar, he thought, gathering up his reins again.

Perhaps he should tell Frederick what had happened. If he didn't see him at the Club that evening, he could always stop at the house the following day. It would be easy enough as the Hunts were in Cedars, which was only a few steps away from the Guest House.

He hesitated. Perhaps not. He might be allowing himself to feel a degree of alarm for no reason at all.

After all, the man might be a beggar who'd had a stroke of luck with some cast-off clothes he'd found. If so, he'd only been doing what any beggar might do if he thought that someone had thrown away an item that could be of use to him, or that might have some value.

And if that were the case, he was unlikely to have lingered there to examine whatever it was, lest someone had seen him rummaging in the bin and had challenged him. Rather, he'd go somewhere less public before he looked at his spoils.

But he hadn't actually rummaged, had he?

He'd appeared to know what he wanted, and he'd gone straight to it.

His brow cleared. He was letting his imagination run away with him.

Whoever it was must have noticed a well-dressed man throw something away, and been curious. He'd have seen that nothing else had been thrown on top of it, so he hadn't needed to rummage.

It clearly wasn't anything more sinister than that, and he'd think no more about it.

Without looking again at the litter bin, he pressed both legs evenly against the horse's sides, and his horse began to trot in the direction of Christ Church and the Club.

9

T *he following day*

THE RAW MORNING air swept down the ice-crusted mountains peaks, and down the dark-green forested slopes, sweeping aside the black curtain of night, and washing the sky with the pale grey light of dawn.

A swell of excited birdsong rose in the air above Cedars, heralding the arrival of the new day.

But inside the house, all was silent.

Frederick stood in front of the sitting room window, the shutters open, staring with unseeing eyes at the sky as it splintered into bands of amber and yellow light.

But the beauty of dawn was drowned out for him by fear, a fear that had haunted his night, denying him the oblivion of sleep, a fear that had shattered the start of the new day.

Throughout the night, images of a crumpled white card

had forced their way into his mind, bringing with them fleeting glimpses of a rage-filled face, of glaring red eyes, of a blood-dripping severed head.

The images came; the images went.

He'd relax, almost. Then they'd loom up again, larger, more lurid in colour, more terrifying.

The moment that the light of day had begun to slide between the shutters, he'd escaped his bed in relief.

Despite it being Saturday, he'd have an early breakfast, he'd resolved as he'd moved quietly across the room to avoid disturbing Constance, and then he'd go into the Secretariat for a couple of hours before it was time to go to the Club.

Work would give him something to do, something to help him forget the card, he'd thought as he'd tied the belt of his dark-blue smoking jacket and then opened the bedroom door.

The card was gone for ever, embedded in the detritus from a Friday night on the Mall. It had been stupid of him to have let the matter unsettle him in the way it had, he rebuked himself as he quietly closed the door behind him.

It had obviously been delivered to him by mistake. If it had been intended for him, he would have had some idea at least of what it was trying to say.

Feeling a welcome lifting of the load that had been weighing heavily on him since he'd first found the card, he'd run lightly down the stairs, the soft pad of his footsteps being the only sounds to be heard in the still of the house.

He'd reached the bottom stair, and stopped abruptly.

It couldn't be!

But it was.

A small white envelope lay on the mat in front of the door.

It was similar to an envelope he'd seen before.

No, it wasn't just similar—it looked to be exactly the same shape and size.

His heartbeat had quickened.

Forcing himself to move, he'd stepped from the last stair, and had gone across to the mat.

His breathing ragged, he'd stood in dread and stared down at the envelope.

What would he find inside it this time?

Then he'd taken a deep breath, bent down, picked up the envelope, and gone with it into the sitting room and across to the window. The envelope in his hand, he'd stood motionless in front of the window while ice-cold fingers crept around his heart, slowly tightening their hold on him.

A few minutes later, muffled sounds of movement came from somewhere at the back of the house.

The servants would soon be starting on their tasks for the day, he realised with a start. He must speedily check the contents of the envelope, and then, unless there was an obvious reason for what he'd been sent, he'd throw it away when he got to the Secretariat.

He pulled open the flap and withdrew a small white card.

His blood froze.

The same hideous image as before was staring up at him.

But unlike the first occasion when he'd seen the depiction of that gruesome goddess, this time the ghastly picture had at one time been crumpled.

It was the same card that he'd thrown away the night before. There was no doubting that. Although the card had been carefully flattened out, it was still creased.

Someone must have seen him dropping it into the bin.

So someone must have been following him.

There was no other explanation.

And this clearly hadn't been delivered to him by mistake —he was the intended target.

Target.

That was the word that had sprung to his mind. Yes, he was being targeted by someone.

But why?

He needed to know.

How could he put something right if he didn't know what he'd done to anger the person in the first place?

And who was that person?

He'd have to find out, but without anyone knowing. It wasn't something for his servants to know, and he certainly wouldn't want to alarm his family.

Frightened, he stood trembling in front of the window, the envelope in one hand, the wrinkled card in the other.

From now on, he must be alert at all times, and he must be aware of the people around him, as one of them was surely responsible for this.

It could be an Indian; it could be someone British.

But it was more likely to be someone with whom he worked, someone whom he'd unknowingly offended, rather than any Indian.

He didn't really know any Indians, for goodness' sake!

There were Indians in the Secretariat, of course. The lower ranks of the administration were filled by a vast army of subordinate clerks and provincial staff that had been recruited in India to do the more humdrum tasks. But as his contact with such people was minimal, it was unlikely to be one of them.

And there were Indians who owned some of the shops

in the Mall or who worked in them. He'd met some of them but there'd never been any altercation with any, and he didn't owe anyone any money.

The only other Indians he really met were his servants, and as far as they were concerned, he was sure they would say he was a good employer. If he hadn't been, he wouldn't have been able to hire the same household staff year after year, apart from one or two housemaids, who tended to change every summer.

It was difficult to believe that he could have inadvertently slighted one of the servants, or had expected them to do an action that demeaned their caste, as if he had done so, Sunil would have told him, and the matter would have been efficiently sorted by Sunil and Constance.

And his *jampanis* had no cause for complaint.

They had a better life with him than they'd have had if they'd been left to be mere coolies, attached to one of the public rickshaw stands owned by the municipality.

Coolies like that were subject to the whims of the *chaudhri* who licensed the rickshaws, and they were lodged in one of the crowded airless godowns the *chaudhri* rented, for which he'd force them to pay him eight annas a month.

The *jampanis* had good reason to be grateful to him so it wouldn't be one of them.

In all probability, therefore, his persecutor—for that was how the man now felt to him—was not an Indian.

He was more likely to be one of the carefully selected ICS officers with whom he worked. He demanded a lot of his staff, he knew, but it was no more than he demanded of himself, and they all recognised that.

At least, he'd thought that they had.

But perhaps he was wrong. Perhaps his uncompromising attitude had given rise to resentment on the part of one of his colleagues.

Or something even stronger than resentment.

To go to the trouble of finding out where someone was going to be living, to come to that person's house in the dead of night to leave a card—not once, but twice—and to follow that person when they left the house, required a feeling that was stronger than mere resentment.

But who could feel that way towards him?

He pushed the card back into the envelope, and slipped it into the pocket of his smoking jacket. When he went to the Secretariat that morning, he'd look closely at all of the projects on which he'd been working, and at the names of everyone working on them with him, and he'd think hard if he could have angered any of them.

But that didn't preclude trying to catch the perpetrator. If he could catch him, it would put an end to his harassment, so trapping him was a priority.

What he should do was tear the card into pieces and throw the pieces into one of the street bins near a place from which he could surreptitiously watch what happened.

If he used the same bin near Scandal Point, he could go into the Coffee House, and keep an eye on the bin. Then if anyone attempted to retrieve the card, he'd be close enough to catch the person, and that would put an end to the whole thing.

He gave an exclamation of annoyance. No, that would never work.

The person was sure to be suspicious if he used the same bin again. And anyway, if the man was watching him, he'd see him go into the Coffee House and he'd realise what he was planning to do.

And while he didn't know how the man would be able to

do it, he was pretty certain that there'd be an envelope on the mat the following morning and inside it he'd find the pieces of card put back together again.

He couldn't risk it.

And since he was being watched, there was no point in throwing it in any bin. He must destroy it completely, and in a way that it couldn't be put together again. It meant that he'd have to burn it.

'Can I get you anything, *sahib*?'

He jumped in surprise, and turned to see Sunil.

He forced a smile to his lips. 'I'm sorry, Sunil,' he said, trying to steady his voice. 'I didn't hear you come in. Yes, as a matter of fact, you can. I'm up early today as although it's Saturday, I need to look in at the Secretariat this morning. Will you tell my wife that I'll be back well before it's time to leave for the Club?'

'Certainly, *sahib*.'

'And you can ask Cook to prepare my breakfast—an omelette will suffice, and toast with some of Cook's excellent strawberry jam. If the *khitmatgar* will serve it in thirty minutes, I'll leave as soon as I've eaten.'

Sunil inclined his head. 'Certainly, *sahib*,' he repeated, and he left the room.

Frederick stared thoughtfully after him, and then shook his head. It wasn't Sunil and that was for sure. He'd bet anything that Sunil knew nothing about it.

No, the person behind the charade was most likely to be a colleague whom he'd slighted. Well, hopefully destroying the card would put an end to the matter once and for all.

He took the envelope from his pocket, checked that the card was inside, went across to the mantelpiece, picked up a box of matches, took out a match and struck it against the side of the box.

He lit the corner of the envelope, dropped it on to the grate and stood watching as the card and envelope dissolved into a heap of ashes.

Done, he thought, wiping his hands, and he turned and left the room.

10

T *he same day*

NOT LONG NOW TILL their first lunch in the Club that summer, Lilian thought happily as she lay on her side, waiting for it to be time to get up and go downstairs.

Looking back, she was so glad they hadn't changed their plans the evening before. The way things had turned out, she now had time to give thought about what to wear for lunch, instead of arriving at the Club in clothes intended for a late-afternoon walk, which would by then have lost their freshness.

She'd ask the *bheesti* to see that there was hot water in the bath tub for after she'd had her breakfast, and she'd drop a couple of her special Chanel No 5 bath tablets into the water so that she'd exude an aura of jasmine and sandalwood when she emerged for the rest of the day.

And she'd wear her primrose-yellow chiffon dress, with

matching gloves and shoes, which was a colour that went very well with her dark brown hair and eyes, she'd been told.

Mentally, she hugged herself in glee.

A large number of those who'd already arrived in Simla were bound to be at the Club, and of particular interest would be the young men they'd regularly encounter in the round of parties, dances and lunches that would fill the following six months.

It might even be the day when she met the person with whom she'd fall in love!

A quiver of excitement ran through her, and she rolled over on to her back and stared up at the ceiling.

Meeting someone attractive was naturally at the forefront of her mind, but she mustn't forget what she'd planned with Daisy.

She'd feign just enough interest in Eric for her father to feel sufficiently hopeful of her agreeing to marry Eric that he encouraged them to meet as often as possible. And obviously, Daisy would go, too.

It was foolproof, she thought as she threw back her bed cover. Nothing could possibly go wrong.

THE MIDDAY SUN was shining down on the Royal Club, Simla, mellowing the tone of the solid grey stone and wood two-storey buildings that stood on extensive lawns surrounded by dark-green forested slopes, as the Chatsworths and Hunts stepped from their rickshaws, crossed the forecourt and went up the few steps to the entrance to the Club.

Turbaned servants, each in a high-buttoned white shirt above loose white trousers, led them through the high-ceilinged wood-panelled hall, past the doors leading to the billiards' room, cards' room and bar, and past the stairs to the library, reading room and spacious panelled dining room, where on Saturday nights the members and their guests gathered for dinner.

On such nights, the Honorary Secretary would sit at one end of the long table, beneath a portrait of the Club's President, and the diners would line the sides of the table, while enjoying wine from the Club's extensive cellars and food served to them by liveried servants. On most occasions, a band would play.

But lunch was taken at round tables set out on the wide expanse of lawn that lay between the main building and a much smaller building, referred to always as the Hut, which was famous for the parties held there on Tuesday and Thursday nights.

To the side of the main building there were four lawn-tennis courts, a couple of which were covered, two squash courts, and stables for eighty horses.

As the two families stepped out of the main building on to the lawn, they were hit by the lively chatter and gales of laughter that emanated from the members and guests who were already seated at the white wrought-iron tables, which were shaded from the sun by large black umbrellas set in the ground between the tables.

At the sight of the vibrant scene in front of them, Lilian and Daisy paused and exchanged delighted glances.

'Lilian!' she heard a voice call.

And a young woman whom she'd met a few times in New Delhi, who was wearing a bright orange dress and matching straw cloche, rushed up to the group, and thrust a card into her hand and Daisy's.

'You *must* come,' she said. 'It'll be the first dance in the Hut this season. It's on Tuesday.'

Before they could thank her for the invitation, she'd hurried off to another group.

'Well, that's a highly satisfactory start to the summer,' Lilian remarked as they hurried after their parents who were heading for one of the large round tables.

'I hope Eric's invited, too,' Daisy said anxiously.

'I'm sure he will be,' Lilian reassured her. 'And he could go anyway even if he wasn't. It'll be the sort of thing where everyone's welcome.'

'We'll be nine for lunch,' Frederick told the waiter hovering at his elbow, and he indicated that they should sit. As he did so, he glanced with studied casualness at the tables in the immediate area.

The waiter inclined his head. 'Certainly, *sahib*.'

Wilfred pulled out one of the wrought-iron chairs for Gladys.

Before Frederick could do likewise for Constance, a waiter had pulled out her chair, and also chairs for Lilian and Daisy, who sat down next to each other.

'What was the card that young woman gave you, Lilian?' Frederick asked.

'Just an invitation to the dance on Tuesday. I can go, can't I?'

He nodded. 'Of course. But you must be suitably chaperoned.'

'She will be, darling,' Constance said calmly.

'I imagine that Stephen and the other two will be here at any moment,' Wilfred said, taking the chair between Constance and Gladys. 'In fact, here they come.'

They all looked towards the entrance and saw Stephen, Eric and a third man approaching them.

Lilian glanced at the third man, looked back at Daisy, and slightly raised her eyebrows.

Daisy lifted her starched white napkin to her lips. 'He's very good-looking,' she murmured into the fold of her napkin.

Wilfred and Frederick half rose from the table.

'Do sit down, gentlemen,' Frederick said, waving his hand in the direction of the three empty chairs.

The three men chorused their thanks.

Frederick and Wilfred sat back down again.

'Allow me introduce you to Jack Leighton, who's staying in the same guest house as Eric and me,' Stephen said. 'He's assigned to the Revenue Department.'

And he introduced Jack to everyone at the table.

'It's a pleasure to meet you all,' Jack said. 'It was most kind of you to invite me to join you today, Mr Hunt.'

Frederick waved his hand dismissively. 'It's a pleasure, Mr Leighton. Or Jack, if I may call you that. After all, we'll be working together in Revenue.'

Jack inclined his head. 'Of course, sir.'

'I gather this is your first time in Simla, Mr Leighton,' Lilian said.

'That's right. But I've heard so much about the place since I joined the ICS that I feel as if I already know it well.'

'Of all the places we visit in Simla, this will probably be a favourite,' Daisy said with a smile. 'Wouldn't you agree, Mr Stanford?'

Eric beamed. 'Definitely, Miss Chatsworth. And it's not just the sporting facilities here that are so impressive, Jack, it's the accommodation, too. All the blocks have long been furnished with hot and cold running water, and all the rooms have electricity. A private electric plant was installed some thirty years ago, long before other such clubs got round to doing likewise.'

'That's quite something,' Jack said.

Frederick glanced towards the entrance to the main building, and then shifted his position a little to look in the direction of the Hut.

'It's good to know about the accommodation,' Jack added. 'I imagine that returning along the ridge late at night could be quite daunting, so the idea of being able to stay here overnight is most appealing.'

'A number of young men stay on Saturday nights when there's a band,' Wilfred said, 'so it's wise to reserve a room in good time if you want to be sure of getting one. There's less demand after the dances on Tuesday and Thursday nights, of course, as there's work the following day.'

Daisy moved slightly to face Eric. She opened her mouth to speak.

'Are you comfortable in your guest house, Mr Stanford?' Lilian asked brightly.

Eric's eyes moved from Daisy to Lilian. 'Very much so, Miss Hunt; thank you. My parents have taken their usual house close to Viceregal Lodge, but I wanted to be near the Secretariat. I feel extremely fortunate to have found such a comfortable place to stay, and with such pleasant company.' He smiled at Jack.

'I'm sure that Mr Leighton would say the same about you, Mr Stanford,' Lilian said. And she treated Eric to her most winning smile.

He coloured.

A couple of waiters started moving round the table, taking the orders for their drinks.

When they'd finished, Wilfred sat back in his chair and looked across the table at Jack. 'Obviously, you weren't deterred by the grievances that some of our ICS colleagues seem to think fit to be aired in public, Mr Leighton. You must surely have heard them, but you joined the Service, nevertheless.'

'It's Jack, please, sir. No, I wasn't put off. When the Royal Commission's report was published eight years ago, proposing improved conditions of service, ICS officers received an immediate pay rise. That seemed to signal an intention to work towards putting ICS salaries and conditions of service on the same footing as those offered by business houses and other comparable professions, and that was good enough for me.'

'It *was* their first pay rise since Lord Cornwallis instituted the scales a hundred years ago,' Eric remarked mildly. 'And they really didn't have any choice in the matter. I understand that officers were finding it difficult to make ends meet, and a significant number were thinking of leaving India. With it becoming harder to interest men like us in a career in India, vacancies were growing.'

Lilian moved slightly forward in her chair, and beamed at Eric. 'That's so interesting, Mr Stanford.'

Eric cleared his throat, unfolded his napkin and put it on his lap.

'How pleasant to meet a young woman interested in something other than clothes and local gossip, Miss Hunt,' Jack said.

'I'm very interested in anything that affects the government in India,' she said, a trifle primly, glancing at Eric from beneath long eyelashes. 'After all, Papa works for the government, so it provides for Mama and me.'

'She's been well educated at that school of hers,' Frederick said with pride in his voice.

'Since you're so interested in colonial matters, Miss

Hunt, may I ask your thoughts on the growing scale of
Gandhi's non-co-operation movement?' Jack said. There was
an unmistakable challenge in his eyes, she noticed. 'A
woman's viewpoint would be most interesting.'

Wondering frantically what she could possibly say about
something about which she knew absolutely nothing, she
went red, and coughed.

'Lilian thinks the same as most of us,' Frederick said
quickly. 'She's frustrated at the government's failure to deal
with it. Aren't you, Lilian?'

'Yes, Papa. That's just what I was going to say.'

She glared at Jack, and took a sip of the gin gimlet that
the waiter had put at her side.

'What about you, Miss Chatsworth?' Eric asked. 'Are
you, too, interested in colonial matters?'

'Not really, Mr Stanford,' Daisy said, going pink. 'I'm not
clever enough to understand such matters like you do. And
to be honest, I find them a little boring. I'd rather go for a
walk than listen to men talk about politics.'

'And women, too,' Jack corrected her gently. 'When Miss
Hunt is around, that is.'

'Yes, of course,' Daisy said.

Lilian dropped her napkin to the ground. Before the
waiter could reach her, she'd bent down to retrieve it.

'He's a pig,' she whispered to Daisy, her head beneath
the table.

Daisy bent down as if to help Lilian. 'But a very good-
looking pig,' she whispered back. 'You must admit, he's an
extremely attractive man.'

'Are you looking for anyone in particular, Frederick?'
Constance asked mildly. 'You seem to be glancing around a
lot.'

Frederick turned back to face the table and smiled at

her. 'I'm sorry, my dear. Put it down to my curiosity about who else is here. It's partly general interest, I admit, but also because some of our friends who've invited us to a luncheon are likely to be here today, and if so, I thought I might thank them in person. One of those people is your father, Eric. We received a couple of kind invitations from him and your mother.'

'I'm sure he's looking forward to meeting you on a more social occasion than is usually the case,' Eric said. 'But he rarely visits the Club, so I'm afraid you're unlikely to meet him here.'

'Ah, yes, I remember.'

He smiled at Eric, and then found himself looking surreptitiously again at the occupants of the nearby tables.

Though why he should do so, he didn't know.

That damned card had been reduced to a small pile of ashes that morning, so he knew he'd seen the last of it.

11

C*edars*
  Later that afternoon

FREDERICK LEANED back in his wicker chair on the upper back verandah and picked up his glass from the small table between his chair and Wilfred's.

Glancing at Wilfred, he raised his glass. 'Your health, Wilfred,' he said. He took a sip of his gin gimlet, put the glass back on the table, and turned again to look at the distant gold-capped mountains. 'Yes, we're well and truly back.'

Wilfred glanced quickly at Frederick, and lifted his glass. 'Your health, too, old friend.' He paused, and changed his position to look more directly at Frederick.

'You seem a little out of sorts, Freddie. I hope it's not because I've dropped in on you unexpectedly this afternoon, even though we've just had lunch together. Daisy was agitating to see Lilian. And you know what the girls are like.

She was probably anxious to know if anything interesting had happened since lunch.'

Frederick nodded. 'She and Lilian are two of a kind.'

Wilfred cleared his throat. 'Actually, it wasn't just Daisy who wanted to come across. I did too. I was somewhat worried about you, old friend. And seeing you now, so clearly anxious, has added to my concern.'

The sound of the two girls laughing together reached them from inside the house.

'Whatever the reason, I'm pleased you came over,' Frederick went on. 'While the view from up here is very beautiful,' he said, gesturing in front of him, 'it's no substitute for interesting conversation.'

Wilfred pulled a face. 'I'm not sure about interesting. I'd set my sights lower if I were you.'

Frederick gave him a wry smile. 'Oh, I'm sure it'll be interesting. I know you, Wilfred. You wouldn't have cut short your siesta without a reason, and one you thought a good one at that. And a bit of concern about the mood I was in after a long journey, and settling in again, isn't a good reason.'

Wilfred took a deep breath. 'You can tell me to mind my own business, but it's more than being in a mood. There's something that's causing you real anxiety, and I'm wondering if I can help. Or perhaps to say you're distracted is a more accurate. Yes, that's it. You've seemed unusually distracted since we got here.'

Frederick gave an awkward laugh. 'I don't think I have.'

'You have,' Wilfred said firmly. 'During our walk along the Mall, for example, you seemed quite tense. And also at lunch today. You were so busy looking at the other tables that you hardly said a word to anyone.'

'I told Constance the reason why.'

'I don't believe what you said, and I don't think she did, either. I suspect that like me, Constance is worried about you. You appear to be on edge, and I'd like to help.'

Frederick raised his glass, swirled the gimlet around its depths, and then put the glass down again.

'You're right about me having something on my mind. Rather, it's several little things,' he said at last. 'For example, you know how much I want a senior position on the Central Board of Revenue, and that Cecil Stanford could clinch it for me.'

'I know that.'

'Well, apparently, his son, Eric, has shown an interest in Lilian.'

'In Lilian!' Wilfred exclaimed. 'That does surprise me. Not that he's interested in Lilian, of course,' he said quickly. 'She's a beautiful woman. But they're very different. In fact, I would have thought Eric had more in common with Daisy.'

'I know what you mean, and I must say, I was surprised, too. But I've encouraged her to look favourably on him. I don't really feel I have a choice, although it's fraught with pitfalls.'

Wilfred stared at him in amazement. 'In what way?'

'I can't help remembering how she initially dismissed him when I raised the subject. In fact, I'd go as far as to say that she was actually rude about him.'

'Well, all I can say is, she seems to have overcome her dislike. At lunch today, I thought she seemed quite taken with him.'

'That's just it!' Frederick exclaimed. 'She *does* appear to be showing an interest in him. But this could just be because I've asked her to do so. Eric wouldn't know that, of course. But if it came to the crunch and he proposed, I can't see her going as far as marrying a man who wasn't genuinely to her liking, just to please me.'

'In that case, she'd turn him down,' Wilfred said.

'But if she'd given him reason to hope, and had then turned her back on him, he could be distraught. Cecil would be less than pleased, and it could seriously damage my career. So I risk hurting my career if I don't encourage Lilian to favour Eric, and also if I do!'

Wilfred shrugged. 'Many a girl has married a man to help her father. Lilian's a good girl. I can see her subduing her natural inclination and agreeing to this.'

Frederick raised an eyebrow. 'Are we talking about the same Lilian?'

Wilfred looked across at him. A smile turned the corner of his lips. 'Maybe not,' he said. 'So what's the next little thing?'

'Well, it's not really my province—it's Constance's. But I can't help being concerned about possible discord in our household this summer. We've a new housemaid, a girl called Asha, and I'm not sure how well she's fitting in.'

'I think I caught sight of her yesterday. She wasn't anywhere to be seen today, but I remember thinking how pretty she was, and that I was relieved she wasn't our maid. Not with Stephen at home. Not that he'd look at her, of course. He's been well cautioned about what's permissible and what isn't.'

Frederick nodded. 'Quite so. I know it's early days, but our *ayah* clearly doesn't like Asha. And you know our *ayah* —if she takes against the girl, that could lead to friction. I think that's why Constance has been finding things for Asha to do in the servants' compound, but there's a limit to what she'll be able to come up with.'

Wilfred shrugged. 'As you say, it's for Constance to deal

with. And like Gladys, she runs a household with supreme efficiency, so she'll know exactly how to handle it.' He paused. 'So, what's the real reason for your disquiet, Freddie?' he asked quietly. 'I've known you long enough to know that you haven't yet told me.'

'You're right, of course.' Frederick put down his glass, sat back and fixed his gaze on the distant peaks. 'If you must know,' he said after a moment or two. 'I think I'm being followed.'

'Being followed!' Wilfred sat upright in surprise. A few drops of his gimlet splashed over the rim of his glass, and he put it back down on the table.

'Surely you're mistaken. Why would anyone follow you?' He frowned. 'Is it that you saw someone on the Mall yesterday and also in the Club today—someone you wouldn't have expected to see?'

Frederick gave a dry laugh. 'That would almost be a relief as then I'd know what the person looked like. Unfortunately, it's just a feeling. But I'm convinced I'm being watched.'

'When you're out, d'you mean? Or when you're inside? At the Secretariat this morning, did you feel it then? Now that you're home, d'you feel it here?'

'I can't be that specific,' Frederick said. 'I'd like to, but I can't.'

Wilfred stared hard at him for a moment. 'You can't, or you won't?' His voice softened. 'Come on, Freddie,' he coaxed. 'This is me, your oldest friend. There's nothing you can't tell me.'

Frederick gave a heartfelt sigh, and shook his head. 'You're right, of course, Wilfred. I don't know why I didn't tell you everything from the start.'

And he told Wilfred what had happened from the

moment that Sunil had handed him the small white envelope containing the card, to the moment he'd burnt the
card.

'And there's something else,' he added. 'When we got
back from the Club today, I was the first to approach the
house. It's residual nervousness, I suppose—I'm nervous
that I might find something else on the mat. But I wanted to
get there before the others, and I did.'

He stopped.

'Well?' Wilfred prompted.

Frederick gave a heartfelt sigh. 'There was a horseshoe
hanging from the door knocker. It was hanging upside
down, Wilfred, and the tip of each end had been painted
bright red.'

'I see. And anyone superstitious would believe that that's
unlucky,' Wilfred said slowly. 'That good luck will drain out
of your home.'

Frederick nodded. 'Exactly. Fortunately, the others didn't
see it. I don't want them to be alarmed. But added to the
incidents with the card, it's made me quite nervous about
what else could happen.'

'That's certainly understandable.'

'And I'm worried about being followed,' Frederick
added. 'I must be or I'd never have seen that card again. And
the person wouldn't have known we were out today.' He
looked at Wilfred. 'Well, now you know absolutely everything,' he said wanly. 'Hopefully, that's the end of it.'

'One would think so,' Wilfred said. He sat back, looking
thoughtful. 'But they're all fairly harmless things, aren't
they? I mean, a picture on a card, and an upside down
horseshoe.' He waved dismissively. 'And I very much doubt
you were being followed.'

Frederick frowned. 'How d'you work that out?'

'First of all, it would be virtually impossible for someone to watch the house all day and all evening, ready to follow you when you left. And secondly, they'd know that they risked being spotted if they attempted to follow your rickshaw. Either you'd see them or your *jampanis* would. And ours might, too.'

'Yes, that's right,' he said slowly. 'And as we've both had the same *jampanis* for the past few years, they'll have a degree of loyalty to us, and they'd tell us if they noticed anything amiss.'

'Just so. And when you think about it, all anyone needs to know is that you're back at Cedars,' Wilfred continued. 'We always leave our rickshaws at Scandal Point and stroll along the Mall before dinner. Everyone does. The Mall's like a club on the move.'

Frederick nodded. 'That's very true.'

'So if anyone was interested in you, they need only go to Scandal Point late in the afternoon and wait for you to turn up. We can assume that they did that, and that when they were there, they saw you throw away the card, and that will have given them the idea.'

'Of course!' Frederick exclaimed. 'Why didn't I think of that? Thanks, Wilfred. I feel much better already.'

'As for today, we usually lunch at the Club soon after our return, so it was almost a certainty that we'd be out,' Wilfred went on. 'They only had to wait for the servants to take their siesta, and then slip down the drive and place the horseshoe.'

'You're right again, old friend.'

'But as to who might do this, is there anyone at all you could have offended, either in Delhi or here?'

Frederick shook his head. 'I've racked my brains to think if I've wronged anyone, but I truly don't think I have. I don't have much contact with Indians, other than in the house, or in cafés and shops. And in the Secretariat, of course. Every year we seem to employ more Indians and Anglo-Indians than the year before. But I know what Indians are like about status, and I make a point of treating everyone equally, down to the lowliest messenger in the Secretariat.'

'So you don't think it's anyone you've worked with?'

'It can't be. But at the same time, it must be! Who else could it be? I must have criticised a report someone wrote, and they're bearing a grudge. Or failed to appoint a person to a position he thought he deserved. Who knows? I'm not aware of giving offence, but I must have done.'

'Well, whoever it is, you've destroyed the card, and it's in the past now.' He paused. 'All the same, I'd be somewhat cautious for a while.'

'Oh, I definitely will,' Frederick said, picking up his glass. 'I intend to be on the alert. And I'd be grateful if you kept your eyes open, too. Nothing too obvious. You know what I mean.'

'Of course I will. But I wonder if for the next month or so, it might not be an idea to enlist some extra help.'

Frederick paused, his glass mid-air. 'What d'you mean?'

'I was just thinking that Lilian's going to be doing some painting in and around Simla, and Daisy, too. It means that on occasions they're likely to be in isolated places with just their *ayahs*.'

Frederick looked at Wilfred in surprise. 'Well, yes, I suppose so.'

Wilfred gave him a half-smile. 'The girls were always able to twist their *ayah* around their little fingers, and I'm sure that's still true. The *ayahs* may no longer have the care of the girls, but they're still close to them, looking after their clothes as well as the clothes of their mothers.'

'So you're saying that if the girls asked the *ayahs* to go for a walk on their own for a while, the *ayahs* might obey them?' Frederick said thoughtfully. 'And that could put the girls at risk?'

'Absolutely. If by any chance your enemy's not yet finished, and intends ill will to you, and possibly your family, too, the girls would be an easy target. Even events like the dance at the Club next week could carry an element of risk. If that person were a young colonial officer, he'd probably be at the dance.'

Frederick put his hand to his head. 'God, that's a thought!' He stared in despair at Wilfred. 'I can see what you're saying, but what do I do?'

'Go to the police?' Wilfred suggested.

'Definitely not! I want to keep this between us, and it would certainly get out if the police were involved. Anyway, they'd be useless. These days, they're too busy keeping watch on those who are lower in the departmental hierarchy to be interested in ordinary detective work or protective duties.'

'What about Eric? You wanted to bring him and Lilian closer to each other, and that would push them together, so to speak. A man protecting a woman has a certain romance to it.'

Frederick shook his head vigorously. 'Absolutely not! Apart from the fact that I can't see him in such a role, gentle man that he is, I'd hate Cecil to know that there was any suggestion of a threat to the family. Even though we've done nothing wrong, it could taint us all.'

'Yes, I can see that could happen. Well, what about Jack Leighton, then? He seems a very capable young man.'

'That's true,' Frederick said slowly.

'Obviously, you wouldn't tell the girls why he kept

accompanying them as we wouldn't want to alarm them. Better they just look on him as a friend. As he's staying in the same guest house as Eric, it would be natural for him to be part of their group. You could have a word with him, see if he'll be their guard, in effect.'

'You don't think that someone as personable as young Leighton might overshadow Eric?' Frederick asked anxiously. 'You know how much I want a match between Eric and Lilian. I'd hate to see someone come between them.'

Wilfred raised his eyebrows. 'Didn't you see Lilian and Jack at lunch today? They clearly didn't take to each other. To say instant dislike isn't too strong. And I'm not surprised at Lilian's antipathy towards him. It rather looked as if he went out of his way to make her appear silly. Why Jack took the line he did, I don't know, but he did, and I don't think you need have any worries on that score.'

'Now that you mention it, I did think they seemed at odds with each other. I'll have a word with Jack tomorrow.' He smiled broadly at Wilfred. 'Thank you, my friend. You've gone a long way towards putting my mind at rest.'

12

That same afternoon

'WHAT's the matter with you, Daisy?' Lilian asked, getting up from her chair on the lower front verandah and going across to sit on the hammock sofa next to Daisy, who was swinging gently as she stared in the direction of the town.

She followed the line of Daisy's gaze. 'Are you hoping to see Eric? If so, you need not watch quite so intently—you'll hear his horse.'

Daisy turned away from the view and smoothed down the skirt of her dress. 'I'm not watching for him. Why would I? I expect he's still at the Club. They're bound to have had more than one game of billiards.'

'Or they could've returned home while we were having a siesta. Perhaps you should start looking up towards the guest house instead,' Lilian said in amusement.

'I'm not interested in what they're doing, so there's no

point in looking anywhere.' Daisy fixed her gaze firmly ahead.

Lilian put her foot on the deck of the verandah and stopped the hammock sofa from swaying. 'Did you enjoy the lunch today, Daisy?'

Daisy shrugged. 'It was all right, I suppose.'

Lilian raised her hands in feigned shock. 'Only all right? When you were sitting so close to Eric? Surely it was better than just all right?'

'But Eric didn't exactly pay me any attention, did he?' Daisy snapped, her blue eyes glistening with tears. 'I might just as well have not been there. He was clearly far more anxious to talk to you. It's you he's keen on, not me. And it's obvious you're interested in him. Anyone can see that.'

Her voice caught in a sob, and she turned back towards the road.

Lilian caught Daisy's hand. 'No, you're wrong, Daisy,' she said earnestly. 'That's what I wanted everyone to think. Every time Eric started to talk to you, I deliberately put on an interested face and jumped in. I told you I was going to do that. It's to satisfy Papa. But you're the one Eric wants. Not me.'

Daisy sniffed. 'Well, it didn't look that way today. And it didn't yesterday evening, either. I *do* understand what you're doing, Lilian, but you didn't give me any time at all to speak to him. Not once.'

Lilian giggled. 'You would have relaxed if you'd seen his eyes every time politeness forced him to look my way.'

Daisy's brow wrinkled. 'What d'you mean?'

Lilian giggled again. 'He looked absolutely terrified, poor thing. He was clearly stricken at having to respond to me. And even more so at the thought that I might genuinely be keen on him. He was all but physically cowering.'

Daisy's lower lip trembled. 'D'you mean it? You're not just saying it?'

'Of course, I'm not. He's completely wrong for me. I know it, and so does he. But Papa would like nothing more than for me to marry Eric, and I'm trying to take advantage of that so as to help you. I told you I was going to do that.'

'That's very kind of you, Lilian, it really is. I suppose I got upset because it's one thing to know something's going to happen, and another to see it happen. And you were so convincing.' Another sob escaped her.

'It meant nothing, Daisy, believe me.'

Daisy frowned in puzzlement. 'But what about you, Lilian? You want to meet someone, don't you? If you're forever talking to Eric when we're in company, you won't find anyone for yourself?'

Lilian waved her hand dismissively. 'Don't worry about me. There'll be plenty of occasions when I won't need to appear dewy-eyed over Eric—such as at parties and dances. In places like that, we'll be lost in the crowd. I've no intention of becoming an elderly spinster, and as there's no better place than Simla in which to find a husband, I won't be wasting the summer.'

'I know what they say about Simla,' Daisy began hesitantly. 'But between the bored women whose husbands stayed on the plains, and the husband-hunting fishing fleet girls, there's a lot of competition. Should you be wasting your time on me?'

Lilian stared at Daisy with mock outrage. 'Daisy Chatsworth! Are you saying that an eligible bachelor would prefer those women to me?'

'Of course not.' Daisy hesitated, and then giggled. 'Well, yes, I am, in a way. It depends on what the bachelors want.'

'No man who'd go after a married woman would be of

interest to me. As for the fishing fleet girls...' She shrugged.

Daisy stared at Lilian doubtfully. 'I'm still worried that you might be deterring the right sort of person from pursuing you.'

Lilian put her foot on the ground and pushed, making the hammock sofa start swaying gently again. 'Anyone who gives up that easily isn't worth having.'

'Well, I hope you find the perfect man. It would be ideal if we were both in love at the same time.'

Lilian beamed at her. 'Yes, it would. And if I *did* meet someone special, we'd rethink the Eric thing. But maybe it won't be necessary by then. You and he might already have come to an understanding.'

'You know who might be just the person for you,' Daisy said, reaching behind her to tighten the blue ribbon that held her hair back from her face.

Lilian stopped the hammock from moving. 'Who?' she asked. 'I haven't yet seen anyone remotely possible. Who've I missed? Oh, no, you aren't going to say Stephen, are you?' She threw back her head and laughed.

'No way! I can't imagine anyone falling in love with my brother, least of all you. No, I was thinking of someone else.'

'Well then? Don't keep me in suspense.'

'Jack Leighton. The man at lunch today. The one who's staying at Rose Bank Guest House, where Eric's lodging.'

'Never!' Lilian exclaimed vehemently.

'He's extremely good-looking in a rugged sort of way,' Daisy murmured, glancing slyly at her. 'And he's got amazing blue eyes.'

'That may be, but he's also a pig. He went out of his way to make me look stupid, and I'll never forgive him for that. I'd rather be that elderly spinster than marry someone like him.'

'Then we'll just have to see who else there is. We'll both keep our eyes open, starting with church tomorrow. And there's the dance in the Hut next week. You might meet someone then.'

Lilian wrinkled her nose in disgust. 'I'd forgotten it was Sunday tomorrow. I hope the vicar's sermons aren't as tedious as the ones we had to endure at school. Aha! Talking of men, there's Stephen!' She jumped up, went to the balustrade, leaned over and waved at Stephen, who was walking down the drive.

'Are you coming to see Daisy and me, Stephen?' she called to him. 'Or are you looking for your father?'

Seeing her, he smiled broadly and came across the small lawn.

'Tempting though the idea of joining your coven is,' he called up to them, 'and discussing with you the best ribbons to encircle a hat, and the most suitable frock to wear for the Viceregal Ball, and who looked truly ludicrous at the Club today, I think I'll restrain myself and find Father.'

'You don't know what you're missing, Stephen,' Lilian said laughing.

He tapped himself on the head. 'Silly me. I was forgetting what you said at lunch today. Such trivia belongs to the old Lilian, and has no place in the mind of the new one. The new Lilian's more concerned with matters pertaining to politics and government than with fripperies such as clothes.'

Daisy snorted. Lilian glared at her.

'No doubt, you'll have been discussing the Report of the Indian States Enquiry,' Stephen continued breezily. 'But as I'm not yet *au fait* with its finer points, I shall leave you to your discussion of the financial implications it raises, and make do with a less profound conversation with Father.'

Lilian made as if to throw a cushion down at him.

Jumping lightly to one side, he gave them a cheery wave and headed for the front door.

Lilian sat back and glared up the road in the direction of Rose Bank Guest House.

'When I called that man a pig, I was being too kind,' she said bitterly.

FREDERICK SWIRLED the brandy in his snifter, took a sip and returned the glass to the small oak table next to the upholstered armchair.

'It was very kind of Vera to offer me some refreshment,' he remarked to Jack, who was sitting in the armchair opposite him.

Jack smiled. 'Eric and I are very lucky to be lodged in such a pleasant house, and with such a kind landlady.'

Frederick nodded. 'Indeed, you are.' He picked up his glass again. 'I hope you don't mind me dropping in on you like this.'

'Not at all, sir. It's a pleasure. Eric will be sorry to have missed you. He's with his parents, I believe.' He paused. 'But I suspect you're not here to exchange pleasantries,' he added with a wry smile, 'delightful though that would be. Is there anything I can help with? Or have I missed a departmental task I should have done?'

'Not at all, dear boy,' Frederick said quickly. 'I'm sure you'll be an asset to Revenue.' He coughed, and looked around the room. His gaze lingered a moment on the painting of Simla that hung above the cabinet, and then he looked back at Jack.

'I've always enjoyed my summers in Simla. This year, however, summer seems to have got off to a bad start.' He shifted awkwardly. 'Perhaps, bad start is the wrong way to express it. But the first few days haven't been as easy as they usually are. And that's a matter of concern. Well, not concern, as such, but I do feel a degree of anxiety.'

Jack leaned forward. 'Something's clearly worrying you, sir, if you don't mind me saying so. If you've thought of a way in which I could help with whatever it is, and that's why you're here, you only have to say the word.'

'That's very kind of you, Jack. Yes, enlisting your help *is* why I'm here. It's a somewhat delicate matter.' He coughed again. 'But I'd better start at the beginning.'

And he began to tell Jack what had happened since the moment that Sunil had handed him the small white envelope.

When he reached the point in his story where the card, which had been unfolded and pressed flat, appeared again on the mat the following morning, Jack gave a sudden exclamation, and sat up sharply.

Frederick stopped in the middle of the sentence, and stared at him in surprise.

'I think I may have seen the man who sent you the card!' Jack exclaimed.

And he told Frederick what he'd seen the night before on the Mall.

'And you don't know if he was an Indian or British?' Frederick asked.

Jack shook his head. 'I wish I did, but I couldn't see his face. The most I can tell you is that he was slender in build and had dark hair. But please finish the story.'

'There's not much more to tell. I burnt the card and as far as I'm concerned, that's the end of it. I don't expect there to be anything on the mat tomorrow morning.'

'But you're still worried, I take it?'

Frederick nodded. 'It's Lilian. And Daisy, too, of course. Lilian's going to be painting places of interest in and around the town. And Daisy will be with her. Wilfred felt that I shouldn't assume that the matter was closed, and he suggested I ask for your help.'

'If there's anything I can do, just tell me,' Jack said.

'When they're outside the town, there'll be few people around, if any. And if there's more behind this sending of cards than I realise, and it isn't over yet, they could be at risk.'

Jack nodded. 'I can see how that would be a concern.'

'The girls will have only their *ayahs* with them. That's fine for the town, but not for isolated areas. I'd be less worried if Constance went with them, rather than an *ayah*, but I'd have to tell her why I wanted her to do so, and I don't want to alarm her. Also, she has a busy life, running the house and her charity groups, and I'd rather not give her anything else to do.'

'I understand.'

'You're only a few years older than Lilian and Daisy, and you're a friend of Eric's. I was wondering if you'd make an effort to get to know them, and perhaps go on the occasional painting expedition with them. Perhaps you could come upon them unexpectedly when they're outside Simla. They mustn't know you're there to protect them, though. It would just be till we were sure that no harm was intended to the girls.'

Jack thought for a moment. 'How would I know where they were going, and when?' he asked at last.

'That's easy. I'd ask Lilian, and then I'd let you know.'

'One other question. As you know, I was recently promoted, and I'd like to continue on an upward trajectory. However, if I take time out in the day to indulge in what my colleagues could feel was frivolity, I can see a demotion in the future, rather than any further promotion.'

'That's a fair point, Jack. And since I'm effectively your boss, I'll give you a task that will act as a cover. Perhaps something relating to the forests or agriculture. After all, Revenue and Agriculture used to be one large department, and even though they're now separate, there are overlaps. I'm sure I can come up with something to justify you being away from the Secretariat fairly frequently. Your career won't suffer, I can assure you.'

'Then I've only one other concern. Your daughter took an immediate dislike to me,' he said drily, 'and I think it very likely that she'll refuse to have me anywhere near her.'

Frederick smiled. 'You strike me as a man who has reserves of charm on which he could call. I'm sure that with a little effort, you could undo the unfavourable impression you made on her.'

Jack nodded. 'I'll do my best, sir.'

'I'm not talking about encouraging Lilian to feel a romantic interest in you,' Frederick added quickly. 'Most definitely not. She and Eric Stanford seem to have a rapport. That could result in a most suitable marriage, and I wouldn't want anything to unsettle her. If you get my drift.'

'I do, sir. You can be sure that I'd never entertain romantic thoughts about your daughter. I prefer women who are more docile, if you don't mind me saying so.'

'Not at all, dear boy. That's understandable. Lilian's a good girl, but a lively one.' He finished his brandy and stood up. 'I'm most grateful to you, Jack. You've taken a weight off my mind. Even though I doubt there's anything to worry about—it's probably just me being silly.'

13

_____

S*unday morning*

DAWN WAS CREEPING up from the horizon when Frederick slipped from his bed, threw a robe around his shoulders and made his way out of the bedroom and on to the wooden landing.

Walking as quietly as possible so as not to disturb Constance, Lilian or any of the servants, he went to the head of the staircase, and stood there.

Silence echoed around him.

He had to know. But at the same time, he dreaded knowing.

Was he about to find another small white envelope on the doormat?

Steeling himself to go down into the shadows below, he took a deep breath, and stepped on to the top step. And then on to the next. And the next.

He stopped a few steps from the bottom of the staircase. His heart racing, he squinted through the darkness to the mat.

But he couldn't see anything there. Nothing at all.

Not that there would be such an envelope, he scolded himself. Having burnt the card the previous day, it was out of the question that he'd see it again.

A sense of elation coursed through him. Of course, it wouldn't be there. And if it had been, he would have seen it by now.

He stopped himself short.

It was possible that there *was* an envelope there, but one that was different in colour—one that was closer in colour to the doormat.

He went down one more step, stopped, and peered again into the gloom. No, there really wasn't anything there.

Straightening up, he stepped off the bottom step and walked across to the mat.

There was nothing there.

A wave of relief engulfed him, momentarily weakening him. It made him aware how terrified he'd been.

Saying a silent prayer of thanks, he went quickly back up to his bed and minutes later, for the first time that night, he fell into a deep sleep.

THE LATE MORNING air was redolent with the heavy scent thrown out by the pine trees that grew beyond Christ Church, and was warmed by the heat from the sun that shone down on the clock in the centre of the creamy yellow bell tower.

The doors of the church swung open, and moments later, the congregation streamed through the arched portico that fronted the entrance and out on to The Ridge. Small groups gathered instantly and conversation filled the air.

'Thank goodness that's over. I thought we'd never get out —the sermon seemed endless,' Lilian said as she and Daisy stepped out into the bright light, with their parents just behind them. 'It's a relief to be out here and able to chat to people again. Stephen had the right idea, pleading pressure of work as a reason not to come. I bet his work is all about improving his billiards game.'

Daisy giggled. 'I think it is.'

'We'll be with you in a moment,' she heard her mother call.

She looked round and acknowledged that she'd heard her mother.

Both sets of parents were standing in a group with Cecil Stanford, his wife and Eric, and she turned quickly back to Daisy.

'Come on, Daisy. Let's go and sit by the railings,' she said, and she walked quickly towards the protective railings around The Ridge.

Daisy hesitated. moment, and then went after her.

'We need to work out what we're doing next week,' Lilian said as they reached the wooden railings and sat down on the cast-iron bench that faced the valley. 'What paintings we're doing, I mean. While they're busy talking, let's decide.'

'We could've discussed it later,' Daisy said sharply, and she glanced wistfully over her shoulder at Eric. 'If we'd stayed with our parents, I might have been able to talk to Eric.'

'Oh, Daisy, I'm so sorry,' Lilian said, and she hugged her. 'I didn't think. Don't look so upset. I bet he comes over to us in a minute.'

'Well, if he does, make sure you give me a chance to speak to him, won't you?'

Lilian glanced quickly at Daisy's profile, and saw that her lower lip was trembling.

'Of course, I will. I promise,' she said, and she hugged Daisy again. 'Now tell me where you'd like us to go this week.'

'Good morning, girls.'

At the sound of Vera Gillespie's voice behind them, both girls stood up and turned to face her.

'Hello, Mrs Gillespie,' Lilian said, struggling to swallow her irritation. 'We were too far away from you in church to say hello.'

Vera smiled. 'I was about to say the same thing. I've been trying to work out how long it is since I last saw you, but I've had to give up. It was certainly a number of years ago. And if you'll forgive me for making a personal comment, you've both grown into lovely girls.'

Lilian laughed. 'You can make as many personal comments as you like, providing they're all as kind.'

'It's a pleasure to see you again, Mrs Gillespie,' Daisy said. 'We were so sorry to hear about Mr Gillespie. You must miss him terribly.'

'Even though it's ages since we saw him, we still remember him as the kindest of men,' Lilian added. 'Would you care to sit with us?' she asked, indicating the bench. 'We were admiring the view.'

'Thank you, both of you,' Vera said, sitting down.

The two girls sat again.

'You're very kind,' Vera continued. 'Yes, I do miss Harold. He was a very special person, and that's why I can't bring myself to leave the town where we spent so many happy years. You'll know, I'm sure, that I've turned my home into a guest house.'

Lilian nodded. 'We *did* hear that. Mr Stanford and Mr Leighton told us they were staying with you.'

Vera nodded. 'That's right. I couldn't be luckier with my first guests. They're both delightful men.'

Daisy gave Lilian a slight smile.

'Your parents have very kindly invited me to join you for lunch today,' Vera went on. 'Since both of my guests will also be at the Club, and don't need me to provide a lunch, I was delighted to accept. There's something I wanted to tell your parents, and I'll do so later, but when I saw you there, I thought I might as well tell you, too.'

'How intriguing,' Lilian said with a smile.

'But firstly, I'd like you to know that if you're ever in need of a chaperone, and none of your usual chaperones is available, I'd be happy to accompany you.'

Daisy beamed at Vera. 'That's really kind of you, Mrs Gillespie. Thank you.'

'Not at all. You'd be doing me a favour. There's a certain monotony to my life these days, and a change of scene would occasionally be welcome. I should not, however, expect to sit with you on every occasion. I'd be at a table nearby, or I might visit a shop. I'm sure you'll have private things to talk about that don't belong in a stranger's ears.'

'You're not a stranger, Mrs Gillespie,' Lilian said, 'you're a friend of the family. But we appreciate your offer, don't we, Daisy? It's very kind of you.'

Daisy nodded. 'We certainly do.'

The two girls smiled at each other, and then at Vera.

'Good. That's decided then,' Vera said briskly. 'Now, how are we doing for time?'

As she glanced round to look up at the clock, she saw that Frederick and Wilfred were walking towards their *jampanis*, leaving Constance, Gladys and Eric still in conversation.

'Oh, I wonder,' she said suddenly, and her hand flew to her mouth. 'Yes, perhaps I shouldn't. If you'll excuse me, girls, I think I'll have a quick word with your fathers.'

Clutching her bag, she jumped up and went hastily after Frederick and Wilfred.

'That was funny,' Lilian said, frowning. 'When she offered to be our chaperone, she began by saying firstly. I wonder what secondly would have been. And what she decided she shouldn't say. I'll ask Papa. And you must ask Uncle Wilfred.'

VERA CAUGHT up with Frederick and Wilfred just before they reached the rickshaws. Hearing footsteps behind them, they'd turned, seen her, and waited.

'I'm sorry to rush up to you thus,' she said, breathlessly. 'But just as I was about to tell the girls, I had second thoughts. It occurred to me that you might prefer that they and your wives don't know about this in case it alarms them. But it's something I think you both should know.'

Feeling a leaden premonition that he wasn't going to like what Vera was about to say, Frederick shot an anxious glance at Wilfred.

'What's this something?' Wilfred asked with a smile.

'It's just that I've seen a man—at least, I think it was a man, but it's hard to be sure—near your houses on a couple of occasions since you took up residence. Because of the view it affords, I tend to leave the upper back balcony for my guests, and I sit on the front balcony for a short time before going to bed. That's how I saw him.'

'Indeed, it's a very pleasant place to sit,' Frederick said.

Vera nodded. 'Yes, it is. Anyway, I couldn't see him clearly as he kept to the shadows on both occasions, and he didn't come up as far as Rose Bank. He stayed near your houses—especially yours, Frederick.'

A chill crept through Frederick.

'I didn't think anything of it the first time I saw him,' she went on. 'After all, it's not unusual for someone to get lost. But the second time was a different matter. I'm sure it was the same person. And again, he seemed to be trying to avoid being seen. I called Jagat and asked him to investigate. But by then, the man, if it was a man, had disappeared.'

Frederick frowned. 'I can't imagine why anyone would hang around like that,' he said. 'Unless, of course, he was planning to steal from us. But as the servants are always in the house, that doesn't sound very likely.'

'Could you tell if it was an Indian?' Wilfred asked.

Frederick looked at him approvingly. 'Good question, Wilfred.'

Vera shook her head. 'I'm afraid not. I'm not even completely certain it was a man.'

'Perhaps it's a suitor for one of the servants,' Wilfred suggested. 'For your new housemaid, perhaps, Frederick. She's very pretty, and I'd be amazed if there wasn't someone in town who was keen on her. Asha's more likely to be the object of male admiration than either of our *ayahs*,' he added with a wry smile.

Frederick's smile was tinged with relief. 'You could be right, Wilfred. She grew up in Simla. Her mother lives in Lower Bazaar, I believe.'

'That sounds the most likely explanation,' Vera said. 'I was sure it was nothing, but I thought you ought to know what I'd seen.'

Frederick nodded. 'And you were right. We'll be a little more alert than usual, just in case. And the servants must be reminded that such friendships are inappropriate for anyone in service. I'll ask Sunil to have a word with them.'

'It might be an idea to let Asha go,' Wilfred suggested. 'Just to be on the safe side. After all, you said there'd been a degree of disharmony since she started. It would be easy enough to replace her.'

'That's true. It's certainly something to think about. I'll see what Constance says.'

'We gave up waiting for you to come back to us!' Gladys said coming up to them, with Constance and Eric at her side. 'It's time to go to the Club. Eric was telling me that he's arranged to meet Stephen and Mr Leighton there.'

'I think we're all ready, so let's go, then,' Frederick said briskly. 'Thank you, Vera. Vera was telling me something about Asha, Constance. Remind me to tell you later.'

14

A t the Club
   Later that day

As she glanced around the lunch table, Lilian inhaled deeply the peppery fragrance of the deep pink cosmos that grew in abundance around the Club. 'I love cosmos,' she said to no one in particular. 'If it grows in England, I never saw it. In my mind, it belongs to India.'

Jack leaned back in his seat and fixed his eyes on Lilian. 'I didn't realise that you were interested in flowers, too, Miss Hunt,' he remarked.

Lilian glared at him across the table. 'I'm not going to ask what you meant by "too". It's only too obvious, given the remarks you made last time I saw you. I'm afraid that you're most predictable, Mr Leighton.'

Inwardly kicking himself, Jack straightened up and assumed a contrite air. 'I'm sorry, Miss Hunt. I didn't mean to upset you. It was a genuine comment, with no underlying intention.'

'You didn't upset me, I assure you. It's far worse than that —you bored me.'

Her nose in the air, she glanced at Eric, who was sitting next to her. He was engaged in conversation with Daisy, so she turned to Stephen, who was on her right.

'How are you enjoying being back in Simla, Stephen?' she asked.

'Aha! Good choice!' Jack exclaimed, forgetting the need for contrition. 'The answer to such an original question is sure to alleviate the boredom into which I plunged you.'

Lilian threw him a look of intense dislike.

Jack laughed, and turned to Gladys, who was on his left. 'I must thank you for providing me with such an entertaining companion as Stephen for my first summer in Simla, Mrs Chatsworth,' he said. 'For a start, it's going to be a pleasure to play billiards with someone much better than I am. I love a challenge, and it'll be that.'

'He won't be too entertaining, I hope,' Gladys said with a smile, 'for the sake of both your careers. Did you hear that, Stephen?' she called to him.

'Indeed, I did, Mother,' he replied with feigned solemnity. 'With only Aunt Constance between us, and with your voice being artificially raised, it would have been difficult not to do so. I assure you that I'll do all I can to eliminate any elements of entertainment from everything we do.'

Gladys laughed. 'Perhaps you'd like to tell me something about what you did before you were sent to Delhi,' she said, turning back to Jack.

· · ·

'WHAT D'YOU like to do when you are not working, Mr Stanford?' Daisy asked Eric.

He gave her a shy smile. 'I'm reluctant to tell you, Miss Chatsworth, as I'm afraid you'll think me a dull sort of fellow.'

'I'm sure, I won't. Pease tell me,' she said in a cajoling voice.

He went pink. 'I go for a walk whenever I can. I love being out in the open air among the flowers and trees. I enjoy everything that's native to whatever area I'm in. But I think that's not a thing that would appeal to many ladies. I'm sure ladies would rather party or be with a group of people.'

'*I* wouldn't. I love the beauty around us. I just wish I knew more about the natural world. What's your favourite flower? In this area, I mean.'

Eric thought for a moment. 'I think I'd have to say the rhododendron. I know they're prolific in Simla, but this prevents people from really seeing them. It's a shame as they're truly a glorious flower. They are a highlight of the Himalayan spring. Our entry into Simla is always greeted with crimson and scarlet rhododendrons. Did you know that their colour depends upon the aspect and elevation?'

Daisy shook her head. 'No, I didn't.'

'In the cold, high altitude ravines that face the north, there are more deep crimson blooms than any other colour. And where it's sunny and dry, you'll find more light pink flowers.'

'I didn't know that,' she said in wonder.

'It flowers twice,' he added, 'as those of us who've been in Simla before will know. It really is a lovely flower. As is the daisy,' he added quietly. 'That, too, is a beautiful flower, and one which blooms in the early spring and continues to bloom until autumn. Some people think it's a weed, but I think the daisy is quite lovely.'

For a long moment, they stared at each other, and neither said a word.

'You're very observant,' Daisy said, finally breaking the mood with an awkward laugh. Then she sat up. 'I've just had an idea,' she told him with a nervous smile, and she put her hand to her mouth. 'Don't hesitate to say no. But Lilian and I are going to be doing some small watercolours of places in and around Simla. Perhaps, you would like to come and see what we're doing at times.'

He went a deep shade of red. 'I certainly would.'

'And you might give me some advice,' she added. 'Lilian won't need any, but I'm useless at painting. I hope to improve over the summer, but with you so observant, you could point out what I've missed.' She bit her lip. 'It might be a little presumptuous of me to ask. If so, please be honest and say if you don't want to do this.'

'Oh, but I do,' he said fervently. 'Very much.'

She blushed. 'Then I'll see that you always know where we'll be.'

They beamed at each other.

'What are you two talking about?' Frederick called across the table, his smile not quite reaching his eyes.

'Nothing,' they chorused in unison.

Both laughed, and each turned away from the other.

What a lovely day it's been, Daisy thought to herself. She couldn't remember feeling happier.

The Club had never looked lovelier. The sun was bringing out the warmth of the solid stone walls, and enhancing the lush green carpet that lay beneath a sky that was a deeper blue than she'd ever seen.

The birds in the trees were singing. The flowers were a glorious profusion of every colour, their fragrance heavenly.

And Eric liked her.

He really liked her.

She was sure that she wasn't wrong. He said he would join her and Lilian whenever he could. He hadn't had to agree to that, but he clearly wanted to. And she was certain that she was the one he wanted to see, not Lilian.

Life couldn't be more perfect.

But it would be better if Uncle Frederick didn't know that.

From the expression on his face, despite his attempt not to show it, he wasn't best pleased by the fact that she and Eric were getting on so well together.

That must be because he wanted Lilian to marry Eric, she realised, and although there was no reason why he should mind terribly if that didn't happen, it would be sensible to remember what Lilian had said. She certainly didn't want him to insist on their mothers accompanying them, which Lilian had thought might happen, so she'd better placate him.

She smiled across the table. 'We were talking about flowers, Uncle Frederick,' she said. 'Mr Stanford knows so much about nature. It was most interesting.'

WHILE THE TWO families and Eric were strolling towards the exit at the end of lunch, Frederick managed to draw Jack slightly away from others.

Realising what Frederick was doing, Jack glanced at him and raised his eyebrows questioningly.

'Mrs Gillespie told me something that's slightly added to the concern I mentioned yesterday,' Frederick said quietly, and he told Jack about the person who had been seen near their houses late at night on a couple of recent occasions. 'It makes it all the more imperative that you keep an eye on the girls.'

'I'll do my best, sir,' Jack assured him.

'If you come to me as soon as you get to the Secretariat tomorrow morning, I'll assign you a task that will account for you regularly leaving the building. It'll be to do with the agricultural revenue. I'll make sure that everyone in the department knows you're working on something for me, so there's no question of anyone thinking you're shirking your duty.'

'Thank you, sir. That puts my mind at ease.'

Frederick coughed. 'It's also occurred to me that it might be prudent to encourage Miss Chatsworth to welcome your visits. Daisy's a very sweet girl so that shouldn't be too painful. Should Lilian take against you and forbid you to go anywhere near them—I'm not saying that she would, but knowing Lilian, anything's possible—it might be an idea to have Daisy in the frame of mind to argue for you to continue joining them whenever you can.'

'I understand, sir. I'll do that.'

'Good. Now all you've got to worry about is how to get my daughter to receive you in a civil manner. Note that I didn't say to receive you in a warm and friendly manner,' Frederick added with a dry smile. 'I wouldn't be as optimistic as that. But at least to speak to you without accompanying every icy comment with a glare. When you've done that, you'll be able to work on Daisy.'

'If I ever get married in the future,' Jack said as they neared the others who were waiting by the rickshaws, 'I think I'll insist on fathering only sons.'

. . .

As he'd got into the habit of doing, Frederick made sure that his rickshaw was the first to arrive back at Cedars after they'd lunched at the Club, and as had also become his habit, he got out of the rickshaw ahead of Constance, and was the first to approach the house.

Each time, he did so with a sense of trepidation lest there was some new cause for disquiet on the door.

As he approached the front door, he saw that he'd been worrying needlessly.

Maybe it really was finished, he thought. He certainly hoped it was. The constant worry was making him into someone he was not. And he didn't like that someone.

So Frederick Hunt now expected him to woo Daisy Chatsworth, Jack thought in anger, lying back on his bed and staring through his unshuttered windows as the deep crimson sunset yielded to the velvet blackness of night.

The faint sounds of music, laughter and conversation drifted up the steep hillside from the Lower Bazaar.

It was an absolute cheek!

Although Frederick Hunt hadn't said as much, that was obviously what he had meant. And the reason was apparent. Anyone at the lunch could have seen how much Daisy and Eric were enjoying talking to each other.

Frederick Hunt had certainly seen it. And it had angered him.

His demeanour whenever he'd looked at the two of them spoke volumes, as did his visible annoyance with Lilian, who was so busy ensuring that he, Jack, understood how much she disliked him, that she failed to make any effort to draw Eric's attention away from Daisy and direct it to herself.

As a result, he was supposed to switch Daisy's interest from Eric to him. Mr Hunt's meaning couldn't have been clearer.

But quite apart from the fact that Daisy's heart clearly belonged to Eric, and his to her, they were so completely right for each other that it was difficult to see how Cecil Stanford could possibly have thought that Eric was interested in Lilian.

He would have to go along with it, though, both for the sake of his career—instinct told him that Frederick Hunt would be a bad enemy to make—but more importantly, he would need to keep close to the two women if he was going to protect them from anyone who might intend to hurt them.

And much as he disliked the pushy Miss Hunt, he wouldn't wish harm to befall her.

15

M onday
The Lower Bazaar

TRAILED BY THEIR *AYAHS*, each in a colourful sari and white blouse, with bangles on their wrists and ankles, Lilian and Daisy left their rickshaws and ambled down the Mall, stopping every so often to look in the shop windows.

'Coming here this afternoon was inspired, Daisy. It was just what I needed. Papa's been in a horrible mood all weekend,' Lilian said as they stood outside a milliner's, studying the window display of jauntily angled berets interspersed with cloches made of straw or felt.

'I like that one,' she said, pointing to a straw cloche with a rolled brim. 'It would fit snugly round my face. You could get one, too, Daisy. We could each buy a different colour.'

'Are you going to buy it now?' Daisy asked.

Lilian shook her head. 'No, not today. If we leave it too

late to go to Peliti's, there won't be any cakes left. But I'll get it before Sunday.'

'Don't you want to wear it for the dance tomorrow?'

'Not really. I was thinking of for when we go to lunch with the Stanfords.'

'You're so lucky to be seeing Eric at the weekend. We haven't been invited. We're going to a friend of father's, which'll be extremely boring,' Daisy said mournfully as they continued down the Mall.

'You haven't warned me off Eric yet,' Lilian said teasingly. 'Is that because you've finally accepted that he's no interest at all in me, and never will have?'

Daisy laughed. 'That's right.'

Lilian stopped walking. 'Don't tell me you and Eric have come to an understanding!' she said in excitement.

'Of course we haven't. He'd speak to Papa first if he wanted anything like that, and he hasn't.'

'I'm not so sure. People are doing things in a different order these days. They decide to get engaged, and then the man asks the father for permission to marry his daughter. Asking for the father's consent is becoming little more than a formality.'

'Not for someone like Eric.'

'You know him better than I,' Lilian said, and they resumed walking. 'Has he mentioned the future?'

'Not as such,' Daisy said. 'But I'm sure he likes me, and I feel the same about him.'

'Well, you must be sure to warn me before your engagement's announced,' Lilian said. 'I'll beg Mrs Gillespie to let me move into the guest house. Father will be unbearable. He'll say it was my fault for being too reticent.'

Daisy laughed. 'No one could ever describe you as reticent, Lilian.' She paused, and again stopped walking.

'Assuming we *do* get engaged—and I don't want to take that for granted—I'm worried what Eric's father will say. He's obviously keen on Eric marrying you as he clearly likes your father and thinks very highly of him.'

Lilian shrugged. 'I suppose he must do, but I'm sure he likes Uncle Wilfred, too.'

'I wouldn't know. I seldom see him with Papa so I can't judge. And he's only spoken to me once. I was so nervous when he addressed me that I couldn't think what to say to him. Since then, I've caught him staring at me a few times, but not in a friendly way.'

Lilian gave an awkward laugh. 'How could he not like Uncle Wilfred? It's just that Papa's worked on several projects for him so he knows him better. When he gets to know you, he'll see you for the lovely person you are, and he'll be thrilled that you're marrying Eric.'

Daisy went pink. 'You don't have to say that,' she said in embarrassment.

'I know I don't. I'm saying it because it's what I think. You're a much nicer person than I am.'

Daisy put her finger to her chin, and pretended to think. 'Now who's the person who's jeopardising her chances of meeting her ideal man because she's trying to help me? I'm so lucky that you're my friend, Lilian.'

'We both feel the same about our friendship, then,' Lilian said with a warm smile. She tucked her arm in Daisy's. 'Come on. We'll go just beyond the fork in the road as that's where most of the shops we like come to an end. Perhaps we'll look at the first few Indian shops beyond that, and then we'll go back to the rickshaw and go to Peliti's.'

As she finished speaking, an Indian came up the hill and passed them by. Lilian dropped her arm and looked back at him.

'What's the matter?' Daisy asked.

'Nothing,' Lilian said, turning back to her. 'It's just he looks a bit familiar.' She shrugged. 'I've probably seen him in town before or he might be one of the waiters at the Club.'

They reached the fork in the road, the swell of noise growing louder with every step that they took, and paused.

The dry smell of sawdust and pinewood drifted up from the lane that ran down the steep slope to Lakkar Bazaar.

And a spicy, peppery smell, mingled with incense, wafted up the other lane, which wound down through the Lower Bazaar, vibrant with colour and crowded with people walking between the flimsy, open-fronted Indian stalls.

'The smell's making me quite hungry,' Lilian murmured as they started to amble down the narrow lane towards Lower Bazaar, dodging the children who ran circles around them, and trailing behind women in brightly coloured saris and men in white turbans and shirts.

On either side of them, vendors were shouting their wares from stalls displaying grain, fruit and vegetables in colourful round shallow baskets, and stalls where brass and gleaming tin-ware hung from the wooden framework, reflecting the rays of the afternoon sun.

And from stalls that sparkled with cheap jewellery, trinkets and delicate glass bangles, some heaped on the table in front of the stall, others hanging from metal structures in a glittering array.

They paused in front of a textile stall that was exploding with colour from the bales of cloth, some plain, some printed, that were piled high in an ascending mass of pink, scarlet, emerald and cerise.

And then they moved on, glancing on either side as they

passed stalls selling medicines, toys, and everything needed for the home.

Skeletal pariah dogs ran in and out of the open door-ways, defying the vendors, who repeatedly pushed them away, and ignoring the angry kicks from people streaming along the alley.

The monkeys, too, were an irritant as they snatched at grain that had been piled in mounds on tables in front of the stalls, and sprang with it on to the corrugated tin roofs. Some sat there in companionable family groups, the mothers crooning to their babies, while others searched their neighbour for fleas, lice or parasites.

Above the noise that rose from the cramped narrow lanes could be heard the shrill whistling of the kite-hawks as they wheeled above the bazaar.

'I really am hungry,' Lilian said as they neared a stall half-hidden by a cloud of steam, and a strong smell of curry hit them. 'Shall we go to Peliti's now?'

Daisy agreed and they turned and went back up the steep hill.

When they reached the fork, they paused to get their breath. Daisy stood staring down the lane to Lakkar Bazaar, where carvers, joiners, repairers and furniture-makers plied their trade.

'We must go there some time,' she called over her shoulder to Lilian. 'Just to have a look. From what I recall, lots of the shops had wonderful carvings on the doors and window frames, and also on the eaves and lintels. I'm sure it's somewhere that Eric would enjoy.'

'I expect he would,' Lilian replied.

'It's like Simla's made up of three worlds,' Daisy added. 'There's the world of wood down in Lakkar Bazaar, the frantic bustle of the Lower Bazaar, and our world, which although very social, is more stately, I suppose you'd say.'

Turning back to the place where the road divided, her gaze fell upon an emaciated beggar who was sitting cross-legged at the corner of the fork.

In front of him he had a wicker tray displaying nuts, chapatis, sweetmeats, oranges and bananas. Black flies hovered above the sweetmeats, buzzing noisily.

She shuddered. 'Let's go now, Lilian,' she said, staring at the beggar in a mixture of pity and disgust. As she started to walk back up to Scandal Point, she glanced back at Lilian.

And stopped.

Lilian was standing a little way down the road leading to Lower Bazaar, staring towards an open-fronted shop, her back to a row of stalls selling clothes.

Curious as to what Lilian was looking at, Daisy went back to her.

'Look, Daisy,' Lilian said. She moved closer to the wooden-framed shop, and beckoned to Daisy to follow. 'They're selling paintings. Let's see what they've got. Not to buy. Just for fun.'

Daisy wrinkled her nose. 'They're not my taste at all. They're much too garish.'

'Exactly,' Lilian said, staring at the paintings.

Varying in size, and mainly in oil, they had been set out on a table that ran along the back of the stall. Some stood on the ground, propped up in front of the table in piles that were several paintings deep, while others were fixed to the back wall.

Most of them depicted places in Simla itself, but there were also a number of scenes in the forests and mountains around the town, scenes that had been the subject in many of the paintings they'd seen over the years.

Panoramic views of the Himalayas at sunrise predominated.

'It's the same sort of thing as we're going to do,' she told Daisy. 'But our paintings will be different. Those are much too bright and artificial.'

'I agree,' said Daisy. 'I much prefer watercolours. I can't see anyone who's not Indian buying anything as lurid as those.'

Lilian turned to Daisy. 'You're right, Daisy; they wouldn't if they had a choice. In fact, I haven't seen anywhere that sells the sort of paintings that the British would choose to hang in their Simla homes, and there's certainly nothing they'd want to take back to Delhi or England.'

Daisy nodded in agreement. 'I haven't either,' she said.

'But we know they like to have pictures of Simla on their walls because we've seen them. And that's given me an idea,' Lilian went on in mounting excitement. 'We'll be doing more watercolours than we'll need for the school, ourselves and our families. Why don't I give some of our spare paintings to the stallholder, and he can sell them?'

Daisy paled. 'You can't. Our parents would be furious. And I'm sure Eric wouldn't be pleased. It'd be like going into trade.'

Lilian laughed dismissively. 'I'm not talking about them selling the paintings for me. They could sell them and keep the money. It'd be helping the stallholder, and also helping the British who'd be able to have the sort of pictures on their walls that they'd enjoy looking at. What do you think?'

'I can't imagine anyone wanting anything of mine, but they'd love yours. I think it'd be a very kind thing to do.'

'I prefer to have a reason for painting, and I'm not really keen on joining Simla Fine Arts and exhibiting with them. That's taking it all too seriously. Sending some watercolours to the school gives me one reason, and helping the stall-holder another.' She looked at Daisy in glee. 'Let's go in and see if the owner likes the idea.'

Lilian turned and gestured to their *ayahs* to remain where they were, and she and Daisy took a couple of steps forward.

But hearing the sound of an approaching horse, they stopped abruptly and glanced up at the rider.

'Stephen!' Lilian exclaimed. 'What're you doing here?' she asked as he reined in his horse and dismounted.

'I could say the same thing to you,' he said. 'Daisy said you were going to Peliti's.'

'We are,' Daisy said. 'But we wanted a short walk first. How did you know we were here?'

'Seeing the livery of Lilian's *jampanis* at Scandal Point was a weeny clue, and I thought I'd come and say hello. But if I'd been a moment later, I think I might have missed you. It looked as if you were about to hide among the paintings. Oh, naughty, naughty,' he said, his eyes opening wide in mock horror.

'I've just realised, you're hoping to pass some of them off as your own in order to have more time to play. Tut, tut.' And he waggled his finger at them.

Lilian giggled. 'Why didn't we think of that? But no, you've got it completely the wrong way round.' And she explained what they were planning to do.

'What do you think?' she finished by asking.

'I can't see anything wrong with your idea, provided you approach everything in the correct way,' he said. 'You'd be helping someone who could use some help, I'm sure, and also helping the British to avoid sore eyes.'

Lilian and Daisy exchanged glances.

'In that case, will you come in with us, Stephen?' Lilian

asked. 'You know what Indians are like. They take men more seriously than women. If you were with us, we'd be less likely to be dismissed as silly little girls.'

He nodded. 'All right. But that's because I should. You shouldn't go in there on your own. Your *ayahs* should be with you. Instead, they're nowhere to be seen. You obviously made it clear to them that you didn't want them with you, but they should have ignored your wishes and stayed at your side.'

Daisy went red and glanced back at the *ayahs* who were standing between the railings of clothes on the other side of the lane.

'They're only over there, so it's not as if we're on our own.'

'But effectively you are, and anyone who saw you would think you unchaperoned. Apart from your reputation, it's a matter of safety. You shouldn't be going into any shop on your own. Suppose the owner's a man. It would be most unsuitable for two young women to be in there alone with him. It could be dangerous for you, but also you put him into a risky position.'

'I hear what you're saying,' Lilian said slowly. 'You're right, of course, Stephen. I'm afraid I got carried away.'

Stephen smiled warmly at her. 'There's no harm done. And I'm sure your parents would approve of the idea. I suggest we talk to the stallholder now, and if he agrees, we can ask one of the servants, Sunil perhaps, to bring them your surplus paintings. That way, there's no need for you to come here in person.'

Lilian clapped her hands in delight. 'Thank you, Stephen. That's a brilliant idea. I henceforth take back every horrible thing I've said and thought about you in the past.'

All three laughed, and they went beneath the wooden supporting frame and into the shop.

There was a hand bell on the corner of the table at the back of the shop. Stephen picked it up and rang it. Instantly, a beaded curtain at the back of the shop was pulled aside, and a middle-aged woman in a multi-coloured sari came into the shop.

She put her palms together in a *namaste*, and bowed at the small group.

Stephen asked if she spoke English. She nodded, but looked hesitant.

Undaunted, he started to explain Lilian's idea.

The woman put up her hand to stop him. Her daughter spoke better English, she told him haltingly, and she moved back to the beaded curtain and shouted something into the living quarters.

A moment later, a young woman slipped between the vertical strips of coloured beads and entered the shop, her head bowed. As she stepped into the rays of light that streamed into the shop, she raised her eyes.

'Asha!' Lilian exclaimed. 'You're here!'

Stephen took an involuntary step forward. His back to Lilian and Daisy, his gaze on Asha, he caught his breath.

Beautiful dark brown eyes stared back at him from a truly lovely face, each feature of which had been drawn with the finest of pens.

His world stood still.

16

L ong after Lilian, Daisy and Stephen had left the art stall and gone in the direction of Scandal Point, Lilian and Daisy on foot, their *ayahs* behind them, and Stephen on his horse, Kamesh remained in the shadows.

Deep in thought, his gaze was focused on the open-fronted art stall that was now empty of people.

So the British women hadn't been told about the card he'd sent to Miss Hunt's father, or about the horseshoe fore-telling bad luck, he mused.

Had they known that someone wished ill to the head of the family, they would not have moved so freely along the road without male protection, nor been so unconcerned about who might be watching them.

Which was lucky for him.

It had been most fortunate that when he'd been returning home after buying some food in Lower Bazaar, he'd passed the Hunt woman and her friend. They'd been walking down the Mall, with their servants some distance behind them.

As he was eager to learn all he could about the family, this was an opportunity not to be lost, and he'd immediately turned back and started to follow them, keeping well behind the servants, who were engrossed in talking to each other.

After a short stroll in the bazaar, the women had turned and started to go back towards the fork. He'd swiftly slipped into one of the shops, and waited for them to pass him by.

Then he'd left the shop and followed them.

To his surprise, they had stood talking in front of the art stall.

Hugging the shop fronts, he had managed to find a place of concealment between two lines of colourful saris hanging from the railings in front of a stall opposite the art shop, and he'd strained to hear what they were saying.

Luckily, he'd been close enough to catch one or two of their words, and he'd heard them mention Peliti's.

He knew that Peliti's café next to the Combermere Bridge was a favourite with the British, who regularly gathered on the terrace overlooking the valley, so that was obviously where they'd be going next.

He had watched them in surprise. Earlier, they'd shown an interest in hats, but it was nothing compared with their excitement at the display of paintings in the art shop. They'd even gone closer to examine the pictures.

So they liked paintings, did they?

That was good to know.

Anything that with a little imagination could be used to unsettle Frederick Hunt and wipe the smug self-satisfaction from his face, was important knowledge, and he'd store it away until he could use it to his advantage.

Just as he was deciding that there was no point in staying for any longer, Stephen Chatsworth had ridden up, dismounted and joined his sister and the Hunt girl. He'd recognised him at once from seeing him in the Secretariat.

His curiosity renewed, he'd sunk further behind the clothing and watched as the three of them talked for a few minutes, and then went into the stall.

Strange, he'd thought. Indian paintings were generally not to the taste of the British.

And he'd moved cautiously to the adjacent stall and placed himself behind a row of white trousers, from which he had a clearer view into the art shop.

Moments later, he was greatly surprised to see an Indian girl, whose name he knew to be Asha, enter the shop from the family's living quarters at the back. He was so surprised that he actually exclaimed aloud.

Not so long ago, he'd seen the girl at the Hunts' house. She'd left their house by the back door, gone through the gate in the latticed fence and had walked the short distance along the ridge to the Hunts' servants' compound. So she must have worked for Frederick Hunt.

Yet now she was there, on the fringe of Lower Bazaar, apparently living with her family.

He frowned in puzzlement. It must mean that she was no longer working for the Hunts. But surely she wouldn't voluntarily have left the comfortable position she'd had in their house to work in an art stall on the edge of the bazaar!

Of course, Frederick Hunt could have given her permission to stay a night or so with her family, if this was indeed where her family lived, but that would be very unusual.

No, the most likely explanation for her being back with her family so soon after the Hunts had returned to Simla, was that she must no longer be employed by them.

Shaking his head in bewilderment, he glanced at Stephen Chatsworth, who had his back to him. He was clearly looking at Asha. And then he'd actually taken a step towards Asha, before stopping abruptly.

With Asha being very pretty, it wouldn't be surprising if Mr Chatsworth was attracted to her. Asha's mother—for the stall owner must surely be Asha's mother—seemed to think so, too. And she'd moved closer to her daughter, who was in conversation with the English women.

The conversation came to an end, and everyone smiled at everyone else. The British left the shop, and Asha and her mother returned to their living quarters.

He had remained in his hiding place until Mr Chatsworth had untethered his horse, mounted it and ridden back up the slope, and the girls and their servants had disappeared from sight.

He'd allow sufficient time for the women to look at one or two shops, he decided, before they got back to their rickshaws, and only then would he leave his hiding place.

How could he use Asha, he wondered as he waited there.

Now that he knew she was no longer in the servants' compound, breathing the fragrant air found high on the ridge, enjoying the benefits that came from working for the arrogant British, but was back in the bustling, cramped Lower Bazaar, among the unpleasant smells and ever-present clouds of flies, possibly made unwelcome by her family to whom she'd become another mouth to feed, what would she be thinking?

His every instinct screamed that she wouldn't be happy.

Everything about the way she dressed and carried herself, about the superior way in which she looked at people, suggested that she would have revelled in the status of being an employee in the household of one of the British rulers.

Being forced to return to her lowly background was bound to have made her angry.

And an angry, resentful woman would surely want her revenge on the person who'd caused her to lose face in the eyes of her community, who'd forced her to return to such humble surroundings.

Which brought him back to Frederick Hunt, and how he could use this new piece of knowledge.

While he was giving the matter some thought, he noticed a movement in the shop.

Asha had come back into the shop carrying a couple of paintings. She dumped the paintings on the long table, went out into the lane and stood staring up the slope towards Scandal Point.

Then her shoulders slumped and she went back inside and started arranging the paintings on the table.

Right, he thought, smoothing down his oiled dark hair. She was clearly interested in getting to know Stephen Chatsworth, and that could give him the opening he needed.

He'd begin by saying that he'd just seen Mr Stephen Chatsworth, whom he knew from the Secretariat, come out of the shop, and he'd ask Asha if she had any idea where he'd gone.

He could mention billiards or squash, as that would imply a closeness between them. Of course, a friendship between one of Heaven-born and a lowly messenger in the ICS would be completely impossible, but Asha was unlikely to realise that.

He was pretty sure that her desire to know more about Mr Chatsworth would cause her to loosen her tongue. If he was right, he should be able to establish fairly easily if she was in the frame of mind to want to punish Frederick Hunt for dismissing her, if that's what had happened.

Smiling in satisfaction, he smoothed down his hair again and went across to the art stall.

WHILE THEIR *AYAHS* chatted to each other at one of the round wrought-iron tables on the far side of the terrace, Lilian manoeuvred a piece of nurmahal cake on to her fork.

'Who'd have thought that Stephen would be so helpful?' she said, struggling to stop the three layers of the cake, held together by three different flavours of jam, from separating and sinking into the custard-filled well in the centre.

'I couldn't believe it when he volunteered to take our paintings to the art shop,' she went on, 'rather than let Sunil do it. He was right, of course—Sunil already has more than enough to do.'

Daisy nodded. 'I, too, thought it very kind of him, especially as he'll have to go out of his way to take them there. It shows he's got a good heart.'

'Which isn't a surprise—your parents are very kind people.'

'So are yours.'

Lilian laughed. 'You don't have to be polite. We both know what Papa is like.'

Daisy smiled. 'You're too hard on him.' She finished her meringue, put her fork down on her empty plate, and glanced over the side of the terrace at the forested valley below.

'It's such a beautiful view,' she said with a sigh. 'D'you think they'd let us do a painting from up here if we asked?'

Lilian laughed and put her hand to her stomach. 'It's a nice idea, but I dread to think what would happen to my waistline if we were faced with several days of such delicious cakes.'

'Good afternoon, ladies.'

Startled, they turned and saw Jack Leighton standing by their table.

'What are you doing here?' Lilian exclaimed in annoyance.

'As Peliti's is known for their coffee and cakes, the same as you, I imagine.' He indicated one of the two empty chairs at their table. 'May I join you?'

'If I said no, would you go away?'

'I doubt it,' he said with a grin, and he sat down facing the view, on the chair between Lilian and Daisy. He took off his solar *topi,* reached across and put it on the empty chair opposite him.

'Were you looking for us?' Daisy asked.

'Indirectly, I suppose I was,' he replied, loosening the collar of the white shirt he was wearing under his pale light-weight suit. 'But not you specifically—you, generally.'

'You clearly delight in cryptic utterances, Mr Leighton,' Lilian said acidly. 'No doubt you think they reflect a level of intelligence beyond that of the average mortal. However, as we've no intention of gratifying your vanity by attempting to work out your meaning, you might wish to explain yourself with greater clarity.'

'I do apologise for seeming to challenge the mental agility for which you're renowned, Miss Hunt. Believe me, that wasn't my intention.'

She glared at him.

'All I meant,' he went on smoothly, 'was that I've heard quite a bit about the popularity of Peliti's, so when your father insisted that I'd done enough for the day on my new project, I thought I'd stop by on my way home and enjoy some social interaction. That was what I meant by you generally.'

He glanced around the terrace. 'But I see I'm out of luck,' he added. 'There's no one here of interest. Apart from you two ladies, of course,' he said with exaggerated haste, and he smiled at them both.

Daisy giggled.

Lilian gave him an artificially bright smile. 'What are you *really* here for, Mr Leighton? You're hardly on the way home. The Secretariat is on the opposite side of Simla from here. So, too, is Rose Bank Guest House.'

A rueful expression on his face, he held up his hands. 'I admit it—you've caught me out. I wasn't on the way home. But this *was* about finding company. My fellow lodger, Mr Stanford, is dining tonight with his parents, and Stephen left the Secretariat ahead of me to go I know not where. It left me feeling somewhat lonely and in need of company. I thought I might find Stephen here, and if not, I might come across other congenial company.'

'If it's congenial company you want, I suggest you try the Club,' Lilian responded.

'It's a little early to go to the Club, or somewhat too late.'

'What a quaint characteristic,' she said sweetly, 'to be unable to frame a simple coherent sentence. But a frustrating one, too, I should imagine, if the aim of engaging the other person in conversation is to communicate with them. How do you get round this?' She cocked her head to one side as she gazed at him expectantly, her eyes exuding feigned curiosity.

He laughed. 'I'm going to let you have the last word, Miss Hunt. I expect you're used to having it, anyway, so you should feel quite satisfied with the outcome of our brief discussion.'

'Unless I'm mistaken, Mr Leighton, *you've* just had the last word. But I'm content to let it remain in place,' she added lightly, 'thereby warming your male ego, of which we seem to have seen quite a lot in the short amount of time we've known you.'

'If I said ouch, would you accuse me of going after that prized last word? But I suppose it's a moot point as to whether such an exclamation is a proper word.'

They stared at each other for a moment.

Then Jack turned away. He beckoned to the waiter who was standing in the doorway to the terrace.

'Since I'm in such charming, welcoming company,' he told the girls as the waiter came towards them, 'I'll stay a little longer. To justify my place at the table, I intend to have a cup of tea and a piece of cake. Would you like anything else to eat or drink?'

They declined the offer, and Jack ordered himself a tea and a ferozepore cake, to be served warm.

'You'll like the cake,' Daisy told him. 'They steep the almonds and pistachios in cream, and add green citron. It's really delicious.'

'That's what I've been told. It sounds quite decadent, Miss Chatsworth,' he said, smiling at her. 'I'm impressed that you managed to get them to tell you their kitchen secrets.'

'I didn't. It was Lilian who got them to tell her. She can be very persuasive, you know?'

'You *do* surprise me!' He glanced at Lilian, raising an eyebrow.

She stared pointedly over the railings that encircled the edge of the terrace.

Daisy cleared her throat. 'So Mr Stanford is with his parents this evening, Mr Leighton, is he?' she said with studied diffidence. 'Are you and he planning to go to the dance in the Hut tomorrow? Not that it matters,' she added quickly. 'I just wondered.'

He nodded. 'Indeed we are. And he said only this morning that he hoped he'd be seeing you and your family there.'

Daisy went pink. She put her hand to her mouth. 'Did he really?' she asked, her eyes shining.

Jack smiled. 'He did, indeed.'

He paused as the waiter poured his tea and put a piece of cake in front of him. 'So what have you both been doing this afternoon?' he asked when the waiter had left.

'We've been to the art stall near the fork,' Daisy volunteered.

Lilian turned sharply back to the table. 'Daisy!' she said, a warning in her tone, and she gave Daisy a slight frown. 'Mr Leighton won't be interested in such a cultural pursuit.'

Jack looked at Lilian in surprise. 'Surely you aren't planning on buying some paintings?' he exclaimed. 'I've heard that you're quite the talented artist, Miss Hunt. Wouldn't you prefer to paint your own pictures?'

'That's what I intend to do. And Daisy, too. We were getting ideas about the sort of scenes that people like to hang on their walls as we'll be giving some of our paintings as presents this Christmas.'

'And what conclusions did you arrive at?'

'That the buildings in town are less popular than scenes in the mountains and valleys. That's a surprise as although you've probably not noticed, some of the buildings have a very interesting structure. Those paintings we'll keep for ourselves, and the views around Simla will be our gifts. Next week, we're making a start on our gifts. You'll see us sallying forth, armed with paints and brushes.'

Jack looked up from his last morsel of cake, and sat back. 'I've just had an idea,' he said.

'Pray, don't risk overstraining your mind,' Lilian said tartly.

'Your father's given me a task which means I shall be out and about in a number of places around Simla, Miss Hunt,' he continued, ignoring her comment. 'It could be quite lonely, being on my own so much. If I knew where you were going to be, I could stop by and say hello. I could look at the paintings you're doing, and give you the benefit of my non-cultural eye. And my lonely task would be a little less lonely.'

'A tendency to loneliness seems to be an affliction of yours, Mr Leighton,' Lilian said coldly.

'I can't disagree with you there,' he said cheerfully.

'Well, I'm afraid you'll have to learn to live with it, or ask Papa for a different task. Our mothers may well be our chaperones on occasions, and both of them would be somewhat askance at the implication of you joining us regularly in such a way. As indeed should I.'

He threw up his hands in mock surprise. 'You're seeing a romantic purpose that just isn't there, Miss Hunt. Nothing could be further from my mind, I assure you,' he said with exaggerated fervour. 'Heaven forbid!'

Daisy started to laugh, then quickly smothered her laughter.

'But now that you've made it clear you dislike the idea so much, Miss Hunt, I'll most certainly avoid going anywhere near you,' he went on. 'And if by chance I should happen upon you, I'll immediately shut my eyes, turn and retrace my steps. But it's a shame,' he added, shaking his head and adopting a mournful tone, 'that I can't use your situation to help me with a problem.'

'Not another convolution!' Lilian exclaimed.

'It's about my fellow lodger, Eric. I've been trying to think how to persuade him to come with me on my trips outside Simla. Not every time, of course. Just occasionally when his work permits. It would be helpful if I could learn from him.'

'Eric!' Daisy exclaimed. And she stared at Lilian.

Lilian straightened up. 'You mean Eric Stanford?'

'That's right. His breadth of knowledge of flora and fauna far outstrips mine, and it suddenly occurred to me that if I could tell him there was a chance of meeting up with you ladies, he might be persuaded to join me. But of course, I wouldn't dream of holding out such a carrot to him, not now that I know your feelings.'

Daisy made a slight exclamation.

Jack glanced quickly at her.

'And indeed,' he went on smoothly, 'there could have been a bonus for you in having Eric's company. He would know of some beautiful places that have escaped most people's notice, and are thus less frequently the subject of an artist's brush. I'm sure he'd have shared them with you, generous soul that he is. But I respect your concerns so that's clearly not to be.'

He leaned forward, picked up his cup and finished the last of his tea.

Daisy threw Lilian an anguished look.

Lilian cleared her throat. 'Having a gentleman like Mr Stanford with us at times, able to deepen our knowledge of our natural environment, overrides the less attractive part of your plan, Mr Leighton, which is that you'll be with him.'

His lips twitching, Jack inclined his head. 'You're too gracious,' he murmured.

'I'll make sure you know where we'll be on the days

when we go out to paint,' she continued. 'On the evening before, I'll either telephone you or one of our servants will go to Rose Bank with that information.'

'Excellent, Miss Hunt,' he said, rising to his feet, and smiling. 'I'll have a word with Eric. For now, I'll bid you goodbye. I imagine we'll bump into each other again at the dance tomorrow, and I look forward to it.'

'How delightful that one of us is,' Lilian said, and she turned her face to the view.

17

T*uesday*

FROM THEIR TABLE in a corner of the Club's card room, surrounded by the stern faces of former Club members that hung from the teak-panelled walls in gilded plaster frames, Frederick and Wilfred listened to the distant strains of music and laughter that emanated from the other side of the lawn.

Frederick leaned forward and picked up his glass of whisky.

'It sounds as if they're having a good time in the Hut,' he said, nursing his glass as he settled back in his armchair and stretched his legs.

Wilfred nodded. 'It does, indeed. And I'm sure their mothers are, too, though perhaps in a somewhat more sedate manner.'

Frederick took a sip of his drink, and returned his glass to the highly polished oak table between them.

'I'm happy to say that after a difficult start, the summer is shaping up to be an enjoyable one,' he remarked in satisfaction. 'The women were obviously delighted to be sitting with the other mothers, talking about clothes and things that women like to discuss.'

'And while they chaperone, we get left to our own devices as a result,' Wilfred said with a smile. 'This could be the first of many such occasions in the Club and elsewhere. I thought both girls looked really lovely this evening. It's no surprise that they've already received a bevy of social invitations.'

Frederick nodded. 'I'm sure their dance cards were full very early on. Constance and Gladys may not have quite as much time to relax as they think they will.'

'Talking of relaxation, I'm glad to see you looking more your old self, my friend. I take it you've put what's been happening behind you.'

'Not entirely, but I do feel easier in myself. I've great confidence in Jack Leighton's ability to keep the girls safe, and nothing else untoward has happened.'

'Let's hope that's the end of it, then,' Wilfred said fervently.

'Indeed so. I don't want anything to keep them from painting in Simla, and to stop Eric from joining them. He's an intelligent man, and I can't see him being drawn to a woman with nothing more serious on her mind than what she's wearing for the next dance. I'm hoping Lilian's talent will impress him.'

'Lilian has a lot of thoughts in her head, serious and otherwise, and an enthusiasm for expressing them no matter where she is,' Wilfred said with a wry smile. 'I wouldn't worry on that score, Frederick.'

Frederick laughed. He picked up his glass and cupped it in his hands. 'Yes, you're right about Lilian's determination to be heard. Nevertheless, I'm relieved that they'll be embarking on their paintings fairly soon. Ideally, I'd like to be able to announce their engagement before the summer is out, and so would Cecil.'

'I'm pleased that Daisy's going to be painting, too. It's a highly suitable activity for a young woman.'

'And more than that, it shows an interest in the area in which they're living. With Eric fascinated by the world of nature, they'll have something to talk about.' He gave a sudden laugh. 'Did you know that Lilian's planning on using me as a warm up?'

Wilfred raised his eyebrows. 'Meaning?'

'She's going to paint my portrait. I've promised to sit for an hour each afternoon, starting tomorrow. She wants to give the painting to Constance for her birthday.'

'Well, I very much hope that Daisy doesn't feel she must do likewise! Lilian has talent; Daisy doesn't. The last time she attempted a likeness of me, I resembled an aged rhinoceros. This is not a humiliation to which I intend to subject myself again.'

Frederick laughed. 'I remember it well. I don't think I've ever laughed as much. But she may have improved. She and Lilian are taking this very seriously.'

'Out of interest, how's this going to work with Jack?' Wilfred asked. 'Are he and Lilian getting on better?'

'I wouldn't put it quite as strongly as that. In fact, how he persuaded Lilian to let him join them, I don't know. But although she's still highly critical of him and seems to dislike him, she's agreed to let him know where they'll be going.'

Wilfred whistled. 'That will have taken some impressive smooth-talking.'

'He must certainly have a way with words. It's worked out well. Constance's extremely busy, and she wasn't keen on chaperoning them for anything other than social events at the Club, so knowing that Jack will be with them, I'm not worried about them having their *ayahs* as chaperones. Both *ayahs* must go, though, rather than just one.'

'I'd volunteer Stephen's services, too, but he's anxious to succeed in his job. At the stage he's at, he still needs to prove himself, and it wouldn't be fair to distract him.'

'Come to think of it, I've not seen him yet this evening.'

'He said he'd ride over when he was ready. He had something to finish off.'

Frederick nodded approvingly. 'With a work ethic like that he'll go far.'

A waiter dressed in white appeared at their table.

'You'll have another whisky, won't you, Wilfred?' Frederick asked.

'I could be persuaded. But just a *chotapeg*. Two fingers of whisky are quite enough on top of what I've already had.'

'We'll each have a *burrapeg*,' Frederick told the waiter. 'I think another three fingers are called for,' he told Wilfred with a smile. 'After all, we need to be fortified for later on, when we're joined by our four chattering females.'

THE SNOW-CRUSTED MOUNTAIN peaks were cold blue against the darkening sky.

Night was falling fast, blurring the fork in the two roads,

one leading down to Lakkar Bazaar and one falling sharply through Lower Bazaar.

Just south of the fork on the road, Stephen sat on his horse and stared down the road that wound through Lower Bazaar, cutting a path through alleys that ran in parallel lines along the side of the steep slope, one alley above the other, each row of houses looking down on the tin roofs of the houses that lined the alley beneath them.

From the bead-screened doorways and lightly curtained windows of every house on every tier, emanated pinpoints of light that sparkled in the night—a panoply of lights that seemingly mirrored the star-filled sky.

But Stephen's gaze was fixed on the art stall, and not on the beauty surrounding him.

The stall was in darkness, but an amber glow shimmered behind the beaded curtain, and his gaze was riveted on that rectangle of light as he waited, hoping.

Time passed slowly.

Night blackened further, and the specks of light from the tiers of houses grew more numerous.

He was just starting to think that his wait was going to have been in vain, and that as he wasn't minded to join the others at the dance in the Hut, he might as well go home, when he heard the rattle of beads.

His heart missed a beat.

The light in the doorway flickered, and a slender shape appeared in the rectangle of light, a black silhouette framed by amber-gold.

It was Asha.

His heart beating fast, he slipped from the saddle, coiled his reins around the water hydrant in front of the shop, hastily moved forward and placed himself in the doorway where she couldn't fail to see him.

She let the bead curtain fall behind her, and glided through the darkness that filled the shop until she reached the doorway.

She paused, inches from Stephen, and faced him.

He stepped into the shop, and stopped.

Both stood still, their features veiled by dusk, their eyes glittering as each gazed upon the other.

Then he heard a woman inside the living quarters shout out. Asha turned slightly and answered. The woman called again, her voice insistent.

Asha looked towards Stephen, and shrugged.

She turned and went back to the rectangle of light. Putting her hand on the curtain of beads, she glanced fleetingly over her shoulder at Stephen, gave him a slight smile, then pushed the curtain aside and went into the living quarters.

The curtain rattled shut behind her and she disappeared from sight.

Elated, he stood motionless, his heart racing.

He knew it!

He'd felt an immediate connection with Asha the day before. And his every instinct had told him that she, too, had felt the same.

And that evening, it was as if she'd known he'd be there, and had come out to speak to him. Because of her mother, they'd been frustrated that night, but they wouldn't be the next time.

And there *would* be a next time.

As soon as Lilian and Daisy started painting, and had done sufficient pictures to hand some over, he'd have an excuse to come to the shop in the daytime and speak with Asha.

And until then, he'd come back the next night, and the

night after that. He'd come back for as long as it took to see her again. Because from the moment he'd first seen Asha, he'd known what love was.

And that was true for Asha, too, he was sure.

And a love such as theirs promised to be was too strong to be denied.

18

T he Hut
Tuesday evening

LILIAN SMILED TO HERSELF—THEY were halfway through the evening and it was going so well.

This was the first moment since she'd arrived in a cloud of pale green organza that she'd had to herself, and that had come about only because she'd given the slot for her second dance with Eric to Daisy, who had an empty line on her card for that dance.

She looked down with pleasure at her little gilt-edged card, folded in half like a book-cover. There was a name written on every dotted line opposite the list of dances and their accompanying tunes.

Eric had been one of the first to write his name on her card using the slender pencil attached by a thin silk cord.

He'd signed Daisy's card first of all, putting his name on two of the dotted lines, and then, seeing Lilian standing beside him fingering her card, he'd blushed and signed hers, too. He'd hesitated, and had then signed on a second line.

But his eyes had been on Daisy even as he'd been signing Lilian's card, and they had been on Daisy all evening, no matter with whom he'd been dancing.

In fact, she'd been quite worried that her mother would see him and Daisy together, and would realise that Cecil Stanford had been completely mistaken about where Eric's affections lay.

But whenever she'd glanced towards their mothers, they'd seemed to be enjoying themselves with the other mothers, and weren't paying the slightest attention to who was dancing with whom, and that was why she'd felt able to let Daisy take over her second dance with Eric.

'A rupee for them.'

She looked up and saw Jack standing in front of her.

'That's rather mean, isn't it, Mr Leighton?' she said archly. 'A rupee is worth considerably less than a penny.'

'You never fail to surprise me, Miss Hunt,' he said, sitting down on the empty seat next to her. 'I would never have had you down as mercenary. However, I'm perfectly willing to add a few rupees to my offer if that's what it takes to be privy to your innermost thoughts. I noticed you dancing animatedly with Mr Stanford. Perhaps your thoughts were on him.'

'Good gracious, how vigilant you are, Mr Leighton! You put the most determined of chaperones to shame.'

He inclined his head in acknowledgement. 'Any praise from you, after the criticism generally heaped on my head by your fair self, is indeed worth having.'

'It wasn't meant as praise, I assure you, Mr Leighton. But I'm happy to humour you and allow you to bask in admiration of yourself, if that's what you wish.'

He leaned back in his chair, and stretched out his legs. 'So what *were* you thinking about?'

'A suitable pose for Papa.' She looked at his face, and burst out laughing. 'I can see you struggling about what to say. Yes, that does sound rather strange, doesn't it? But it isn't really. I'm going to start on a portrait of Papa tomorrow. I shall seat him on the lower back verandah, and I've been wondering whether to ask him to sit or stand.'

'What time of day will you be doing this? If it's at the end of the day, he'll be tired, and sitting would probably be his preference.'

'He's coming home for lunch every day for the few days it'll take, and he's going to give me an hour after lunch before he goes for his siesta. I'm going to paint him outside the room between the dining room and pantry. That room's going to be my studio. I'll be keeping everything there.'

'By everything, I take it you mean your brushes and paints?'

She nodded. 'And paper. The paper's very important. Papa's got me some Cox's paper and Whatman's Rough. They're the best papers for watercolour paints as although they're very absorbent, the colour's still strong after the paint dries.'

'Why two kinds of paper?'

'You choose the paper according to what you're doing. The Whatman's Rough has a textured surface, but it isn't too rough. You don't want it too rough as the paint would settle in what I call the valleys. That's no good for fine details. Papa's nose might come out like a formless blob, for example.'

He laughed. 'I can see that. Well, you certainly seem to be taking this seriously. You do surprise me, if you don't mind me saying so.'

'Since you've said it, regardless of whether or not I mind, your qualification is rather redundant, don't you think,' she said, a tinge of amusement in her voice.

'Touché.'

'But you're right. I like painting and I *do* take it seriously. And as I'm giving the portrait to Mama for her birthday, it must be good. I've already amassed everything I need, such as my paints, pencils, brushes, a palette, cloth and two small bowls for water—one for cleaning my brushes, and one if I need clean water.'

'What's the clean water for?'

'If I make a mistake, I must lift the paint before it dries.'

'I see.'

'It means that I'm now ready not just for Papa's portrait, but for when we start to paint around Simla, too.'

'Well, I'm very impressed, Miss Hunt. I hope you'll allow me to see your pictures.'

'Since you and Mr Stanford intend to join us at times, I imagine you'll see the pictures, permission or not. Unless you plan on keeping your eyes tightly shut throughout your visit, that is,' she added.

'Ouch,' he said, and with a wry smile, he rose to his feet. 'I'll leave you to enjoy your thoughts.'

'Aren't you going to ask me to dance?' she exclaimed, sitting upright. 'I thought that was really the reason you came over.'

'Then I'm afraid you were mistaken, Miss Hunt. You've already bested me once this evening, so I shall leave you to someone with a hide that's thicker than mine. Good evening.' With a slight bow, he walked away.

Lilian stared after him. How rude, she thought.

And a bit annoying, if she was being honest with herself.

It might have been quite pleasant to have danced with

him. Not because he was very attractive—a good-looking face was no more than a veneer—but because it was fun to spar with him. And so far, she hadn't met anyone else about whom she could make the same comment.

But it was early days, of course.

He wasn't going to be the only person she'd enjoy engaging in conversation.

Well, not exactly enjoy. It was more that she relished the challenge of exchanging remarks with someone who could keep her on her toes, and who could respond with a touch of humour.

But there would be other men in Simla who had a liveliness of mind. All she had to do was find them. Which she would do when she started to look for them. Something she must soon begin to do.

Eric and Daisy spun into her line of vision. Eric was gazing warmly into Daisy's face. Daisy was looking up at him in adoration.

She wanted someone at whom she could stare with the same sort of love with which Daisy was looking at Eric, and who would look at her in the same way.

She glanced quickly at their mothers. Both her mother and Daisy's had stopped talking and were staring fixedly at Eric and Daisy.

She felt a sudden panic.

She jumped up and went across to Daisy and Eric.

As she reached them, both turned towards her, surprise on their faces, and a trace of displeasure.

With a slight motion of her head, she indicated their mothers. Daisy understood at once, and drew back from Eric to let Lilian take her place.

As Lilian and Eric joined the dancing, Lilian's head was slightly closer to Eric than Daisy's had been as she sought to

erase from their mothers' minds the memory of Daisy and
Eric's closeness.

FROM HIS POSITION at the back of the Hut, Jack stared
towards the dance floor, his gaze moving from Lilian to Eric,
and then to Daisy, who was sitting at the side of the room in
the chair vacated by Lilian, her eyes cast down.

He looked back again at Lilian, and his blue eyes were
cold.

19

*he Secretariat
Wednesday*

THE LARGE ROOM in the Secretariat that was awash with telephones, tables, paper and files, buzzed with early morning activity as the senior clerks arrived for the start of day and took their seats behind their desks.

Envelopes were piled high in the in-tray on the corner of every desk, and in the trays lodged between the telephone and typewriter, one for the outgoing post and one for the documents that were to be distributed within the Secretariat itself by the *chaprassis.*

Once settled, the senior clerks summoned their secretaries and juniors, to run through with them the tasks on which they'd be working that day, and to dictate any necessary memos, as well as to acquaint them with any recently received information from New Delhi.

As he made his way through the rows of tables to his

private office, which was flanked on one side by the office used by Cecil Stanford on the occasions that he visited the Secretariat, and on the other by Wilfred's office, Frederick nodded to one or two of the senior clerks as he passed their desks, and to any *chaprassis* in the process of delivering messages for the various officials.

When he reached his office, he went straight inside.

Hearing Frederick arrive, Wilfred came out of his office. He paused to let a *chaprassi* pass between him and Frederick's door, and then went and stood in Frederick's open doorway.

'You're very keen to start work today, I see,' he said. 'Normally, you arrive about an hour after me.'

'It's not exactly keenness,' Frederick said with a rueful smile. 'This is about the hour after lunch I've promised Lilian. I'm now wishing I hadn't agreed, but it's too late to back out. It wouldn't be fair on Lilian. Or on Constance, who, for some reason, seems quite keen on having a painting of me, despite the fact that she sees me every day.'

'Perhaps you can persuade Lilian to paint you while you're sleeping. That way, you wouldn't lose siesta time,' Wilfred suggested with a smile.

Frederick pulled a face. 'Not a chance, I'm afraid. I'll be sitting, wide awake, on the lower back verandah outside her studio. It's the most convenient place for her.'

'It'll be a lovely setting. You'll be surrounded by wild lily-of-the-valley and by climbing roses, which are glorious at the moment; their scent's quite heavenly. There are worse places in which to pass an hour.'

'You're right, of course. It means, though, that if I'm late getting home for lunch, I won't have time for a siesta. So I must stop for lunch at the appointed hour, which I seldom do. Until she's finished, therefore, I'll be starting work earlier than I usually do.'

'How long do you think it'll take?'

Frederick shrugged. 'She said she'll need me to pose for three days, and then she'll be able to do the rest by herself. I think she's being a little optimistic, but we shall see.'

'I'll leave you to it, then,' Wilfred said. As he stepped back, he collided with a passing *chaprassi*. 'I do apologise,' he said, turning hastily to the man.

The *chaprassi* lowered his head, put his hands together in a *namaste* and made an inaudible comment.

'Good chap,' Wilfred said, and he went back to his office.

THERE WAS a knock on Frederick's office door.

'Come in,' he called. 'Ah, Jack!' he exclaimed as Jack opened the door. 'Good to see you.'

'Good morning, sir,' Jack said, going into the office.

'You're just the person I wanted to see.'

Jack raised his eyebrows in surprise. 'I am, sir?'

'Indeed, yes. Constance mentioned that she saw you talking to Lilian last night. I was worried that Lilian might be regretting her decision to let you accompany them on their painting expeditions.'

'There's no need to worry, Mr Hunt. That's been satisfactorily settled, and there's no question of her changing her mind.'

Frederick looked at him in relief. 'I don't mind telling you, it's a weight off my mind. Wilfred and I were wondering how you did it? If you don't mind me saying so, you and Lilian don't seem to get on very well. I rather thought she might refuse to have your company.'

Jack grinned. 'Saying that I could bring Eric Stanford with me might have helped.'

Frederick smiled broadly. 'Well done, lad. And well done, Lilian, for being so receptive to my wishes. So you'll be able to entertain young Daisy while Eric and Lilian get to know each other better. According to Constance, Daisy and Eric spent rather too much time together last night. It'll be good for Daisy to have a distraction.'

Suppressing a moment's irritation at another attempt to link him with Daisy, Jack leaned forward and placed a file on Frederick's desk. 'I've drawn up a list of strategies with which to approach the forest survey you require,' he told Frederick.

'Excellent.'

'You'll see that while I'm covering all the essential areas, I'll have a degree of flexibility as to which place I visit on any given day. Where I go will be determined by your daughter's plans. But despite that element of uncertainty, within a couple of months, you'll receive a survey conducted with a range and thoroughness that won't have been negatively affected by the purpose for which you've set me this task.'

'Thank you, Jack. I appreciate your dedication to your job. Lesser young men might have shirked the work side of things, knowing that they'd ultimately get the promotion they sought, regardless of that. But not you. You can be sure that whatever the outcome of our subterfuge, this will enhance your career, not damage it.'

'Thank you, sir.'

Picking up Jack's file, Frederick glanced up at him. 'How is Lilian going to let you know where she'll be painting on any given day?'

'Either she'll send me a message by one of your servants the evening before, or she'll telephone. If I haven't heard from her by breakfast, I'll know they won't be painting that day.'

'I see you've got it all sorted out,' Frederick said in satisfaction. 'Asking for your help was clearly fortuitous. I need not worry any longer.'

TIMING WAS ALL IMPORTANT, Kamesh congratulated himself.

It hadn't been chance that had placed him outside the office of Frederick Hunt that morning—it had been the outcome of his forward thinking.

He'd inveigled himself into the position of being the *chaprassi* who collected and distributed the messages for Frederick Hunt and for those who worked in his division, and thus he'd had reason to be near the office on several occasions recently when Frederick Hunt arrived for work.

He hadn't been noticed by anyone, of course. One Indian looked like another, and one Anglo-Indian looked like the next Anglo-Indian. Likewise, one *chaprassi* looked like any other *chaprassi*.

They were all invisible to the arrogant British.

But that was a stroke of good fortune for him. He could go anywhere, be anywhere, and not rouse any suspicion since none of the British would realise that they'd seen him before.

He'd been wondering what to do next to discomfort Mr Hunt, and as a result of what he'd heard that morning, he now knew.

It had been handed to him, as the British would say, on a plate. There was no need to follow him, or watch the house. As a result of Mr Hunt's conversation with his friend, he'd heard all he needed to know.

All he had to do was wait until the time was right, and then take action.

And since the British met each other every weekend, be it in the Royal Club or in the home of one or other of their friends, he could safely assume that there'd be a time on any given Saturday or Sunday, if not on both days, when the Hunts would not be in their house.

And the servants always had a siesta.

Admittedly, their siesta was shorter than that of their employers, but it would be long enough for his purposes. There was no need, therefore, for him to rush at anything or risk being seen through a lack of caution.

Careful planning was needed, so it would be too soon to make a move this weekend.

Frederick Hunt had clearly decided not to involve the police or Service officials. If he had done so, they would have been seen making enquiries.

It meant that there'd be no surveillance on the Hunts' house, so before doing anything else, he could take a closer look at the back of the house, being very careful not to arouse suspicion.

It was also too soon to make another move because he hadn't yet discovered if Asha's resentment could be used by him in any way.

She had been somewhat reticent when he'd first spoken to her, as if suspicious that he might be trying to disguise an interest in her, an interest that it was obvious she wouldn't have welcomed.

Someone like Asha would be determined that the beauty she'd been given should not be wasted, and that meant marrying the right person. A lowly office messenger like him was about as far as you could get from being the right person.

She'd warmed up slightly after he'd referred several times to Stephen Chatsworth, and she'd let slip the fact that she was furious at Constance Hunt for asking her to leave.

She'd done nothing wrong, she'd insisted vociferously, but the Hunts' *ayah,* an ugly woman, had taken against her, and had blamed her for a feeling of disgruntlement in the household.

Instead of the trouble-making *ayah* being asked to leave as she'd obviously spoken out of jealousy, it was Asha who had been made to go. It was so unfair, she'd complained.

So Asha was clearly resentful, as he'd hoped. But unfortunately, as he'd soon realised, it wasn't going to help him.

Her focus wasn't on revenge—it was on herself, and on how she could meet someone who would give her a better life than the one she'd have on the art stall. And if she'd had any desire for revenge, it had clearly passed.

And he'd soon understood why.

When he'd sympathised with her for being fired for no good reason from a job that had offered her excellent prospects, she'd agreed.

But she'd added with a sudden surprising coyness that although she'd thought at first that her best chance of meeting a suitable future husband would be by working for a British family, she thought she might have been wrong.

It had been obvious that she'd already set her sights on someone. And that someone he knew to be Stephen Chatsworth.

But there was no point in telling her that she was wasting her time, that Stephen Chatsworth would never marry her, and in saying that she'd do better to try to make headway with one of the prosperous Indians who owned some shops on the Mall, as he'd sensed that Asha was the sort of person who was sure that she always knew best.

So resentful though she was, it was highly unlikely that he'd ever be able to encourage her into the frame of mind to want to act vengefully against the Hunts.

In the light of that, he'd had to re-think the Asha situation, now that her only use to him was going to be her connection with Stephen Chatsworth.

At first that had been a depressing realisation.

But the more he thought about it, the more he'd begun to see that this could present an opportunity that would possibly be more fruitful even than that of a vengeful Asha.

The more he knew about the Hunts' plans, the better.

Because he worked in the same building with Stephen, he had the advantage of being able to see him most days, should he wish to do so. Being an office messenger, there'd be no surprise if he were frequently in the vicinity of Stephen's desk.

It shouldn't be too difficult, therefore, to insinuate himself into a position whereby he could act as a messenger between Stephen and Asha, if matters were to progress as far as she hoped.

And if he had anything to do with it, matters *would* progress that far.

With the Chatsworths and Hunts close friends, if he succeeded in making himself indispensable to Stephen and Asha, he should be able to elicit from Stephen more details about the Hunts and their intentions than he could find out through being their *chaprassi*.

Time was on his side. The British would be in Simla until the leaves turned brown, curled at the edges and fell from the trees. And that was some way off.

Smiling to himself, he slipped an envelope into the in-tray that was closest to him, and moved on to the next desk.

20

L*ater*

'ARREN'T YOU USING YOUR PAINTS?' Frederick asked in surprise.

'Not today,' Lilian said. 'All I'm going to do is sketch you. I'll start to fill in the sketch tomorrow. Watercolours dry more quickly than oils, and I don't want to make any mistakes.'

She turned and looked at Daisy, who was sitting behind her, watching what she was doing. 'What do you think so far, Daisy?'

Daisy got up, went and peered over Lilian's shoulder at the piece of paper taped on to a thin square of wood. 'You're so talented, Lilian. It's already a really good likeness. You're going to be very happy with this, Uncle Frederick,' she said straightening up. 'And so is Aunt Constance.'

'I hope you're right, Daisy. Remember, Lilian, when

you're painting my face, a little flattery wouldn't go amiss,' Frederick said with a smile. 'You could lose a few of those anxiety wrinkles that you've caused me over the years.'

'Very funny,' she said. 'About next week, Daisy. I thought we could leave the buildings for a few more days, and make a start on somewhere outside Simla,' she said as she outlined in pencil the shoulders of her father.

'That sounds lovely,' Daisy said with a wide smile. 'Where did you have in mind?'

'Nothing as yet. I thought I'd ask Mr Stanford's advice when we lunch with his parents on Sunday.'

Frederick beamed. 'That's an excellent idea, Lilian.'

'Please don't move, Papa.'

'I'll keep still for the next ten minutes, but then you'll have had your hour, and it'll be siesta time. After that, I intend to return to the Secretariat. I'm hoping to have finished my latest project for Cecil by Sunday.'

LILIAN PAUSED in her conversation with Daisy, and waited until the *khidmatgar*, supervised by Sunil, had placed the cutlery, plates and a cake stand on the small wicker table between the chairs on which she and Daisy were sitting, and both servants had left the front verandah.

'I'm so glad you were able to stay on for tea this afternoon, Daisy, and that Mama was agreeable to us having tea by ourselves. Now that Papa's gone back to the Secretariat, she'll be on her own.'

'She probably realised we'd be talking about the dance last night and what we're doing next weekend, and both subjects would bore her.' She gave a loud sigh. 'Talking of next weekend, you're so lucky to be seeing Eric.'

'Don't worry, you'll be seeing him soon after that,' Lilian

said firmly. 'I'll have almost finished Papa's portrait by the end of this week, so we can start on some scenes next week. I bet Eric will join us.' She hesitated. 'But before that, there's something that's been worrying me. I hate to bring it up, but I must.'

'Worrying you?' Daisy echoed, and she frowned. 'What's that?'

'Last night, when you and Eric were dancing, he was gazing at you adoringly, and you were looking at him in the same way.'

Daisy went red. 'We weren't, were we?'

'Yes, you were, and our mothers were watching. Eric is supposed to be interested in me, not you, and I'm supposed to reciprocate. That's what his father wants, and mine, too. I don't know why his father's so set on it, but he is.'

'It's so unfair,' Daisy said in despair.

'If Eric comes out with us,' Lilian went on, 'you'll get some time together away from our parents' eyes, so it's important that he does. When he's confident about your feelings for him, he'll get over his shyness and propose. When he does, his father will have to accept it.'

'I know that, Lilian, and I'm so grateful for your help. I just wish Eric's father liked me better.'

'He will when he gets to know you, and when he sees how right you are for Eric. But that's only going to happen if we're careful. All we need is sufficient time for Eric to propose to you. As soon as he does, we can stop pretending.'

'I can't wait for that day!'

'But it might not come for some time if you give the game away, as you almost did last night. Our mothers will now be keeping a closer eye on the three of us in future.'

Daisy's hand went to her mouth.

'It would be awful if they told Papa,' Lilian went on. 'If

he knew the truth, he might be so anxious about keeping on the good side of Eric's father that he'd forbid me to allow you to do any painting with me if Eric was going to be there.'

Daisy gave a sharp gasp. 'D'you think he would?' she asked, a tremor in her voice.

Lilian nodded. 'I'm afraid, I do. Papa's a very kind father, but there's another side to him, too. He's very ambitious, and he'd never let anything stand in the way of something that could advance him.'

Daisy bit her lower lip. 'What do you suggest we do?'

'What we planned at the start. For as long as it takes, it must look as if Eric and I are interested in each other.'

Daisy nodded. 'I suppose I could make a point of ignoring Eric, even though I'd hate to do so. He might be upset.' Her eyes filled with tears.

'You should certainly stand back from him a little, and I should move forward to him. I did that when we first got here, but recently I've rather relaxed.' Lilian paused for a moment. 'Of course, there's always another way.'

Daisy looked at her with eyes full of hope. 'There is?' she asked.

Lilian nodded. 'We could take Eric into our confidence. If he knows why I engage him in conversation when he'd rather be talking to you, he might play along with that as I'm sure he's as keen on spending time with you as you are with him.'

Daisy vigorously shook her head. 'I don't like that idea at all. He's an honest person, and not at all devious. I'm sure he'd be really unhappy to be asked to take part in subterfuge.'

'You'd be amazed at how devious most people can be, Daisy, if it's the only way of getting what they want. And I'm certain it wouldn't be for long. I'm sure that Eric will soon declare his feelings. Then he'll ask Uncle Wilfred for your hand in marriage, and uncle will say yes.'

'I really don't want to do that,' Daisy said quietly. 'Apart from thinking he'd hate the idea, there's another reason, too.' She fell silent.

'Well?' Lilian urged.

A pink haze spread across Daisy's cheeks. 'Our plan is based on the assumption that Eric feels for me what I feel for him. But we don't know for sure that he does.'

Lilian laughed dismissively. 'Of course, we do! Just think of the way he looks at you, Daisy.'

'That doesn't necessarily mean that he's anxious to marry me, and that his feelings are such that he'd go against the wishes of his father. We've only met a few times. It's much too strong an assumption to make at this stage. I'd be telling him, in effect, how much I regard him, when he hasn't made a similar declaration to me. No, if he knows about our plan, it might frighten him off.'

With her mouth set in a firm line, she looked down at her plate.

'Well, you know Eric better than I, so we must do what you think best,' Lilian said after a moment or two.

'Thank you, Lilian.'

'We'll stick to our plan, and we won't tell Eric. But rather than you acting coldly towards him, I'll try to elbow you out of the way. As I did in our first few days here.'

'I must admit, I prefer that idea.'

'Good. We'll start tomorrow night when we go to the Hut. Our mothers are bound to go with us again as they enjoy chatting to the other mothers, so it'll be the perfect occasion to present a different picture of you, me and Eric.'

'He might not go to the dance. Two dances in one week might be too much for him.'

'I'll ask Mr Leighton to make sure that he does. And when I'm talking or dancing with Eric, I'll make a great effort to keep his back to our mothers so they don't see the terror in his eyes whenever he looks at me.'

Daisy giggled. 'You do exaggerate, Lilian.'

Lilian shook her head, 'Not in this, I don't,' she said cheerfully. 'Now that it's all decided, perhaps you'll take a piece of gingerbread. Cook's gingerbread is delicious.'

And she pushed the cake stand closer to Daisy, picked up the pot of tea and filled their cups.

SHADOWS WERE COLLECTING in the dust-filled cracks between the cascade of ramshackle shops and dwellings that formed the Lower Bazaar, and mingled scents of sawdust and sandalwood, garlic and ghee, rotting vegetables and sewage, hung heavily in the air.

From every tier, the sounds of music and laughter, of talking and crying, of pans rattling and bedsteads creaking, rose up and joined the ever-present rattle of the cicadas and insects of the night, and the occasional howl of a jackal guarding its territory deep among the forested slopes.

Kamesh stared in irritation in the direction of the art stall.

However, he was staring not at the shop itself, but at two figures shrouded in darkness as they sat close together on a flight of steps a little way down from the art shop.

He should have been the one with Asha, not Stephen, he thought in annoyance.

But not in the way that Stephen was. Stephen had obviously more than a simple friendship in mind. No, he would have sat with Asha as her friend, not as a suitor.

Ingratiating himself with her had been all he'd been

thinking about since the moment he'd realised that he could hardly approach Stephen and suggest that he carry messages between him and Asha.

Stephen would have instantly wondered how his friendship with Asha was known, and his suspicions roused, he would be unlikely to leave it at that.

No, if he was going to become their agent, the suggestion would have to come from Asha.

If he could establish a casual friendship with her, based on her knowing that he worked in the same place as Stephen, it wasn't unreasonable to assume that at some point she would suggest he take a message to Stephen.

From then on, they would welcome him into their lives, and he'd have a good chance of getting more ideas about how to hurt Frederick Hunt.

Tonight had been about beginning that process.

He'd planned to tell Asha that he'd heard of a vacancy for a housemaid, and he'd wondered if she'd be interested in putting herself forward for the position.

She wouldn't, of course.

She had a much better prospect in mind.

And that prospect was thwarting his plans that evening.

It was just as well that a slight delay wasn't going to matter. He glared again in Stephen's direction, and then turned to go back up the slope to the house he shared.

He would return the following day, he decided as he reached the few steps leading up to his front door and try to catch Asha immediately after her siesta, when Stephen was unlikely to be there.

And after that, as he already had something in mind, he'd go into Lower Bazaar and get everything he needed.

21

The Coffee Shop
Friday

'I'M glad you suggested we come into Simla today,' Daisy told Lilian.

'Blame my curiosity,' Lilian said with a laugh. 'I was dying to hear what you thought of last night, and I didn't want to wait. So, what did you think of the dance?'

'I'm just glad it's over. I felt tense all evening, and I didn't dare to relax and be myself. And I felt sad at not being able to dance with Eric more than once, while you had several dances. I hope we don't have to do this for much longer. I hate deceiving our parents, and I hate you having to pretend you feel something for Eric.' She paused. 'You are pretending this, aren't you?'

'Of course I am, silly. The only reason we danced as often as we did was because I had him locked in a vice-like grip. He couldn't escape my clutches as he was too gentlemanly to forcibly pull away from me. He would have much rather been with you.'

'I hope that's true.'

'It is,' Lilian said firmly. 'I wish there was an alternative, but I can't think of one. I, too, dislike misleading our parents, and I hate falsely raising the hopes of Eric's parents. It feels very wrong, but I don't know what else to do. You must try to get him to declare his feelings for you as soon as possible.'

'I'll do my best.' Daisy hesitated a moment. 'I was surprised that Mr Leighton didn't stay longer at the dance.'

Lilian shrugged. 'I didn't realise he'd left early. I was too busy paying attention to Eric, thereby gratifying my mother, who was watching me like a hawk. Mr Leighton's only importance to me last night was in making sure that Eric turned up. What he did after that was of no interest to me at all.'

'It's very kind of Mr Leighton to be so helpful about Eric,' Daisy remarked after a moment or two. 'Most men wouldn't want to be involved. Not unless they were anxious to please a certain person, that is.' She glanced slyly at Lilian.

Lilian laughed. 'I hope to meet someone interesting before the summer is out, but it won't be him, I can assure you. He and I will never get on. He's far too sure of himself. So, tell me what you're doing on Sunday while we're at the Stanfords.'

'Having lunch at one of Papa's friends. They live on Summer Hill so it'll be a long journey. Papa said that he and his wife are very pleasant, and that I'll like them. But whether or not I do, it'll take my mind off Eric, and it'll stop Mama and Papa from dwelling on the fact that they've been so obviously excluded by Mr Stanford. He must really dislike my family.'

'I'm sure this has nothing to do with your family. It's about pushing Eric and me together.'

'But Papa and Uncle Frederick are such good friends that it's very obvious when one is invited and the other isn't. It's making a statement. At least, that's the way my parents look at it.'

Lilian shook her head. 'I'm certain you're mistaken,' she said. 'It's because they're such good friends that they're less likely to be invited at the same time.'

Daisy frowned. 'What d'you mean?'

'Well, Mr and Mrs Stanford probably want to get to know Papa away from the office. But if Uncle Wilfred was there, too, he and Papa would talk to each other, and it would be difficult for the Stanfords to get to know either of them. I'm sure you'll be invited another time.'

'I hope so,' Daisy said. 'For Stephen's sake, as much as for anything else. He'll want a promotion, too, when he's been in the Service for long enough, and that would be harder if Eric's father didn't like him.'

'What's Stephen doing this evening?'

Daisy shook her head. 'I've no idea. When we got back from lunch, he muttered something about the Club, so I imagine he's gone to play billiards yet again.'

22

T *he Stanfords' house*
Sunday

THEY LEFT their rickshaws at the foot of the gravelled drive that sloped down from the road to the Stanfords' house, which had been built on a large clearing hacked out of the densely forested hillside, and levelled.

The house was just as Lilian had remembered from all those years ago.

It was a half-timbered, two-storey house, topped by a pitched roof, gables, four chimney stacks, and eaves into which a decorative design had been carved. The same design had been etched into the wooden verandah that encircled both of the floors.

She knew that the servants' compound lay back from the house, screened from sight by a voluminous mass of pink and white cosmos. Over the passage of time, their strong heady aroma had become ingrained in the wooden structure of the house.

On the area of clearing to the right of the house, there was a tennis court.

It was difficult to imagine Eric in tennis whites, she thought drily as she followed her mother and father up the steps to the front door. Now Jack Leighton was a different matter. Being lean and seemingly muscular, he had the right build, and must look extremely good in them.

Mentally, she kicked herself.

He was one of the most arrogant men she had ever met, and it didn't matter what he looked like in anything he wore as she had no intention of looking at him more than was absolutely necessary.

As Frederick reached the front door, it was opened by the Stanfords' butler.

Frederick gave him their names, and the butler stood aside to let them in. As they did so, the Stanfords' *chaprassi* stepped forward, and the butler indicated that the *chaprassi* should accompany the guests across the lobby to the drawing room and announce them.

Cecil and Margaret Stanford rose to their feet as the Hunts were shown in.

'Good of you to come, Frederick,' Cecil said as he came forward to shake first Frederick's hand, and then Constance's.

'On the contrary, it's very kind of you to invite us, Cecil,' Frederick said. 'Constance and I have been here before, of course, but Lilian will have been too young to remember it. I'm right aren't I, Lilian?'

'Partly, Papa. I remember the outside of the house, but I had forgotten the exquisite detail in the interior.'

Cecil Stanford beamed at her. 'It's kind of you to say so, my dear. Isn't it, Margaret?'

'Indeed it is. It's a pleasure to see you again after these past ten years, Lilian. If you don't mind me saying so, you've grown into a lovely young lady.'

Lilian blushed. 'You're too kind, Mrs Stanford.'

'Do please sit down.' Cecil pointed vaguely towards a grouping of armchairs and sofas. Margaret Stanford sat down on an armchair opposite the sofa, and Constance went and sat on the sofa.

'Now what would you like to drink?' Cecil asked as Lilian sat down next to her mother. 'I can strongly recommend the rum and curaçao cocktail invented by the Club. My *khitmatgar* has mastered the balance of the drink and knows just how much lemon to add.'

They all immediately asked for the rum cocktail, and the butler left to convey their order to the *khitmatgar*.

In the silence that fell, Lilian looked around the drawing room. 'Oh, what a wonderful piano!' she exclaimed, indicating the gleaming grand piano in the opposite corner of the room.

Cecil smiled proudly. 'We're very proud of it. My wife is a creditable player, and sings, too. As do you, Constance, if I recall correctly.'

'That's right, Cecil,' Constance said with a smile. 'Or rather, I sing a little, but I don't play. I bought some sheet music with me, as I always do, on the off chance that there'll be some singing later.'

'That would be delightful. And I know that Margaret, too, is feeling musical and plans to play for us.' He turned towards Lilian. 'Do you play, my dear?' he asked, taking one of the seats opposite her.

'A little, Mr Stanford. I learnt at school in England, but I haven't touched the piano since then. We didn't have one in Delhi and we don't here, either. But be thankful. You would certainly prefer the sound that Mama so effortlessly makes to the discordant noise that rises from the keys as I plead with them to respond to my touch.'

He smiled warmly. 'I'm sure you're just being modest.'

'I'm not,' she said with a laugh. 'And if you look at my school reports, you'll see that my teachers agree with me. I much prefer painting. I'm just finishing a portrait of Papa, in fact.'

'How delightful,' Margaret Stanford said. 'Perhaps you'll allow us to see it at some point?'

Lilian smiled at her. 'Of course, I will,' she said. 'Or perhaps I should say that I'm sure that Mama will be pleased to show it to you. I'm giving it to her for her birthday.'

'What a lovely idea!' Margaret exclaimed.

Lilian smiled again, and then glanced around the wood-panelled room, her eyes returning to Cecil Stanford.

'I think I know what you were about to ask,' he said with a smile. 'Yes, Eric *will* be joining us. I think that's what you were wondering, isn't it, Lilian? I hope I may take the liberty of calling you Lilian?'

Across the room, Frederick beamed.

In the face of the warmth and kindness of Eric's parents, which made everything so much more real, Lilian felt a sudden acute sense of discomfort at deceiving them in such a way.

With difficulty, she managed a smile at Cecil. 'I'd be honoured, Mr Stanford.'

A door opened and closed behind them.

Glancing round, Lilian saw that Eric had entered the room.

Going slightly pink, Eric went across to Frederick and Constance and greeted them. Then he said a stilted hello to Lilian, made a vague remark about the pleasure it had been to see her at the dance on Thursday, expressed his gratitude for being allowed so many dances with her, and then sat down close to his father.

'How are you getting on in Revenue, Eric?' Frederick asked.

Eric angled himself to look at Frederick. 'Satisfactorily, I hope, sir. It's somewhat forbidding when you're in a department in which your father has been so successful, but it would have been foolhardy not to have taken advantage of the knowledge and experience that Father can pass on.'

Frederick nodded. 'A wise decision.'

Constance leaned slightly forward. 'You're virtually our neighbour, Eric. A mere handful of deodar trees separates us from Rose Bank,' she said warmly. 'You must feel free to drop into Cedars whenever you wish. And I promise I won't allow Frederick to talk to you about work,' she added with a smile.

'That's very kind of you, Mrs Hunt. Thank you.'

'And I expect that Lilian would like to show you her paintings,' Constance added. 'She's quite correct in thinking that they're more successful than her musical efforts. I think you missed hearing her say that she's doing a watercolour of her father as a present for me.'

'I've heard that Miss Hunt is a gifted artist,' Eric said, going a deep shade of red. 'And on Thursday, we discussed her plans for painting some of the beautiful places around Simla. My fellow lodger, Jack Leighton, had told me what she intended to do.'

'That was good of him,' Frederick said.

Eric nodded. 'Hearing that, I volunteered to take Miss

Hunt and Miss Chatsworth to some lovely places that are seldom painted. As I understand it, Miss Chatsworth will be improving her painting skills under the direction of her friend.'

'Good lad,' Cecil said, and he beamed at first Eric and then Lilian.

Feeling more uncomfortable by the minute at the deception, Lilian forced a smile. 'It's very kind of Mr Stanford, isn't it, Papa?' She looked across at Cecil Stanford. 'But Eric's made it clear that this won't be allowed to interrupt his work. He's very conscientious.'

Four pairs of eyes looked approvingly at her and Eric, and she inwardly groaned.

'Dinner is served,' they heard the butler say, and they all rose to their feet.

Cecil offered his arm to Constance. 'I hope you'll allow me to escort you in, Constance.'

'I'd be delighted, Cecil,' she said, and tucked her hand under his elbow.

Frederick offered his arm to Margaret.

Eric and Lilian glanced at each other, and then Eric looked quickly away.

Thank goodness they were at the back, she thought in relief as she and Eric followed their parents into the dining room. If their parents could see his desire to escape, they wouldn't be quite as complacent.

But enough was enough, she thought as she walked alongside him.

As she'd listened to both the Stanfords and to her parents that morning, the feeling had grown that they'd reached a position where to deceive their parents for longer would be very wrong, and it was time that the deception was brought to an end.

. . .

'AT LEAST, we managed to avoid any discussion about pay and promotion,' Margaret remarked as she and Cecil sat on the verandah after their lunch guests had gone. 'It's rare to escape the subjects, whether we're in New Delhi or up here.'

'As you say, we avoided them today, my dear. I thought it a most pleasant lunch.'

Margaret nodded. 'I did, too. I do wonder that you're so intent on Eric marrying Lilian, though.'

'What makes you think that's what I want?'

Margaret laughed. 'I've known you long enough to be able to read your mind, Cecil. You've mentioned Lilian several times recently, and the fuss you made about the table seating today. You never normally pay any attention to it, unless it's the most formal of dinners. Also, the warmth you exuded towards the Hunts. You're always an excellent host, but this was more than that.'

'How well you know me, my dear. I must confess, I think that Lilian would be an excellent match for Eric.'

She raised her eyebrows. 'Indeed? Even though they don't have a single thing in common, and Eric looked quite alarmed every time she addressed him?'

He smiled at her. 'I hear a mother who's feeling a degree of anxiety at the idea of losing a child. Your apprehension about another woman taking your place in your son's life is understandable, my dear, but it will pass when you see Eric as happily partnered as I with the wife he needs to fulfil his potential.'

She picked up the knitting that she'd placed on the table next to her. 'Indeed, Cecil. I suspect, however, that his wife won't be Lilian Hunt.'

. . .

'IT WAS GRUELLING,' Lilian later told Daisy when they sat on Daisy's back verandah, gazing out over the hills as dusk crept across the garden and the thick green shadows of the deodars, and slender shadows of the pines, shortened.

The scent of flowers was strong in the evening air, which vibrated with the calls of nightjars, and the noise of the invisible cicadas.

'Poor Eric. I felt so sorry for him,' she went on. 'Every time I spoke to him, he went scarlet. Our fathers were beaming as they took this to be a sign of true love in a man embarrassed by the strength of his emotion for the woman in front of him. But I knew it was abject fear that I might have feelings for him.' She giggled.

'Well, I hope your interpretation of his heightened colour is the right one,' Daisy said, a trifle sharply.

'Believe me, it is. As you will see on Tuesday. He's taking us to a beauty spot that he's never seen featured in any paintings. Mama's going to chaperone us, but she's hoping that your mother will come, too. And Mr Leighton will be there as well.'

Daisy turned to her in excitement. 'That'll be wonderful. Thank you so much, Lilian.'

Lilian cleared her throat. 'I know what we've planned, Daisy,' she began awkwardly, 'and I know what I recently said. But I'm not sure we should continue with the deception.'

'Why not?' Daisy asked in surprise. 'The last time we talked about it, you were still very keen.'

'I know I was. But it's made me think differently, being with Eric's parents and mine and seeing how much they're hoping for this. I think they truly believe that Eric and I will get together. When I realised that, I began to feel so bad. You and your parents should have been the ones getting close to the Stanfords, not us.'

'But we can't if they don't invite us,' Daisy said bluntly.

'If you can think of any way of getting a declaration from Eric, we could end this very soon. I'd feel so much better if we could.'

Daisy nodded. 'So would I, and I'll certainly try. I meant to ask you about the portrait of your father. Have you finished it yet?'

'Almost. It just needs some finishing touches. D'you want to see it?'

Daisy nodded. 'I'd love to. And then I ought to be going. It's getting late now.'

'Come on, then,' Lilian said. 'We'll walk round the verandah. After that, Sunil can take you back to your house.'

They got up and started towards the back of the house.

As they reached the corner of the house, there was a sudden rustle of leaves, and they stopped sharply.

'Did you hear that?' Daisy asked, glancing anxiously at Lilian. She leaned against the balustrade and stared hard into the dense mass of dark green foliage that grew in the corner where the protective stone wall along the back of the house met the latticed fence that screened the servants' compound.

Lilian waved her hand dismissively. 'It'll be an animal looking for food, or one of the servants. Or it could be the wind. Who knows? Come on, Daisy, before it gets too dark for you to see the colours I've used.'

WHAT BAD LUCK that the two women had chosen to go to the back of the house at the moment they had, Kamesh thought in frustration as he sat on his bed in his house.

He'd had to conceal himself so swiftly that he'd jumped headlong into the foliage, and they'd clearly heard him.

Or, at least, they'd heard a sudden unexpected sound.

To his relief, thinking it was an animal, Lilian Hunt hadn't felt the need to call for the servants. Had she done so, it would have been hard to have avoided detection.

But despite not achieving everything he'd intended, going to their house that evening hadn't been a completely wasted exercise. He now knew the only time he'd be able to get up close to the house itself.

He had wanted to see what sort of window and shutter locks they had, and if he'd actually be able to get inside the house. That evening had been his second attempt to find out.

As with his first attempt, though, it had failed. He hadn't succeeded that evening because the two women had chosen the wrong moment to walk along the verandah.

His first attempt had failed for a different reason, and had shown him that it would be a difficult thing to do in the daytime, even when the Hunts were out and it was siesta time.

Having given the Hunts' servants enough time to fall asleep that day, he had then started to make his way down the side of the small front garden, keeping close to the latticed fence.

As he'd been doing so, he'd happened to glance up at the house, and had seen the face of an Indian woman at one of the upper windows.

The face was staring directly down at him.

He'd felt a sudden panic, and had stopped.

Instantly bending down, he'd moved a little further along the fence, making extravagant motions of searching for something among the white flowers of the potato creeper.

Then he'd stopped, straightened up, and acting out a feeling of despair, had returned to the ridge road.

Instantly, he'd turned into the Chatsworths' front garden and had begun to go down the other side of the fence, again giving the impression to anyone who might be watching that he was looking for something, while all of the time fervently hoping that no one would ask him what he'd lost.

Had they done so, he'd have had to say that he'd been bringing some papers for Mr Hunt, but they'd been lifted out of his hand by a gust of wind before he could deliver them, and he was hunting for them.

It had been the only thing he could think of.

After a few minutes, he'd glanced surreptitiously up at the window at the top of the Hunts' house, but the face had gone.

He rifled through the leaves for a couple more moments, just to be on the safe side, and then looked up again. To his relief, there was still no one at the window, so he turned round and hurried back up to the road.

The experience had taught him that he couldn't count on all the servants taking their siesta at the same time, and he'd realised that he'd be too exposed in the daytime. It wasn't just the Hunts and their servants who might see him, but the Chatsworths, too, or their servants.

So for his second attempt, he had waited until darkness was starting to fall.

For his third attempt, he'd almost certainly come in the dead of night, when he could count on the dense cloak of darkness concealing him, should concealment prove necessary.

And that third attempt would take place very soon.

23

T uesday
Late morning

AFTER GAZING from side to side at the beauty they were passing through, they finally emerged from lanes carved through forests of cedars, oaks and pines, where rhododendrons crowded the verges on either side, and white roses hid among bushes and ferns, and came out into a clearing towards which Eric, accompanied by Jack, had been leading them.

As soon as their rickshaws came to a halt, Lilian and Daisy jumped out and ran into the centre of what they saw was a fern-fringed glade backed by a semi-circle of dark-green deodars, poplars, mountain ash and birch.

The central expanse of grass was riven by long golden spears of light that slanted in narrow rays between the trunks of the trees.

Their mothers followed them, and they all stood gazing

around them in delight, inhaling the sweet scent of balsam and wild Himalayan lily-of-the-valley, and enjoying the gentle touch of the pine-laden breezes that blew off the distant peaks.

At the head of the glade, water fell in a slender column from overhanging rocks into a sparkling pool. Iridescent red, green and blue dragonflies swooped and hovered over the water's surface, and darted between the ferns and moss-covered logs that bordered the pool.

'It's so beautiful,' Daisy breathed. Feeling Eric's eyes on her, she smiled at him. Shyly, he returned her smile.

Eager to begin drawing the scene, Lilian asked Jack and Eric to help her and Daisy to set up their stools and wooden easels, and to put a table next to each easel.

Seeing them thus engaged, Constance and Grace said that they'd go for a short exploratory walk and be back before long.

On each table they put a tray of brushes, a cloth, two pots of water, and a paint tin which acted as both a container for their paints and also, in the sectioned lid, a palette for mixing the colours.

They stood a sturdy folder of watercolour paper against the side of each table, and then both Lilian and Daisy sat down, checked the steadiness of their easels, and stared at the view.

After a few minutes getting the measure of what they were going to paint, both started to outline the scene in pencil.

Jack and Eric sat on stools a little way back from the girls.

Jack glanced at the cane chairs that had been set out for the two mothers, and smiled.

'Hats off to you, Eric,' he said. 'You've certainly found them a lovely view to paint.'

Eric beamed with pleasure. 'I hoped they'd like it. I thought it offered everything—flowers of every colour, trees in a variety of shapes, and foliage in different sizes and textures of green. And, of course, the majesty of the mountains.'

'You're certainly right about that.' Jack glanced at him curiously. 'You obviously love the natural world. I wonder that you've chosen a job that keeps you indoors for most of the day.'

Eric nodded. 'I do love it. I come to places like this if I want to relax, or to think, or if I feel under pressure, or if I just want to be by myself. They're such peaceful retreats.' He paused. 'You're right, though. I've chosen an employment which puts me inside an office and prevents me from being outside.'

'So why *did* you make such a choice?'

'I suppose it's because I don't dislike the actual work. In fact, it's frequently very interesting. And there's nothing I'd rather do. So, since I must earn a living—I should hate to have to rely on my father for a home, food, money to spend —this seems as good a job as any. Indeed, it's better than many in that I'll benefit from my father's help.'

'That makes sense.'

'When I'm more experienced, I'll be able to have a better balance between work and play. At the moment, there's a little more work to play than I'd choose.'

There was a sudden wave of laughter from both Lilian and Daisy.

Lilian was leaning across to Daisy's easel, and seemed to have made a comment about an aspect of Daisy's painting, that had caused them both to erupt into laughter.

'More important than the job, though, will be the wife I have,' Eric continued, his gaze on both the girls. 'It's important that I have a wife who shares my interests.'

'I can't think of anything more important,' Jack said. He paused. 'Perhaps you should see if either of the girls could use some advice. You might be might be able to help them with the shape of a petal, for example,' he said with mock seriousness. 'It would be a shame not to take advantage of their mothers having taken a short stroll.'

Eric went red, and beamed. 'I think you're right.'

And he got up with alacrity and walked unhesitatingly up to Daisy.

So, after all her efforts at deflecting Eric's interest to herself, Lilian was going to be disappointed, Jack mused as he watched Daisy's face colour in delight.

Their heads close together, Eric studied Daisy's picture. She indicated the brilliant red flower she was starting to paint, and then pointed ahead to a clump of lush green ferns near the water's edge, through the spiky fronds of which several bright red flowers could be seen.

A moment later, Daisy put down her watercolours, Eric pulled back her chair and Daisy stood up, her drawing pad and pencil in her hand. Both of them smiling broadly, they headed for the ferns.

Surely Lilian could see the situation as it was, Jack thought in impatience, and not as she wanted it to be. If she did, she would realise that the only graceful thing to do was step aside.

Staring at the back of her head, he wondered if such thoughts were running through her mind.

Since the only way to find out was to ask her, he decided to do so. And he stood up, picked up his stool, carried it across to where she was sitting, placed it next to her and sat down.

She glanced sideways at him. 'I don't recall suggesting you sit with me,' she said icily.

'You didn't. Take this as an unbidden kindness on my part,' he said with exaggerated sweetness. 'Seeing that you'd been deserted by your friend, I thought I'd join you. Intuition told me that any company would be welcome in Daisy's absence, even mine.'

'I'm sure Daisy will be back soon, and our mothers won't be gone for long. As for your intuition, I suggest you send it back and ask for a refund.'

Jack pulled a hangdog face. 'Confession time. I'm the person who wanted company, and I was prepared to overlook the fact that the only available company was you.'

'This is not about you being lonely again, is it?' she exclaimed. 'Surely, you aren't falling into the sin of repetition, Mr Leighton!'

He opened his mouth to reply, but got a clear look at her drawing, and closed it.

'That's excellent, Lilian,' he said, his voice taking on a note of surprise. 'You're clearly very talented.'

She turned to him sharply. 'Flattery will only get you so far, Mr Leighton. Possibly I'm entering my dotage at an unusually young age, but I have no memory at all of allowing you to refer to Miss Chatsworth as Daisy, or to call me Lilian.'

'Dotage has much to answer for. But since we now seem to be using first names,' he said cheerfully, 'my name is Jack.'

'Is that so, Mr Leighton?' she said haughtily, and she turned to look at Daisy and Eric.

They had stopped at the edge of the ferns, and Eric was kneeling down, indicating one of the red blooms hidden among the fronds. Then he stood up again, and pointed towards the mountains that rose above the uneven line of trees.

Daisy followed his gaze, and then turned and said something to him.

He looked back at her and made a remark, gazing into her face.

She nodded.

Each smiled hesitantly at the other, and even from a distance, the haze of pink that spread across the cheeks of each was visible.

Jack glanced at Daisy and Eric, and then at Lilian, who was still watching them.

'I'm sorry, Lilian,' he said quietly. 'I know this isn't what you hoped to see.'

She went red. 'I don't know what you're talking about.'

'I think you do. I've seen the four of you together too often not to be aware that you've an interest in Eric. But if you hadn't realised it before, I think you'll see now that Eric is looking in a different direction, and that his feelings would seem to be reciprocated.'

'I've never had the slightest romantic interest in Mr Stanford, if that's what you're insinuating,' Lilian snapped.

'Then I'm very glad to hear it. You would be completely wrong for him.'

'What business is that of yours?'

'Personally, none at all. It's my friendship for Eric that's speaking. He's a gentle, reserved man with a love of the natural world, and for him to be happy in life, he'll need a wife who shares similar interests and who is equally sweet-natured.' He gave her a wry smile. 'That would not be you, Lilian, I'm afraid.'

She turned to him, a livid spot of crimson in the centre of each cheek. 'And how precisely do you see me?'

'As a beautiful woman,' he said quietly, 'with a liveliness of character and wit that would terrify poor Eric. For you to be truly happy, you need someone strong enough to stand up to you and answer you back.'

She gave a mocking laugh. 'Such as you, I suppose!'

He violently shook his head. 'Not at all! Perish the thought!' he exclaimed. 'Our casual verbal contests have been amusing, but I've no intention of marrying a sharp-tongued woman who'd make my life a sparring contest. Not me, and not Eric, either. I want a sweet, docile wife, who thinks I'm wonderful.'

'That's a steep requirement,' she said after a slight pause. 'I'm afraid I foresee a lonely old age for you, Mr Leighton.'

'Better that than an unhappy one,' he retorted cheerfully.

As he finished speaking, he glanced at her. To his great surprise, her eyes had filled with tears.

He suddenly thought back to what he'd said.

His stomach turned over.

Why hadn't he been more careful with his choice of words?

In an instant, he wished he could take back the words that had poured so carelessly from his mouth, words that he wasn't even sure he meant.

Bitterly reproaching himself for the pain he'd unwittingly caused, but helpless as to how to undo the damage he'd done, he stood up and looked down at Lilian. 'I'm sorry I spoke so hastily, Lilian. I gave you the wrong impression.'

'You clearly said what you meant, Mr Leighton,' she said, staring ahead.

He picked up his stool. 'I'm sorry,' he said again. 'It's probably just as well that we go back to our original grouping. Your mothers will soon be back, and they wouldn't be pleased to see us like this, you and me here, and Eric and Daisy over there. Despite my clumsy words, I hope this won't be the last time that Eric and I are allowed to join you.'

'From what you've just said, you'd obviously be quite happy if it were.' Her voice threatened to break. 'Who wants to be with someone whose conversation is sharp and prickly?'

'Of course, I didn't mean that. I enjoy talking to you, Lilian. And that's the truth. I spoke rashly, and I sounded critical of you in a way I didn't intend, and I'm bitterly sorry for what I said.'

'Don't be. I understood you perfectly, Mr Leighton. Your unvarnished words came from your heart, or from what purports to be a heart, and it's good to know what you truly think.'

'It may have sounded that way, but I don't truly think it. Not at all.' He hesitated. 'About us coming out with you like this again. May we?'

She paused. 'For Daisy's sake, yes. Contrary to what you believe, Mr Leighton, I want Daisy to be happy. And Eric, too.'

He nodded. 'Thank you, Lilian. That's kind of you. I'll go and get Eric.'

She watched him return the stool to the place it had been before, and go across to Daisy and Eric, neither of whom looked pleased to see him approaching.

.   .   .

As he walked back to their seats with Eric, Jack felt like screaming in anger at himself.

In trying to be quick with a sharp comeback, he'd offended Lilian, and he hadn't meant to. All he'd wanted to do was make her see that things were better the way they were turning out.

But he should have thought before he spoke, he berated himself. If he had, he would have expressed himself better. As it was, the hurt in her eyes suggested that she'd been deeply wounded by his words.

But it was too late to take them back. What was done, was done.

And his criticism of Lilian, which he wasn't sure even reflected the way he actually felt, would never be forgotten by her, he feared, and would always stand between them.

How *did* he feel about her?

His steps faltered. His unvarnished words, she'd said, showed what he truly thought of her.

But did they?

He didn't know. He'd never thought about it. He'd just known that he always enjoyed his banter with Lilian, and after each session he'd looked forward to the next. And he would be greatly upset if he'd thought there were to be no more such exchanges.

Fortunately, he'd been able to limit the damage caused by his thoughtlessness, and he and Eric would still be able to join the girls on their painting trips. He would never have been able to relax had he thought that they would be in and around Simla without any real protection.

So he could banish any such concerns from his mind, he thought as he saw the two mothers returning. But he couldn't so easily banish from his mind the sight of Lilian's anguished face.

He hated himself for causing her pain.

Not that Lilian was in any way special. He would have felt the same regret had it been anyone else that he'd hurt.

All the same, he was really angry at himself for his thoughtlessness.

24

Later that evening

WAS that really how she came across to the people who met her, Lilian thought, staring up at the ceiling, tears trickling down her cheeks. He had made her sound like a demanding harridan. Yet all she'd been trying to do was help Daisy to have some time with Eric.

That was the action of a good friend.

But thinking about it, all he would have seen, and all anyone else who saw her with Eric and Daisy would have seen, was that every time Eric tried to talk to Daisy, she, Lilian, had intervened, forcibly drawing Eric's attention to her, and away from Daisy.

She mentally cringed.

Why, oh, why, hadn't she given a little thought as to how her actions would make her appear to someone other than her father, she wailed inwardly, gripping her sheet to her throat.

Her father had clearly been delighted every time she'd engaged Eric's attention, but no one else would have been.

And Jack Leighton certainly hadn't been.

He'd formed the opinion that she was determined that Eric should be her husband, irrespective of the fact that Eric was clearly interested in Daisy, and Daisy's affection for Eric was evident every time she looked at him.

And at times, Daisy hadn't been too pleased, either.

Although Daisy had known why she was leaping into the conversation in the way that she was, she'd expressed anxiety on more than one occasion that Lilian might genuinely have feelings for Eric.

It showed how convincing her performance had been.

Oh, why hadn't she taken note of Daisy's words, considered the effect of her behaviour on others as well as on her father, and rethought the whole plan?

It was her pride, she thought, her stupid pride.

In her eyes, she always knew best, and if anyone tried to wrong her, then they were at fault.

On their first lunch at the Club, Jack Leighton had seen through the pretence she'd adopted to make it appear that her interests were similar to Eric's, and he'd made her look silly. She'd taken umbrage, and she hadn't forgiven him.

But while it was true that it wasn't gentlemanly to humiliate a lady in such a way, she'd actually brought it upon herself, and should have assumed part of the blame.

Furthermore, she should have allowed for the fact that as a friend of Eric's, Jack was bound to have been concerned on Eric's behalf.

And then, in every verbal exchange with Jack after that, she'd made things even worse between them. By the acidic way in which she'd responded to his every comment, and by her need always to have the last word, she'd built upon the negative impression he had originally formed of her.

That afternoon at the lovely glade, he'd told her that he viewed his conversations with her as a form of sparring match, and looking back, it was easy to see why he would think like that.

No wonder he fought shy of her.

Yes, he'd talked about her wit. But wit alone was insufficient. For there to be a real friendship, that wit should be accompanied by warmth and friendliness. And the last two had been sorely missing from her side of their exchanges.

It was true that as soon as he'd spoken, he'd tried to soften the effect of his words, claiming that he hadn't meant them to give the impression they had.

But no matter what he said, his words, being spontaneous and unplanned, had come from his heart, and in doing so, they had revealed what he truly felt about her.

And they'd hurt.

Why they'd hurt so much, she didn't know. It wasn't as if she'd entertained any romantic thoughts about him, so it wasn't a case of thwarted hopes.

And yet, she felt an acute sense of disappointment.

It must be that she was dissatisfied with herself, she decided, rolling on to her side, her cheek landing on a wet patch of pillow. It was unpleasant to realise that you'd let yourself down.

She was a warmer person—at least, she sincerely hoped she was—than the picture she'd been giving the world of herself. And for her own self-respect, and nothing to do with Jack Leighton, she was going to try to come across as a more pleasant person in the future.

The false image of Lilian was most definitely being consigned to the litter bin.

And as she would always associate the painting she'd started that morning with the words spoken to her by Jack, and with the pain caused by her sudden self-awareness, she knew with absolute certainty that she wouldn't keep it.

Even though, as Eric had remarked, the scene was so real that when you looked at it, you could almost smell the scent of the pine resin and the heavy blooms laden with fragrant petals, and you could hear the relentless buzz of myriad insects.

Yes, she'd never done a more atmospheric painting, nor one that was truer to the view she was depicting, but this would be the first painting she gave to the woman who owned the art stall.

She'd finish it from the sketches she'd done, and by the following Monday, she would have put it in a modest wood frame and would have given it to Stephen for him to take it to Lower Bazaar.

And from that day on, the new Lilian would emerge.

DAISY'S HEART WAS FULL.

She lay in her bed, staring towards the window.

The shutters were open and she watched a full moon slide from behind the clouds and outline in silver the jagged crests of the distant peaks.

She hoped that the day would never end, and she was going to keep her eyes open in order to make every moment last for as long as possible.

What a wonderful day it had been!

Eric had been so easy to talk to. They'd spoken about the area around Simla, and he'd told her about some of his favourite places, and had said that he hoped he'd be allowed to take her to them.

With Lilian, too, he'd hastily added, but she'd known exactly what he'd meant.

And he'd talked about the deodar trees around the glade, and throughout Simla.

They were also known as the Himalayan cedar, he'd said. The name deodar came from the Sanskrit word *devadaru*, which meant timber of the gods.

The trees were given that name because they were so attractive to look at, with their branches drooping so gracefully, and also because their wood was used to build temples and palaces. The Egyptians had used it to build the sarcophagi for their mummies, he'd told her.

It had all been so interesting.

Her painting had been a complete failure, unable to focus as she was, and she'd consigned it to the bin as soon as she'd returned to the house. But no one would have been able to focus on a painting when they were so close to someone like Eric.

And when in so many different ways, Eric was telling her that he loved her.

She hugged herself in delight.

He hadn't said that in so many words, but he didn't have to. Just the way he looked at her, the tone of his voice, the warmth in his manner—she knew that he felt about her as she felt about him.

And she was equally sure that he knew how much she cared for him.

What a wonderful friend to her Lilian had been!

Without Lilian, she and Eric were unlikely to have grown as close as they had in so short a time. It was the ability to be able to speak to each other without their chaperones hovering about them that had made all the difference.

Instead of exchanging polite stilted phrases under a chaperone's watchful eye, she and Eric had been able to stroll around the glade together, stopping to admire the wild flowers, revealing to each other the way they felt by the words they said, and by those they didn't say.

She could pinpoint the exact moment when their conversation had slipped from being somewhat general into something more personal.

Eric had said that he'd almost not come to Simla that year. An opportunity to spend the summer in England, engaged on government work, had presented itself, and he'd seriously thought about doing that.

But at the last moment, the idea of not coming back to the beauty of Simla, and to the wide variety of glorious plants, birds and animals, had proved too much for him, and he'd turned down the offer.

She'd stopped walking and stared at him in relief.

I'm so glad you *did* come, she'd told him fervently.

Immediately after she'd spoken, she'd realised how forward that must sound, and her stomach had turned over.

But he hadn't seemed to think badly of her.

On the contrary. Rather than berate her, he, too, had stopped walking, and he'd turned towards her and stared intently into her face. Do you mean that, he'd asked quietly. And she'd nodded that she did.

Neither had said anything.

They'd just looked at each other. She could read his eyes. They were saying the words he was too shy to utter, and she knew that hers were, too.

And then they'd smiled.

She'd known in that moment that he truly cared for her, and her heart had been soaring ever since.

Not even the sight of her dismal painting when she and

Eric had got back to her easel and looked at her efforts, and not even the fact that Lilian and Jack seemed out of sorts, with each ignoring the other, could take her mind from Eric.

When would he formally declare himself, she wondered. And what would his father say?

It was a shame that Lilian didn't have romantic feelings for Jack, she'd thought several times that day. Jack seemed really kind. Eric spoke very highly of him, and he would be a good judge of character.

And Lilian was a lovely person. Anyone who really knew her would know that.

Fortunately, as she and Eric now knew how they felt about each other, she was certain that their families soon would, too. They'd passed the need, therefore, for any kind of subterfuge, and Lilian could stop the pretence of feeling affection for Eric and could concentrate upon finding a man for herself.

It was still early enough in the season that Lilian's name wouldn't have been coupled with Eric's, so they wouldn't be considered as paired off. And if anyone thought they were, the fact that she and Eric would soon be known to be destined for each other would put an end to that.

It was all turning out so well. Lilian had been feeling uncomfortable about the deception with Eric, and she'd be pleased to know that they could bring it to an end.

Eric's face filled her mind, his eyes shining with love.

And she slowly drifted into a peaceful sleep.

WITH THE HOUSE behind him in darkness, Jack sat in his cane chair on the back verandah of the Rose Bank Guest House, staring out into the night.

He and Eric had been sitting there from the time the sun

sunk low into the horizon, and clouds of crimson and silver began to streak across the sky, until black night had consumed the remains of the day.

Unusually for Eric, he had talked almost non-stop, and all on the same subject, Jack thought wryly. It was how wonderful Daisy had been.

She'd been fascinated by the flowers and insects he'd pointed out, and she'd wanted to know the origin of the word deodar. She was so much more interesting than any other girl he'd met. There'd been so much for them to talk about that it was infinitely easier to be alone with Daisy than it was to be in the company of others.

Other people always seemed bored by what he had to say, he'd told Jack earnestly, and when he'd try to say something that might interest them, he invariably got it wrong and had felt a complete idiot. People must think him a clumsy oaf, he'd frequently thought.

But not when he was with Daisy.

Daisy made him feel as if he was informative and interesting. He never stumbled over his words with Daisy, nor struggled to find what next to say.

It was quite a relief to Jack when purple and blue-toned shadows rose from the horizon, smothering the reds and ambers of sunset, and Eric, observing the lateness of the hour, bade Jack goodnight and went happily to his room.

But Jack sat longer on the verandah, unable to shake off his despair at the situation with Lilian.

When they'd returned from the painting expedition— he and Lilian morose and hardly speaking, Eric and Daisy blissfully happy, but trying hard not to show it—the two mothers had fortunately been so engrossed in their conversation that they'd failed to pick up on any tension.

But tension there had been between him and Lilian, and

while she'd deserved his rebuke, he was still furious with himself for what he'd said and how he'd said it, and he'd been desperately anxious to say something that would lift the sadness from her eyes.

But he couldn't think what.

Nor could he think why the whole thing should matter so much to him, but it did.

25

T*he Club*
Friday evening

SWALLOWING AN INCREASING nervousness as he sat in the corner of the card room in the Club, waiting for Cecil to tell him the reason why he'd been invited to dine with him that evening, Frederick managed a smile across the table.

'This seems to be fast becoming my seat,' he told Cecil. 'Wilfred and I have rather got into the habit of making a beeline for this corner each time we've come for a drink.'

Cecil nodded. 'I, too, find myself invariably gravitating to the same area in a room. I think we're creatures of habit who feel most comfortable when surrounded by a degree of familiarity.'

'Indeed so,' Frederick said. He took a sip of his whisky. 'It was very kind of you to invite me this evening. It was an excellent meal.'

'Not at all. Since I was going to bring up a non-work

subject, it seemed only right that I should do so in a non-work environment. I wanted to tell you how pleased I was with the way in which a friendship between Lilian and Eric seems to be developing.'

A wave of anxiety swept through Frederick, and he murmured something indistinguishable.

'Yes,' Cecil said, smiling broadly. 'I've never seen Eric as happy as he's been these past few days. I'm most grateful to you, Frederick. By engineering it so that Eric knew of Lilian's desire to find new places to paint, it's meant that the pleasure he takes in being outside the town has been of benefit to Lilian, and has brought them together. Your plan seems to be yielding results.'

'I can't really take credit for this—Eric's roommate, Jack Leighton, suggested it.' He paused, and took a drink of his whisky. 'But I wonder if it's working in the way we want,' he said slowly, replacing his glass on the table.

'What d'you mean?' Cecil asked sharply.

'Just that Lilian was very quiet last night,' Frederick said, 'and was far from her normal lively self, whereas Wilfred remarked in the office this morning how much Daisy had enjoyed the day. It was Gladys who'd drawn Wilfred's attention to Daisy's unusually high spirits when she returned home yesterday afternoon.'

Cecil looked up at the ceiling, and then back at Frederick. He frowned. 'Are you suggesting,' he asked at last, 'that Eric might be taken with Daisy, not Lilian?'

Frederick cleared his throat. 'It's possible, is all I'm saying. The two of them seem to have much in common—more so than Lilian and Eric. And from what Constance and Gladys have said after the dances, both seem to think that Eric's interest might lie with Daisy, and that Daisy feels the same about him.'

Cecil stared down at his glass in silence.

'Would that be so bad?' Frederick asked at last. 'Daisy's a lovely young woman with a gentle nature. And the Chatsworths are a most upstanding family.'

'I will never countenance a union between my son and Daisy Chatsworth,' Cecil said in clipped tones. 'If you *are* correct in your thinking—and I'll speak to Eric when I get back from our short stay in Viceregal Lodge—I'll make it very clear that I forbid it.'

Frederick nodded. 'I understand.'

'But I hope it won't come to that,' Cecil went on, 'and that Eric will be able to assure me that his interest lies with your daughter. After your visit to us, Margaret remarked on how pleasant Lilian was. And how suitable for Eric. Suitable in a way that Miss Chatsworth wouldn't be.'

'It's very gratifying to hear you say that, sir. We think Eric a delightful young man, and would be extremely happy were he to be taken with Lilian.' He rubbed the side of his nose, and attempted to smile ruefully at Cecil.

'It's unfortunate, though,' Frederick continued, 'that we can lead the horses to the water, so to speak, but not make them drink. All I can say is, I hope very much that Lilian's unusual quietness was occasioned by an awareness that Eric was attracted to her, rather than by realising that Daisy was the object of his affections.'

'We'll have to hope that your former interpretation is the correct one, Frederick. As you may have deduced, Margaret and I have been invited by the Viceroy to stay for a few days. As soon as we return, which I anticipate will be Thursday next, I'll speak to Eric. While we're at the Lodge, I suggest you attempt to find out from your daughter whether a union with Eric looks likely.'

'I'll certainly do that,' Frederick said quickly.

'Good. Well, let's turn to our thoughts then to our plans for the Annandale Races. After all, they're not far off. I'm hoping your family will join my picnic group. It would be most appropriate to have you with us if Eric is, indeed, interested in Lilian.'

A cold hand tightened around Frederick's heart, and he felt a gnawing sense of dread.

Leaning forward, he picked up his glass and swallowed the contents in one go.

26

The following Monday
Early afternoon

MORE AND MORE DURING the past few days, Stephen had been thinking that it was time that he and Asha started meeting in daylight.

He wanted to be able to sit and talk normally with her, rather than them always having to skulk around at night, hiding in corners, and he had been wondering how to bring this about.

Now, thanks to Lilian's plan, he had the perfect means of doing so.

He glanced at Lilian's painting, which was propped against the side of his desk, loosely covered with a cloth, and smiled in satisfaction.

What good luck that he had happened upon Lilian and Daisy outside the art stall that day, just as they were deciding to give the owner some of their paintings to sell.

Had he not seen them there, he might never have met Asha.

But he had.

And the moment he'd glimpsed her, he'd known that he had to see her again.

He had realised at once that delivering the paintings on the girls' behalf would give him a reason to see Asha, but until Lilian had given him that morning the first painting to be sold, he had completely overlooked the advantage of being able to go openly to the art stall during the daytime.

Grinning inwardly, he tucked the painting under his arm, and headed for the steps that led down from the Secretariat.

He'd timed it carefully. Most of the officers were either still at lunch or preparing for their siestas as it was close to the time when the whole town seemed to go to sleep. He was unlikely, therefore, to be seen by anyone he knew as he headed towards the Mall.

But should anyone show any curiosity as to what he was doing, he'd indicate the package under his arm, and jokingly say that he'd got embroiled in one of Miss Hunt's madcap schemes. They and he would laugh, and he'd continue on his way.

His timing would also be perfect for catching Asha at the stall.

Hoping that he'd find a way of visiting her in the day, Asha had told him the time at which her mother went for her siesta. She said she would always linger for a short time after her mother had gone in case he should come. But if he didn't, she, too, would have a rest.

His steps speeded up. He couldn't wait to see her again.

And it seemed as if she felt the same way about him.

He very much hoped that she did as he knew already that he just couldn't live without her.

HAND IN HAND, Stephen ran with Asha down the slope that took them away from Lower Bazaar, dodging as they went the pine trees, deodars and bushes of wild rhododendrons.

As they neared the bottom of the hill, the background trickle of water became stronger, and he asked Asha if they were close to a river.

It came from a small spring, she told him, known as Churail Baoli.

Moments later, they were walking across a carpet of tiny blue gentians, violets and star-shaped anemones in order to reach a flight of stone steps that led down to the water.

Removing her hand from Stephen's, Asha ran down the steps ahead of him, and crouched on the narrow band of ground that encircled the glittering water.

Laughing, she looked back up at Stephen, and pointed to a couple of bright yellow butterflies that were chasing each other above the water's surface.

God, she's beautiful, he thought, standing at the foot of the steps, watching her.

'Come,' she called to him, and she beckoned for him to join her, indicating the place on the ground next to her.

He went quickly to her side and sat down.

'In a spot like this,' she said, and she kissed his shoulder, 'we can talk without fear of *Maan*—of my mother, I mean—interrupting us and wanting to know what we're saying.'

He glanced around, and his gaze returned to her.

'But if anyone came upon us, it would look wrong,' he said, and he blushed. 'You shouldn't be alone with me like this.'

She smiled at him. 'I know you mean me no harm, Stephen, so I'm content to be here alone with you. And as for anyone seeing us, it's unlikely anyone will come here.'

'Why not?' he asked in surprise. 'It's lovely, and it's so peaceful. Surely anyone who wants to escape the bustle of the bazaar for just a short time is likely to come here?'

'Ah, but it's haunted,' she said, and she giggled. 'So people are afraid to come.'

'Haunted by what?' he asked, half-laughing.

'By a woman in a white sari. *Churail* means the "spirit of a woman" and *baoli* means "water source". Many people say they've seen the woman here. No one would visit here after night starts to fall, and most people won't come here at any time in the day.'

'But why would a woman haunt a spring?'

'It's women who died in childbirth years ago. They became witches, and they try to kill anyone who comes to drink from the spring, or to rest after walking the steep streets in the town. The witch makes herself look like a young woman who's in need of help, and she traps the man. This is how the spring gets its name.'

'I take it you don't believe this, since we've come here.'

'No, I don't. People have got it wrong,' she said, her voice very serious. 'The spirits in the water holes that are found in the hills are good spirits. Witches are bad spirits.'

Thinking she was joking, he'd been about to laugh, but then he saw the gravity on her face, and he swallowed his mirth.

'My mother will be very pleased with the painting,' she said a few minutes later, breaking into the companionable silence. 'There are many views of Simla's mountains and forests, but the scene your sister's friend has painted is different, and has been very cleverly done. She is a very good artist.'

'Yes, she is. And there'll be many more such paintings. At least I hope there will, as they give me a reason to see you.'

Beneath the delicate hue of her skin, he saw that she'd blushed.

'You don't need a reason to visit me,' she said quietly. 'You can come in the evenings like you've been doing. Or you can come as you've done today, even if there's no painting to bring.'

His heart raced. 'You don't know how happy it makes me to hear you say that,' he said hotly. 'Just to know that you want our friendship to continue means everything to me.' He paused. 'Or is friendship the wrong word. You've no idea how much I hope that it isn't strong enough to describe what you feel for me.'

He stopped talking and stared at her.

Her head was bowed, her gaze again on the water.

Gathering courage from what she'd said, and from the way she'd spoken, he took a deep breath.

'I know that I feel more than just friendship for you. I didn't intend to say this today as it's really too soon—it's the first time we've been alone together in the day—but I can't stop myself. From the moment I saw you, Asha, I've not been able to get you out of my mind. To tell you the truth, I love you.'

She raised her eyes to look into his face, but didn't speak.

'Please, say something,' he urged, impatience overriding his feeling that she would need time to think about his words. 'Even if you don't feel the same about me, say that maybe, just maybe, the day will come when you do.' He fell silent.

'Kiss me,' she said, her voice a whisper.

His heart leaping with happiness, he leaned towards her, took her face in his hands and brought his mouth down on hers, gently at first, and then harder.

Feeling passion in the kiss she returned, he pulled her closer still, trembling as he felt her slender body against his.

Then each drew back from the other, breathing heavily.

She smiled at him. 'And now you have my answer. I, too, felt as though something special happened the day I met you. I love you, Stephen. But I wish I didn't.'

He looked at her, startled. 'But isn't it good that we feel the same about each other?'

'What is not good is that we come from different worlds. No one from my world will want me to be close to one of the British, who think they have the right to rule our country and tell us what to do. And who ignore our demands that they leave. And no one in your world will welcome me.'

'Of course, they will,' he said with a dismissive laugh. 'They'll see you're beautiful, and they'll see how much we love each other, and they'll be happy for us.'

'No, they will not,' she said steadily. 'I am Indian. I look Indian, sound Indian, and think as an Indian. At first, the way I do things, and what I believe, would be interesting for you. And getting me accepted by your people would be an exciting challenge. But such acceptance would never happen, and at some point you would tire of me and want someone at your side who is like all the English girls who come over here.'

'No, I wouldn't.'

'I am sure you would, Stephen, and this is why I wish I didn't love you. But I do, and I want to carry on seeing you, even if unhappiness waits for me at the end. Unless, of course,' she added, her voice taking on a lighter note, 'I come to feel something for a man I've met who seems to have an interest in me.'

Stephen straightened up, and swung himself round to face her. 'What man? Is he British?'

'No, but he works for the British. He works in the Secretariat, and he knows you. He has suggested that if I've a message for you, and give it to him, he'll pass it on to you. He delivers messages, I think.'

Stephen frowned. 'He must be one of the *chaprassis*. But how does he know I like you, and why should he help us?'

'He's seen us together at night when he's been returning to his house. But I think his offer of help might be to give him a reason to visit me.' She coloured slightly. 'I have no interest in him as a man, though.'

'And you say he recognised me?' Stephen said slowly. 'That's strange as I don't know any *chaprassis* by name. But I suppose they're bound to know our names.'

'He knows you go to the Club and play billiards. And he knows you are friendly with Mr Hunt. He's mentioned Mr Hunt quite a few times, so I'm sure Mr Hunt would know who he is.'

Stephen shrugged. 'Well, if the man wants to help us, I suppose we should let him. It means we can plan when and where to meet, rather than me just turning up at your house, hoping you'll be there.'

'I agree.'

'We'll try him out before too long. I hope it won't be long before I see you again. Every minute without you is going to seem never-ending.'

'And for me, too,' she said, nestling up to him. 'But I would also like you to come into my home at night.'

He glanced at her. 'Into your home? What are you saying, Asha?'

His heart beat fast.

She rolled over on to her back. 'I'm not saying that we will share a bed,' she said with a giggle. 'We won't—we're not husband and wife. But I'd rather sit with you inside the house than out on the cold steps in the dark.'

'Surely your mother would not want us to be alone together like that?'

'She will not be pleased that my guest is a British man, but she will understand that we're in love, and she will not stop you from coming. She will sit in in her part of the room, behind the dividing curtain, and we can sit in my part. She doesn't understand English, so we can say what we wish. But because she's there, she'll know we're not doing anything that would be wrong, and she will accept you visiting me.'

'I must say, I do like the idea.'

'Then you should come into my home on Friday,' she said. 'It's more comfortable there than here.' Giggling, she pulled some twigs from beneath his back and threw them in the air. 'And we would have more time together as we wouldn't have to come here, which pleases me,' she added.

'Oh, Asha,' he breathed. 'How I love you! I'll be there,' he said, and again closed his arms tightly around her. 'As far as that man who visits you is concerned, he and I have one thing in common—we're both drawn to the same very beautiful woman. The difference is, she's going to be *my* future, not his.'

27

T*he Hut*
Tuesday evening

THE TREES that were dotted around the lawn between the Hut and the Club building were garlanded with small silver tinsel lights that nestled deep among the dark-green foliage.

Sparkles of light glittered on the surfaces of the tables that had been placed on the grass outside the Hut, along with some sofas and chairs that offered alternative seating for those who were not dancing.

Lilian and Daisy's cards were full within minutes of their arrival, Lilian's card being filled with the names of men whom she'd no recollection of meeting before.

Daisy's card had one name only on it. That name had been written on every line. Minutes after they'd arrived, Eric had claimed every dance with Daisy.

But when Lilian had seen Daisy's card, she'd looked at her in alarm.

'He hasn't yet spoken to your father, Daisy,' she said, moving Daisy to one side so that she couldn't be heard. 'And nor has he spoken to his father. If you dance every dance with Eric, it's making it obvious to our mothers and everyone else, isn't it, that you and Eric have some sort of understanding?'

'Does that matter?' Daisy asked, her face dropping.

'I think it does. To make such a public statement, when neither set of parents has been spoken to, would be frowned upon by everyone. As you once told me, Eric's a man who values tradition, and I think he would be disappointed with himself tomorrow morning when he realised that he hadn't gone about things in the correct way.'

'I suppose you're right,' Daisy said miserably.

'Why doesn't he have the first and last dance with you, and perhaps take you to the refreshment table for the buffet? But let other men have the dances in between.'

Daisy nodded. 'I'll tell him,' she said, and she went across to Eric.

A moment later, Lilian saw that they were erasing some of Eric's names from Daisy's card. As she turned from Daisy and looked towards the dance floor, she saw a short, balding man heading in her direction.

Inwardly, she groaned. Outwardly, she smiled as she allowed him to lead her to the dance floor.

THE DANCE finally came to an end.

Lilian thanked the balding man, whose conversation she'd found devoid of wit and about as far from Jack's repartee as it was possible to imagine, and hastily moved to the other side of the room, hoping to be alone until the music started again and she was claimed by the person who'd signed her card for the next dance.

But instead of the dance music sounding, the lights in the Hut were dimmed.

There was to be some entertainment before the next dance, she realised. At least, that would delay the next dance, she thought in relief.

The lights lowered further still, and the dance floor rapidly cleared. The dancing couples moved to the rear of the room where they either sat or stood in a semi-circle facing the dance floor, laughing and chatting in expectation. Those who'd been outside on the lawn came in and stood at the back.

A single spotlight came on, its focus the centre of the polished wood floor.

The room fell silent.

A woman in a deep-blue satin dress that skimmed her body stepped out of the shadows and into the spotlight.

The music began.

The woman started to sing 'Night and Day'.

The room was silent until the moment that the final note had died away, and then the room erupted as everyone cheered and clapped.

Lilian found that there were tears in her eyes, and she surreptitiously wiped them away.

Feeling a movement of air next to her, she glanced to her side and saw that Jack had sat down beside her.

'You must be a masochist,' she said. Hearing the awkwardness in her voice, she coughed. 'Wanting a further sparring session, I mean.'

'I should never have said that, Lilian. I didn't intend it to come out in the way that it did. I've always enjoyed talking to you, and I didn't make that clear. I want to apologise again for my clumsiness of expression.'

'Apology accepted. Now you may go in search of that docile someone who'll adore you.' She put her nose in the air and turned back to look at the dance floor, which was starting to fill again.

'So what did you think of the song?' he asked.

'I thought it very moving, if you want to know,' she said in a monotone. 'It was perfect for my mood. It's the first time I've heard it.'

'I enjoyed it enormously, too.' He paused. 'What are your painting plans this week?'

She frowned at him. 'Don't you have someone waiting for you to claim them for a dance?' she asked tersely.

'No, I don't. I haven't signed a single card. I came here this evening solely because I wanted to talk to you.'

'How unwise of you to waste time in which you could be searching for a slavering creature who'll readily worship at your feet.'

He gave a theatrical sigh. 'Phew! If that's where she's going to worship, I'm thankful for the ease with which I can order hot water.'

She stared at him, and then burst out laughing.

He laughed, too, and felt himself relax.

'I really am sorry for the way I spoke to you, Lilian,' he said when their laughter had died away.

'I believe you are, and I *do* accept your apology. Genuinely. We both have things to regret about that conversation, and the whole thing's best forgotten.'

He held out his hand to her. 'Let's shake on it.'

With a giggle, she took his hand. As she shook it, their eyes met, and held.

Then both swiftly dropped their hand and turned to look towards the dance floor.

'I see that Daisy's dancing again with Eric, and neither has eyes for anyone else,' he said after a few minutes' silence. He glanced across at the area where the chaperones were sitting. 'For some reason, your mother and Daisy's seem very interested in what's happening on the dance floor.'

She followed his gaze to their mothers. Gladys Chatsworth was smiling, but her mother was grim-faced.

'So they are.' She looked back at the dance floor. 'This is something that Eric and Daisy will have to sort out for themselves.'

'You're not going to advise them, or at least warn them that their closeness has been observed by two eagle-eyed mothers?'

'No,' she said firmly. 'I'm not Daisy's keeper, you know.'

She saw the man who'd reserved her next dance approaching.

Jack saw him, too. 'Do you want to dance with him?' he hastily asked.

'No,' she said bluntly.

Jack got up, intercepted the man and had a quick word with him. The man took a step back, gave a Lilian a slight salute and went swiftly across to the far wall where several women were sitting, hoping for a dance.

'What did you tell him?' Lilian asked when Jack sat down again.

'Just that you were feeling nauseous and it would be wise not to twirl you too fast. He took one look at his polished shoes, and decided against a dance.'

She laughed.

Leaning back in her seat, she smiled at Jack.

'You've cheered me up no end,' she said. 'I would miss it if we were no longer friends and didn't talk to each other.'

He glanced down at her card. 'I see you've no dances with Eric. Is that a concern?' he asked.

'Not at all,' she said cheerfully.

He looked at her in surprise. 'But I thought you were interested in him.'

'As you pointed out, and as anyone who knows us would realise, he would be totally wrong for me. We'd make each other miserable. And that would be such a shame as he's a genuinely nice man. He and Daisy are perfect for each other.'

He frowned. 'But every time I saw you together in a group, you were trying to attract Eric's attention. I don't understand.'

Lilian sat upright. 'I don't know why I should mind you thinking badly of me, but for some unaccountable reason I do, so I shall tell you the truth. But you must promise to keep it to yourself. D'you promise?'

Jack nodded. 'I do.'

So Lilian told him about Eric's father wanting her to marry Eric, and how her father had requested her to try to feel something for him. It was all a sham, though, she explained, and she told him about her attempt at using the situation to help Daisy.

Jack sat quietly until she finished talking.

'And you say that Cecil Stanford is set against Eric marrying Daisy, but you don't know why?' he said at last.

'That's right. It's very strange. Daisy's so nice.'

'I hope then that when he sees them together, and sees how happy they are in each other's company, he'll change his mind.' He paused. 'And you really have no feelings for Eric?'

'None at all, and I never did, except that I like him as a person. As for his feelings for me, they're best described as total fear. You should see his face every time he looks at me, Jack. There's always panic in his eyes!'

They both laughed.

'And haven't you found anyone you *do* find interesting? Apart from me, of course,' he added with a grin.

Again they both laughed.

'Actually, I *do* find you interesting, Jack, and I enjoy talking to you—our sparring matches, you would say. But I've not yet met anyone I find interesting in the way you mean. But when you think about it, I've been completely focused on the Daisy and Eric situation. But now that that's resolved, I can think about myself.'

He nodded. 'You should do that. In the meantime, at the risk of repeating myself, what about your future painting plans?'

'Daisy and I thought to go out on Thursday. I was going to ask if you and Eric would like to come and see us when we're in situ. We're not going far,' she added quickly. 'Just to the Secretariat. All you'd have to do is step outside. Lots of the British will want a souvenir of their time in Simla, and the Secretariat building would be a good symbol for them. After that, we thought we'd do Christ Church. And then we'd like to go somewhere outside Simla again.'

'We'll see you on Thursday morning, I'm sure,' Jack said with a smile.

'Are you not dancing?' Daisy asked coming up to them, a radiant glow on her cheeks. Eric followed close behind her, beaming with happiness.

'We've been talking,' Lilian said.

'You can talk when you dance,' Daisy said. 'Eric and I do.' She looked back at Eric and gave him a wide smile.

He blushed.

A dark-haired young man in a lightweight cream-coloured linen suit approached the group.

'I beg your pardon,' he said, with a slight bow. 'I believe I'm to have the pleasure of this dance with you, Miss Hunt.'

Clutching her dance card, she stood up. 'Please, excuse me,' she said, her gaze embracing Jack as well as Daisy and Eric. 'You'll note that I'm taking your advice, Mr Leighton.'

And smiling at the young man, she gave him her hand.

As she walked with him towards the dance floor, she felt the weight of Jack's eyes on her back every step of the way.

Unaccountably, she felt pleased.

28

T *hursday*

LILIAN AND DAISY stood in front of the Secretariat after their morning's painting and watched the *jampanis* carefully place their art equipment in the rickshaw.

'You've certainly captured the building,' Jack said, glancing appreciatively at Lilian's outline and at the first wash of colour she'd given the prominent four-storey structure. 'I've never before realised how much it resembles a chalet in its appearance, despite having a large portico with a decorative frieze.'

She'd caught the sunlight reflecting from the bay windows at the side of the building, he told her, and the solidity of the grey stone walls surmounted by the high-pitched red galvanised iron roof.

He finished by remarking that all the square and

pointed towers on the roof made it look a bit like a castle in a fairy tale.

'That's how I see it, too, ' she said smiling. 'That's one thing we can agree on, then. I'm glad you and Eric came out earlier on and said hello. We're just sorry that we haven't been able to see Eric again.'

'Believe me, he didn't want to rush off like that—he'd intended to come out here again like I've done. But apparently, his father's been away for a few days, and now that he's back, he sent a message to say that he wanted to see Eric without delay. He didn't say why, though.'

'I hope there's nothing wrong,' Daisy said anxiously.

'I'm sure there isn't,' Jack reassured her. He paused. 'Will you both be at the dance tonight?' he asked, glancing from one to the other.

'Definitely,' Lilian said. 'Won't we, Daisy?'

Daisy nodded vigorously. 'And I hope Eric will be, too.'

Jack smiled. 'I'll see you there. But until then, I must do some work.'

Giving them a slight wave, he went back into the Secretariat.

ERIC STOOD in the sitting room of his parents' house, facing his father, who was standing with his back to the unlit fire, his expression grim.

His mother had risen to her feet and was resting her hand lightly on his father's arm.

'Your father has slept badly for several days, Eric. He spent the whole of our stay in Viceregal Lodge, worrying about you,' she told him.

'About me,' Eric echoed, and he looked at his father in

sudden anxiety. 'Is there anything in my work that has caused displeasure?' he asked in alarm.

'Not at all,' Cecil said hastily. 'On the contrary, I hear nothing but good reports about your application and the tasks you've undertaken. No, there are no problems on that score. Continue as you've been doing, and you have a great future with the British Government.'

'Then I don't understand,' Eric said, frowning.

Cecil shifted his weight to his other foot. 'It's about where your interests might lie outside of work,' he said.

Eric's frown deepened. 'You mean, that I enjoy walking in the hills around Simla?'

'No, of course, I don't,' Cecil snapped. 'I'm talking about your marital future. You're old enough now to be thinking about getting married, and I fear you might be losing sight of what matters.'

Margaret's hand applied some pressure on his arm.

Eric stared at his father in surprise. 'But surely, sir, all that matters is that I love the woman I choose for my wife, and that she loves me. That's what's important.'

'Don't be naive!' Cecil barked.

'Do calm yourself, dear,' Margaret told him. She patted his arm, and turned to Eric.

'Your father has got it into his head that you might be interested in a young woman who would not be a suitable wife for you. And naturally, as he wants the best for you, this is upsetting him.'

Eric stared at his mother in surprise. 'Obviously I wouldn't want to marry anyone unsuitable, but I can't see myself falling in love with such a person.'

'Yes or no. Are you thinking in terms of matrimony with a woman you've already met?' Cecil asked bluntly.

Eric paled. 'Yes.' He heard his voice tremble, and he took

a deep breath and continued. 'I've found someone whom I'd be very happy to have as my wife. I haven't yet asked her, but I'm hopeful that she feels the same way about me. I haven't spoken to her father yet.'

'Is the woman Lilian Hunt?' Cecil barked.

'Lilian?' Eric gave a laugh of incredulity. 'Of course, it isn't.'

'Why not? She's a good-looking woman with a vibrant personality, and she strikes me as eminently capable. You could go far with a woman like that at your side.'

'But I don't love her and I never could. She's beautiful, I agree, and she'd be an excellent wife for the right person, but I'm not the right person. In fact, I find her quite intimidating,' he added, and he went red.

'Then who are you talking about?'

'Daisy Chatsworth. She's absolutely perfect for me, and if she agrees to marry me, I'll be the happiest man alive. I know that's a ghastly cliché, but it's the truth.'

'Never,' Cecil thundered. 'You will never marry Miss Chatsworth. I can't make you marry Lilian Hunt, but I can do everything in my power to stop you uniting this family with the Chatsworths.'

Eric went white. He stared at his father in amazement. 'But why? Both Wilfred and Gladys Chatsworth are charming, and they've shown me kindness on every occasion when kindness was needed. And Daisy's lovely to look at, and has such a sweet nature.'

'She's no dynamism,' Cecil said dismissively. 'Can you truly see her hosting dinners at your house for your colleagues—dinners which would help you further your career? And can you imagine her promoting your career by charming the people she meets at the parties and events to which you're invited? Can you? Because I can't.'

'That's hardly the most important thing,' Eric said, his voice shaking in the face of his father's fury. 'My happiness is. And as far as my career goes, I intend to make my way by hard work. You know me, Father,' he said, his voice taking on a note of despair, and he gestured to his chest.

'Do you really think I'm the sort of person who'd want to marry in order to advance my career, who'd put hosting dinners and parties above everything else? Do you really think I'd list dynamism above every other quality a woman should have?'

'Not if that were her sole good quality, no, but it's a factor to consider. If you had the right woman at your side, it would compensate for the deficiencies in your social manner,' Cecil said impatiently.

'Cecil!' Margaret exclaimed.

He waved his hand. 'You know what I mean. You've many strong points in your character, Eric, and I'm proud of you. But you clearly aren't at ease in office gatherings and among large groups of people. Making a mark on such occasions is more important than you realise, and having a wife who could help you do so shouldn't be ignored.'

'Daisy will be able to give me all the help I need,' Eric said stubbornly.

'You're not marrying her, and that's that.'

Eric turned and walked out of the room. A moment later, they heard the front door slam shut.

Margaret dropped her hand and returned to her seat.

'Sit down, Cecil,' she ordered. And she indicated the armchair Cecil always used.

'Now what's this all about, dear?' she asked when he was sitting down. 'Lilian's a very pleasant girl, with a lovely personality an a lively wit. But she'd be completely wrong for Eric. I saw that from the outset. In fact, I believe I said so at the time.'

'You might have said something along those lines,' he said grudgingly.

'I don't understand, then, why you're persisting in this idea of a marriage between them. She couldn't have made him happy, and her strengths would never have compensated for what you term as Eric's deficiencies, but what others might consider to be good points. She would have flattened him, and he'd have increasingly withdrawn into himself. Surely, you want a better life for your son than that, don't you?'

'He's not marrying Daisy Chatsworth. I won't let it happen. I can't explain why. It's just a feeling I have.'

And he got up and stalked out.

LILIAN WALKED out of the Hut, stood a moment or two looking at the dappled green lawn that lay beneath the silvery arc of the fairy lights, then she went and sat at the nearest table.

A moment later, Daisy came out to join her.

Lilian looked at her in surprise. 'I thought you'd be with Eric. He looked determined to hang on to you for the whole of the evening.'

'He'll be here in a minute,' Daisy said happily. 'He was waylaid by someone from the office when we were on our way to get a lemonade. He said he'd have a quick word with his colleague and then bring out the lemonades.'

'He's admirably attentive,' Lilian said with a smile.

'Yes, he really is. He seems different tonight—more confident, perhaps.'

'You certainly seem to be getting on well.'

Daisy nodded. 'We are. He's so easy to talk to. Papa said that some of his colleagues and their wives think he's too reserved, and a bit proud, perhaps on account of the position of his father. But he's not. He's just shy. When he's relaxed, he starts talking about the things he enjoys, and he's really interesting.'

'I've brought you a lemonade, too, Lilian,' Eric said, coming through the French windows that led from the Hut, and sitting down. 'I knew that Daisy would be with you, and I thought you, too, might like a drink. If you don't want it, just leave it.'

'That's thoughtful, Eric. Thank you. I'm not going to ask if you're enjoying the evening, as you obviously are.'

'You're right. Being here this evening, in such excellent company,' he glanced at Daisy, 'is a most pleasant change from sitting at my desk, going through endless piles of reports.'

His gaze went back to Daisy, and stayed there.

Colouring with pleasure, she looked back at him, adoringly.

'The music is about to start,' he said. 'When you've finished your lemonade, Daisy, perhaps we could dance again? If you wish to, that is. And if you think your mother won't consider me too forward.'

'I certainly do wish. I can drink this later,' Daisy said, hastily getting up. 'And Mama will be delighted to see me so happy.'

Smiling at each other, she and Eric went to the dance floor.

'Have you given up on the dancing?' Jack asked, coming out and sitting down where Daisy had been. He pushed Daisy's untouched glass of lemonade towards the centre of the table. 'If you have, is it because I damaged your feet in the two dances we had?'

She smiled. 'My feet are fine, thank you.'

'Yet, you're sitting out here. There are two more dances before the buffet. You could prove that your feet are injury-free by dancing with me again.'

'I don't think so,' Lilian said, shaking her head. 'Mama would be apoplectic. We'd be dancing together too frequently, like Daisy and Eric. We'd effectively be making a public statement that isn't true. It's different for Daisy and Eric. They're clearly in love. We're not.'

Jack turned to look at her. 'Are you sure of that, Lilian?' he asked quietly, his voice suddenly serious. 'I've not been able to forgive myself for speaking so rashly to you on Tuesday, and for hurting you. I kept on asking myself why I was so upset—so abnormally upset—about what I'd said, and I could only come to one conclusion.'

She stared down at the table, unmoving.

'And I can think of one reason only,' he continued, 'why you would be as upset as you were over what you must have realised was nothing more than an unthinking response, made when I was trying to be too clever.'

Still she said nothing.

'So I wanted to see you, and I've been very much looking forward to this evening.'

She gave an awkward laugh. 'Is this about you feeling in need of mental stimulation, and thinking another verbal contest might do the trick?' she asked. 'Or is it that you were feeling lonely again?'

He shook his head. 'This is only about spending time with you. As much time as possible.'

Her heart leapt.

'Is it really, Jack?' she asked, and she felt a lump come to her throat.

He nodded. 'I've always genuuinely enjoyed our conversations, and each time we parted, I couldn't wait to see you again. But I was slow to realise why that was.' He paused. 'Aren't you going to ask me why?' he said with a half-smile.

Biting her lip, she shook her head.

'Well, I'll tell you anyway. It's because of my feelings for you.'

'Your feelings?' she echoed.

'I care about you, Lilian. More than that.'

'I see.' She looked at him across the table. 'Is that why you wanted to come out with us when we went painting?'

He hesitated imperceptibly. 'Of course, it is. I was drawn to you, just as an iron filing is drawn to a magnet.'

She cocked her head to one side. 'Hm. I don't know how I feel about being compared with a lump of lead.'

He grinned at her. 'Not even though it means that you have so much power over that poor iron filing, that whichever way you go, so does the iron filing?' He paused. 'So, if I'm right in what I'm supposing—in what I'm hoping,' he continued, a smile in his voice, 'and I offer you my hand, will you take it and come back into the Hut and dance the next dance with me?'

He held out his hand.

She stared at it, and then, very slowly, she took it.

For a long moment, each stared into the face of the other.

Then her face broke out into a radiant smile. 'So, iron filing, let's go and dance.'

29

The following day

'I WONDER what Mr Stanford wanted with Eric yesterday,' Lilian said, spreading a lavish layer of butter on her morning toast. 'He didn't say anything about it at the dance last night, and obviously I didn't ask. He didn't tell Daisy, either, or she would have told me, but she said Eric seemed confident and happy, so it can't have been that bad.' She took a bite of her toast.

Frederick glanced sharply at her. 'I'm not sure that we should be discussing someone else's business,' he said shortly.

'Don't be so stuffy, Papa,' Lilian said lightly. 'Anyone would be curious at Eric getting such a summons.'

Constance smiled at her across the table. 'If I know you, Lilian, when you next see Eric, you'll wheedle it out of him, since you obviously want to know.'

She glanced from Lilian to Frederick. 'If you'll both excuse me, I think I'll go to the kitchen and check on the store cupboards. If you remind me tomorrow, Lilian, we'll arrange for the *durzi* to come to the house. I'd like him to make us each a couple of dresses.'

Lilian made as if to get up from the table to follow her mother, but Frederick asked her to stay. She sat down again, somewhat surprised, and not a little anxious.

Frederick rang the bell, and when Sunil came in, he asked him to arrange for them to have a cup of tea.

Unsure about what was on her father's mind, she cleared her throat and picked a neutral topic while they waited for the tea to arrive.

'I'm delighted with your portrait, Papa, and I think Mama will be, too,' she said. 'I went into the studio before breakfast, and had another look at it. It needs one or two little tweaks, but that's all.'

Frederick nodded. 'I can't wait to see the finished work.'

When the tea had been served, he dismissed Sunil and the *khitmatgar*, picked up his cup and stared at Lilian.

'You look very serious, Papa,' she said in sudden alarm as she saw the gravity of his expression. 'Have I done something wrong?'

'I hope not, my dear. It's just that I think I know what Cecil wanted to see Eric about.' He took a sip of his drink. 'And if I'm right, it involves you.'

'Me!' she exclaimed.

'Yes,' he said, replacing the cup on the table. 'He and Margaret have been staying with the Viceroy, and Cecil told me that as soon as they returned, they'd find out from Eric if his affections had been engaged, and if so, by whom.'

'I see,' she said slowly.

He cleared his throat. 'I made my wishes very clear,

Lilian,' he said in clipped tones. 'What will Eric have told his father?'

'Well, he won't have told him that we're planning to get engaged, because we're not.'

Frederick made an exclamation of anger and frustration.

'I don't know where Mr Stanford got the idea that Eric was interested in me,' Lilian went on, 'because he never has been. He's always been keen on Daisy. That's been clear since we met him in Delhi. And Daisy feels the same about him. I'm sorry, Papa. This isn't what you wanted to hear, but it's the way things have turned out.'

'I don't like hearing you sound so defeatist, Lilian,' he snapped. 'But all may not be lost. Cecil has no intention of allowing Eric to marry Daisy. And if Eric is as attached to her as you seem to think he is, he'll need someone at his side to help him overcome his disappointment, someone to whom he can transfer his affection.'

Lilian gave a laugh of derision. 'Eric has a mind of his own, but neither you nor his father seems to realise it. He may be a quiet sort of man, but he's not a weakling, and nor is he a chess piece who can be moved this way and that. He'll do what he wants, not what his father wants him to do.'

'I wouldn't be too sure of that. Lilian. Cecil wields considerable power, and Eric is dependent upon him in many ways. I hope very much that you won't give up on trying to make Eric fall in love with you.'

She gave a loud sigh.

'It's not an unreasonable request,' he snapped. 'Young women from families of our standing are expected to follow their father's wishes when it comes to matrimony.'

'I don't love Eric and I never could. And he could never love me.'

'You have to marry someone suitable, and there's no one more suitable than Eric. What would you do if you didn't get married? Be a governess? The idea's ludicrous.'

'So is the idea of marrying someone I don't love,' she retorted.

'Even if you didn't love Eric when you married him, you could come to do so during your marriage. Many couples fall in love after they're married. And it's not as if you've met anyone for whom you feel an attachment.'

'Actually, I have,' she said. 'It's Jack Leighton, if you must know.'

'Leighton!' he exclaimed. 'He was tasked with getting close to you so that he could protect you. But he wasn't told to engage your affections. On the contrary.'

Lilian went white. 'What do you mean, he was told to get close to me?'

'There've been one or two strange happenings, which suggested that someone might intend me harm. Things that might have unsettled you, and your mother, too, had you been aware of them. I wanted to be sure you were safe, so Jack was commissioned to accompany you and Daisy whenever you went off painting. I gave him a project that would act as a cover.'

'I see,' Lilian said quietly.

'I must admit, I wasn't sure at first that Jack would be able to persuade you to let him join you, but he's an enterprising young man, and he found a way. Needless to say, I shall stand him down at once. He's obviously gone further than his brief.'

'His brief?' Lilian echoed.

'That's right. With him busy ingratiating himself to you, making sure that you continued to allow him to accompany you, it's no wonder that your attention was drawn away from Eric. But with Leighton out of the way, you'll be able to put your focus where it should be.'

She stood up. 'I was obviously mistaken about Mr Leighton. But I'm not mistaken about Eric. It's Daisy he'll be marrying, not me.'

And she walked out.

HALF AN HOUR LATER, Lilian knocked on the door to her father's office, and went inside without being told she could do so.

At her approach, he looked up from his desk. 'Well, this is a surprise,' he said, putting down his pen and indicating that she should go to one of the two mahogany chairs in the corner of the room.

She went and sat down, her face serious, and he went across and sat in the other chair.

'To what do I owe the honour?' he asked, his expression wary.

'You need not worry, Papa,' she said coolly. 'I'm not here to talk about Mr Leighton, in whom I've lost all interest. Nor to talk about Eric. I'm here to ask about the strange happenings you mentioned earlier on.'

He nodded. 'I see.'

'I want to know what these were, and why you didn't tell us. Mama and I ought to have been aware that there could have been an attempt to harm us. It would have made us extra alert.'

'I believe I did the right thing in trying to keep you from worrying about what might have been nothing,' Frederick said, a defensive note in his voice.

'We're not children!' she exclaimed. 'We should be

allowed to judge the situation for ourselves. So tell me, what's been going on, Papa?'

He gave a loud sigh, and then he told her what had occurred since they had come to Simla.

When he finished talking, she remained silent for a few moments.

'Not long ago, after our lunch with the Stanfords,' she said eventually, 'Daisy and I went round to the back of the house to look at your portrait, and we thought we heard someone on the garden. It was getting dark and there was nothing to see, but now I'm wondering if it could have been that mysterious person.'

'Why didn't you tell me that?' Frederick asked.

'Because we didn't give it any more thought. We didn't know there was a cause for concern. We thought it could be an animal, or even the wind. You hear sounds like that all the time at night.'

Frederick smiled at her. 'And I'm sure that's all it was. It's why I didn't tell you what had happened. I knew you'd start seeing things that weren't there. It's a while now since anything untoward has happened, so whoever it was, has probably taken his malice elsewhere.'

'In that case, I don't need Jack Leighton, so you can tell him not to come near us again.'

Frederick hesitated. 'I do believe that the risk has gone, but all the same, I'd rather that Jack accompanied the two of you for a little longer. Just to be sure.'

'Can't you get someone else to protect us?'

He shook his head. 'Not really, no. I don't want word about this to get out. It wouldn't look good for me at work. And it might hurt your chances of matrimony.'

'Surely it wouldn't,' she said, incredulous.

'It might. And if you can't make Eric want to marry you,

you'll need to meet someone else. You don't want young men to think they'd be at risk if they courted you. The fewer people who know about this the better. And that includes Daisy. Why frighten her needlessly?'

'All right, I won't say anything to anyone, and you can leave Mr Leighton as our guard. I don't like it, but I can see the sense in what you're saying.'

30

L ater that day

THE EARLY AFTERNOON sun was bright as the Stanfords' team of *jampanis* pulled up at the foot of the narrow drive leading to Blue Pine Lodge.

Cecil Stanford stepped out of his rickshaw, glanced up at the Chatsworths' house, and hesitated a moment. Then he straightened his tie, took his briefcase from the rickshaw, and walked resolutely up to the front door.

Wilfred Chatsworth was at the Secretariat, he knew, as was Stephen. But he hadn't gone to the house to see them— it was Gladys Chatsworth who was the object of his visit.

And if he'd timed it correctly, she wouldn't have yet gone up for her siesta, and he'd be able to talk with her about a matter that really should have been raised some years before.

But just in case it turned out that he was mistaken in

assuming that the male Chatsworths would be at the Secretariat, he had with him some papers that he could hand over to either Wilfred or Stephen, and a covering story that he'd hastily concocted on the way there.

Grasping the brass door knocker firmly, he rapped loudly three times. Moments later, the butler opened the door.

Cecil handed Mittu his card, and asked to speak with Mr Chatsworth Senior.

Upon being told that the *sahib* was at the Secretariat, and the young Mr Chatsworth, too, Cecil said that since he was there about an issue of some importance, he would speak instead with Mrs Chatsworth.

And without waiting to be invited to enter, he stepped over the threshold and into the house.

Mittu swiftly closed the door, and rushed to walk in front of Cecil and he headed across the oak-panelled hall to the drawing room. Opening the door, Mittu stood with his back to Cecil, blocking his entry into the room.

With a note of apology in his voice that he hadn't first checked to see if the *memsahib* was at home, he then announced that Mr Cecil Stanford would like to speak with her.

'Send him in, please, Mittu,' Cecil heard Gladys say.

Mittu stood to one side, and allowed Cecil to go into the room.

As he went in, Gladys put down the book she'd been reading, and rose quickly to her feet.

'How lovely to see you today, Mr Stanford,' she said, making a poor attempt at masking the surprise she felt at his visit. 'It's been much too long.'

She smoothed down the skirt of her sage-green cotton

dress, pointed to the chair opposite her, and asked him to sit. Then she sat back down.

'May I order some refreshment for us?' she asked. 'Some tea or coffee, or something stronger, perhaps?'

He shook his head. 'Not for me, thank you.'

She indicated to Mittu, who'd been hovering in the open doorway, that he could leave them.

'If this is about work, I expect Mittu has told you that Wilfred's at the Secretariat,' she said. 'And Stephen, too. I don't know if this is anything I can help with, or if you'd prefer to take your leave of me and go straight to the Secretariat.'

'That's very considerate, Gladys.' He gave her a slight smile. 'Our friendship goes back many years, so I trust you'll forgive my informality in using your first name, and I hope you'll be equally informal.'

She inclined her head in acceptance.

'But it's you I wanted to see,' he went on, 'which is why I timed my visit for when neither Wilfred nor Stephen would be here, and you wouldn't have yet gone upstairs.'

She smiled at him. A trifle coldly, he thought.

'How intriguing, Cecil,' she said. 'Yes, it's almost twenty years since we were young things together, and Frederick and Wilfred were on the first steps of their career ladder, somewhat lower down than you. However, we've seen very little of you since then.'

He coughed in embarrassment.

'While not entirely surprising in the circumstances,' Gladys continued, 'the distance between us was possibly a little excessive, and unnecessarily so. Apart from seeing you across the room on official occasions and at Secretariat parties, and colleague farewells in the Club, we've haven't seen you socially. Not at all.'

'It was understandable, though,' he said in obvious discomfort. 'I think you'll agree.'

'I'm not entirely sure that I do. Yet here you are today, Cecil. What can you now want with me, I'm wondering. Unless, of course, this is about Daisy and Eric.'

Cecil wiped his brow and smiled. 'You always were perceptive, Gladys. Yes, it is. Except that there won't be a Daisy and Eric. My son will not be marrying your daughter. I will never countenance it.'

Her eyes glittering, Gladys drew herself into an upright position in the chair. 'I'm not sure that it's your decision to make, Cecil. If I recall the law correctly, at twenty-one years of age, a child no longer needs parental consent to marry. Eric is comfortably past that age. This will, therefore, be Eric's decision, not yours. Isn't that so?'

'I know my son. Believe me, the decision will be taken out of his hands, and he'll do as I wish,' Cecil said coldly.

Relaxing the rigidity of her posture slightly, Gladys stared at him in bewilderment.

'But why, Cecil?' she asked. 'I don't understand your objection to Daisy. She's a sweet-tempered girl, who'll be just right for Eric, who has an equally agreeable nature. The two of them are beautifully suited, and get on very well together, so I'm lost as to what your objection can be.'

'I can't believe that!' Cecil retorted. 'You must know why I'm against such a marriage.'

Gladys frowned, and put her hand to her mouth. 'You're alarming me, Cecil. Is this something Daisy has done? Or Wilfred, perhaps?'

'Of course, it isn't,' he said impatiently. 'It's who Daisy is. Because of that, I'm obviously counting on you to support me in this.'

Gladys's frown deepened. 'What do you mean, who she is? She's Wilfred's daughter and mine.'

'But she isn't, is she?'

Gladys dropped her hand and stared at Cecil in amazement. 'What *are* you talking about, Cecil?'

He went red. 'Surely, you can't have forgotten what happened all those years ago? It might only have been once, but still. When Wilfred and Frederick had been sent north of Delhi for two weeks, and we were left by ourselves? I'm thinking of Henry Musgrove's party. Stephen was ill so Margaret stayed at home. Neither of us had our spouses with us. You can't have forgotten.'

Gladys looked at him in displeasure. 'No, I haven't. But it was a long time ago. It was one night of stupidity in the folly of youth, and I can't even clearly remember it. We'd been partying for several days, and that particular night, we'd drunk far too much before the party even began. It didn't mean anything to either of us, so it was best forgotten.'

He raised his eyebrows. 'Was it? Even though a very few months after that, you and Wilfred announced that you were expecting a child.' He took a deep breath. 'That child was mine, wasn't it? It was Daisy. So Daisy can't marry Eric as he's her half-brother.'

'Oh, Cecil,' Gladys said, shaking her head. 'If only you'd come to me about this sooner. I could have told you that Daisy is Wilfred's daughter, not yours. '

His mouth fell open. 'You mean, she isn't mine?'

'No, she isn't.'

'You could just be saying that,' he said accusingly.

'I promise you, I'm not. If she were your child, do you really think I'd have allowed her to get that close to Eric?'

He slumped in his chair. 'No, you wouldn't. Of course you wouldn't.' He put his hand to his head. 'Oh, what a massive relief!' He paused. 'But how do you know for sure that she isn't mine?'

'Apart from the fact that I had my monthly visitor not long after Wilfred's return, Daisy is very like Wilfred in appearance. And in her mannerisms, too. If you hadn't withdrawn from us in the way you did, you would have seen that for yourself.'

He straightened slightly. 'I've seen her a few times.'

'And each time, you were obviously thinking she was your daughter. You will have expected to find yourself in her face, and been unable to see her features with clarity.'

'Well,' he exclaimed, and again he sat back in his chair. 'Well,' he repeated. 'I don't know what to say.'

'I do. If you seriously thought she was yours, Cecil, why didn't you come to me years ago and ask outright if she was? When she was born might have been a sensible time to ask.'

He was silent for a moment. 'That's a good question, Gladys,' he said at last. 'Funnily, in all these years, I've never asked myself why I'd made an assumption, and didn't attempt to check its validity. I think,' he said slowly, looking down at the floor, 'that it must have been that I didn't want to hear that she was my daughter.'

'I see.'

'Yes, that's the reason,' he said, looking across at her. 'I loved Margaret, and I still do, and I would never have wanted to jeopardise my marriage. Nor to have put yours at risk. If I'd known for certain that Daisy was mine, I might not have been able to stay silent all these years. But believing—as opposed to knowing—left the door open. I didn't need to make any declaration, or take any action such as providing for a child. I could put it to the back of my mind, and get on with my life.'

'I suppose I can understand that, but I still think it folly not to have asked me. Instead, you took an extremely upsetting way out and ignored us.'

'I suppose I kept my distance from you so that I could remain in ignorance of the truth. I took the easy way.'

'Easy for you, but not for Wilfred. I've lost count of the number of times that he wondered at you dropping him from your circle of friends.'

He nodded. 'I'll try to make up for it in the future.' He hesitated. 'If you don't mind, Gladys, I feel a bit shaken, and I think I *will* have a whisky, thank you.'

Neither said a word until Cecil had a whisky in front of him, and Gladys a gin gimlet.

'It's a little early in the day for me,' she said, glancing down at her glass. 'But it's been something of an unusual day.'

'It has, indeed,' Cecil said, and he took a sip of his whisky. 'I can't tell you what a relief this is,' he said, wiping his brow again. 'Not that I wouldn't have been very proud to have had Daisy as a daughter—she seems a lovely girl, and quite charming. But it's better this way.'

'It's gratifying to hear you speak highly of Daisy. And fortunate, too. She'll be your daughter-in-law, after all, will she not, Cecil?'

'I think we can now safely say that she will be.' He raised his glass. 'To Eric and Daisy.'

LATER THAT EVENING, the Chatsworths had a second visit in the day from a Stanford.

When Mittu opened the door, he saw Eric standing there, his face betraying his nervousness.

'I'd like to speak to Mr Chatsworth Senior on a matter of great importance,' Eric said.

Mittu bowed, ushered him into the hall and asked him to wait.

Watching from the landing, Daisy heard Eric's words, and saw Mittu go up to Wilfred's office, knock on the door and enter the office. A moment later, Wilfred came hurriedly out, slipping into his jacket as he did so.

He rushed up to Eric, shook his hand, and led him into the drawing room.

She leaned back against the wall and burst into tears of joy.

She knew what the matter of great importance would be, and she knew the answer Eric would get, and she knew that she had never been as happy as she was at that moment.

When the drawing room door was opened a few minutes later by Wilfred, who was about to call for Daisy, she was already there, standing in the hall outside the drawing room, tears streaming down her cheeks.

Seeing her there, Eric hurried past Wilfred, and ran towards her, a broad smile on his face, his arms outstretched.

In sheer joy, she stepped into them.

nnandale
Saturday, later in June

WHEN THEY REACHED the end of a broad avenue flanked with slender pines, they found themselves at the Annandale Ground, their destination for the day.

Impatiently, they waited as the *jampanis* pulled the rickshaws around the huge semi-circular expanse of grass surrounded by groves of pine trees and deodars, to the place where they intended to stop.

Before they'd set off that morning, Frederick had told Lilian that many years before, the British had seen the clearing as it then was, and had decided to increase its size in order to provide some much-needed space that wasn't too far from the town.

To do that, they'd cut into the hills and made an area large enough to encompass not only a racecourse that was about a mile and a half in circumference, but also a polo ground and a cricket pavilion.

At one end of the ground, they'd built eight or nine decorated pavilions, topped with bright-green gabled roofs, which formed three sides of a quadrangle. The fourth side had been left open to allow people to enter and leave the pavilions.

As the rickshaws came to a halt, Lilian saw that at the far edge of the cricket and polo ground, under a cluster of walnut trees and willows, and shaded by large dark parasols, there were a number of cloth-covered tables and chairs that would have been set out that morning by butlers and *khit-matgars,* sent in advance to get everything ready for when their employers arrived.

'We're so lucky to have a comparatively flat piece of ground of this size in such easy reach,' Constance remarked to Frederick as she stepped out of their rickshaw.

'Absolutely,' he said, giving her his hand to help her down. 'With the town being built on a series of mountain ridges, there's no room for a garden unless you live outside the town. And with the only open area in the town being The Ridge, we need Annandale.'

Constance took a couple of steps and looked around her. 'And very beautiful it is, too. Every year I'm overwhelmed by the marvellous view of the Himalayas and Simla. Like the path through the forest, it's truly breathtaking. Although I'm not particularly interested in the races, I still consider our Annandale visit to be the highlight of June.'

'I do, too,' he said.

She looked back towards the avenue. 'Ah, good, I can see Wilfred and Gladys, and also the girls.' She turned back to Frederick. 'I'm glad that Cecil and Margaret included the Chatsworths in their invitation.'

'I think you'll find that they'll always be invited in future,' he said drily. 'We're the ones who should be grateful for being included.'

He glanced towards the picnic tables. 'Cecil's already here, I see. We'll wait for the others, and all go across together.'

'And Jack, Eric and Stephen have just arrived, too,' Constance told him, seeing the three men hand the reins of their horses to the Annandale *syces*. 'I wonder if Jack is planning to race this afternoon.'

'I asked him yesterday, and he isn't. He said he'd like his first visit to the races to be as a spectator, not a participant.'

'That's probably a good idea,' she agreed, watching the three men head towards Daisy and Lilian, who were standing in front of their rickshaw, deep in conversation.

'I'm pleased that Stephen has joined us today,' Frederick said.

Constance nodded. 'Me, too. We've hardly seen him in the past few weeks as he's been working so hard. Gladys said that Wilfred's very proud of the way in which Stephen's applying himself. Apparently, he frequently stays in the Secretariat and works all afternoon instead of taking a siesta.'

'That's certainly impressive,' Frederick remarked. 'It bears out what Stephen said at the office yesterday. He told me he'd be riding here with Eric and Jack, and that he was looking forward to it as he hadn't had much time for riding recently.' He paused. 'I'm sure it won't hurt his career that Eric will be his brother-in-law.'

'I imagine it won't.' She glanced at him curiously. 'It's strange how suddenly Cecil relaxed his opposition to Eric marrying Daisy, don't you think?'

He shrugged. 'I suppose it is. But I doubt we'll ever know why. I certainly don't, if that's what you're wondering.'

'Well, whatever the reason, it'll give us another occasion to get out our finery. I believe he and Margaret are planning on hosting a ball to celebrate the engagement, but not till after the monsoon.'

Frederick nodded. 'I thought he'd do that. I can't help regretting, though, that the engagement won't be between Eric and Lilian. I genuinely think Eric would have been a good match for Lilian. There's a lot to be said for a marriage between two different temperaments as they'd balance each other.'

'Or one would eat the other alive,' Constance said drily. 'And I think it'd be Lilian who survived.'

He looked at her in amusement. 'Maybe so.'

She glanced at Frederick anxiously. 'Seriously, Frederick, you're not still worried that your career will suffer, are you?'

He shook his head. 'No, not at all. Whatever it was that changed Cecil's mind about Daisy has caused him to mellow somewhat in other respects, too. He's made it clear that there's no reason at all why I shouldn't progress further.'

'I'm delighted to hear that, darling. Since you seem to be having a lucky streak at the moment, perhaps you should place a few bets today.'

She glanced across the ground to the amateur jockeys gathering at the side of the racecourse in front of the stands that sheltered spectators when it rained.

'I see a number of our friends are going to be jockeys today,' she said with a smile. 'What a lively bunch they make with clothes in every colour of the rainbow. And how funny it is to see riding horses decked out as racing horses.'

'It is, indeed. Ah, here come Wilfred and Gladys. Just as well. Cecil must be wondering what we're doing.'

He took a step forward as the Chatsworths reached them. 'I'm glad you're here now. It means we can go over to Cecil's table together. Safety in numbers, you might say.' He laughed.

'Good thinking, Freddie. I'm a bit nervous about this afternoon, I don't mind telling you,' Wilfred said as he and Frederick led the way to Cecil's table. 'After years of being effectively ignored by Cecil, his sudden *bonhomie* is quite hard to get used to. Gladys is delighted, though, as she knows how much Eric means to Daisy.'

They reached the table, and Margaret and Cecil stood up to greet them, and bade them be seated. Cecil indicated that Daisy should sit next to him, and Eric sat on her other side. To Lilian's annoyance, Jack took the seat next to her.

They settled in their chairs to the sound of a couple of loud explosions as the *khitmatgars* opened the first of the bottles that had been sitting in silver buckets filled with ice. The *khitmatgars* stepped forward, bottles in hands, and filled each flute.

'Champagne!' Frederick exclaimed. 'Are we celebrating something, Cecil?'

They all laughed.

Eric and Daisy beamed at each other.

'Just informally at this stage,' Cecil said, picking up his glass. 'We'll do it in style after the monsoon has passed. This is informal, you understand, but welcome to our family, Daisy.'

She flushed.

. . .

As they finished their picnic of truffled hare pâté from the Périgord, tomato sandwiches and *pakora,* puff pastries stuffed with vegetables or cheese, and *samosas* filled with meat, sponge cake with rum butter, chocolate cake, scones and small black grapes, Lilian prided herself on having managed to avoid talking to Jack.

Although he'd been sitting to her right, she had maintained a conversation with Stephen, who was on her left.

Such a lengthy conversation with Stephen hadn't been difficult as he'd been flatteringly interested in knowing the plans she had for further paintings.

He'd bumped into Asha a couple of times recently, he'd told her, when he'd gone down to Lower Bazaar, and she'd said that the first three paintings had sold within minutes of being displayed on the stall, and she'd clearly been keen for more.

She'd reminded Stephen that she still had to do a couple of paintings for the school in England, but she promised to try to give him one more for the stall before the end of the week.

She'd brought her sketchbook to Annandale, she'd added, as she'd thought of doing a picture of the races. The livery of the jockeys would be vivid against the emerald green of the course, and she could see that being a pictorial memory the British would want to take back home with them.

She'd have more time to paint scenes, she'd said, as she'd now finished her father's portrait, and was going to show it to her mother later that day or the following day. But after the next picture for the stall, she'd do one or two for her family to keep.

Stephen's attention was then claimed by Constance, who was on his other side.

Out of the corner of her eye, she saw Jack starting to angle himself in his chair so that he was facing her.

'Do people go to that little temple we passed on the way here, Mr Stanford?' she asked, turning hastily to look at Cecil, positioning her back to Jack.

Cecil, she'd noted earlier, had seemed to be making heavy weather of a conversation with Daisy. So she'd be rescuing poor Daisy as well as showing Jack what she thought of him.

'Not any longer, Lilian,' he said, and she thought she detected relief in his eyes as he turned from Daisy. 'At least, I don't think they do. Margaret and I have been here on occasions other than for the races, usually for dog shows or flower shows, but there's always been a paucity of visitors to the shrine.'

'How strange,' she murmured.

'Yes, it is. And years ago, when we used to come to the annual fair that took place between the first and second days of the races, it was always deserted even then.'

'I wonder why that should be,' she said. 'It looks as if a lot of skilled work went into the making of it.'

'Yes, it did. It's not to our taste, of course, but it would be attractive to Hindus, I would have thought. I've heard that it's now considered a spot of little or no sanctity owing to a silly prejudice to the effect that the presence of Christians desecrates Hindu places of prayer. Rubbish, if you want my opinion. But it could account for the lack of worshippers there.'

'How interesting,' Lilian said. 'Thank you.'

Cecil inclined his head. 'A pleasure, Lilian.'

There was a flurry of air on her right as Jack shifted again to face her.

'May I trouble you further, Mr Stanford,' she said swiftly,

'and ask why the place is called Annandale? There doesn't seem to be any house here which would have given its name to this piece of ground.'

He smiled warmly. 'Another good question, my dear. A Captain Pratt Kennedy, one of the first people to explore the region, discovered this valley, and was struck by its beauty. As anyone would be. He named the valley after his child-hood sweetheart, whose name was Anna. And he put the word dale with it, as dale means valley. Thus you have Annandale.'

She clapped her hands in glee. 'That's perfect. I shall now always associate Annandale with love.'

'I think that's very appropriate,' Gladys said, her smile embracing both Eric and Daisy. 'Don't you, Margaret?'

'I do, indeed,' Margaret said warmly. 'You, Wilfred and Daisy must come to us for Sunday lunch one day soon, and we can talk about plans for the wedding. Stephen, too, of course. And obviously, Eric will be invited.'

They all laughed.

Stephen leaned forward. 'May I say here and now that I've no intention of donning a Victorian page boy suit, and walking down the aisle in front of my sister, bearing a silk cushion with either a ring or a prayer book on it.'

They all laughed again.

'What a shame, Stephen. You would have looked remarkably sweet,' Wilfred said.

'We shall take your request into account, Stephen,' Margaret said, with a smile. 'Our first decisions will be about the place for the wedding, and the date. It'll be in New Delhi in the spring, before the move to Simla next summer, I suggest. Cecil has business friends in Delhi that he'd wish to invite, who remain on the plains during the summer. It'd be good for Eric's career if they were included. And we need to think about hymns, and bridesmaids.'

'I'm sure that Daisy will want Lilian as her bridesmaid,' Gladys ventured. 'Won't you, Daisy?'

Daisy smiled at Lilian. 'Yes, Mama. She's my closest friend.'

'Of course, she will,' Margaret said, a trace of impatience audible in her voice. 'But we'll want more than one bridesmaid for a wedding that I hope will be impressive,'

'Daisy looks overwhelmed,' Gladys said with a quiet firmness. 'You were kind enough to mention us all having a lunch together, so perhaps we should leave further discussion till then.'

'Good idea!' Cecil said briskly. 'These are women's concerns, after all.'

He gave a slight cough. 'But before we leave the subject, I'd like to say that Margaret and I hope you'll allow us to help with the wedding. I realise this breaks with convention, but it is obviously something that, if done correctly, will help Eric in his career.'

Wilfred flushed. 'It's very kind of you. Perhaps we could talk later.'

Margaret smiled across at Stephen. 'Listening to all this excitement, I imagine you're hoping it won't be too long before you're in the same position as your sister, Stephen,' she said pleasantly.

Wilfred laughed in dismissal. 'Stephen's thoughts are only on work at the moment, I'm happy to say. There'll be plenty of time for all that other business in the years to come. Isn't that so, Stephen?'

'If you say so, Father,' he said evenly, the tone of finality in his voice bringing that line of conversation to a close.

Lilian leaned slightly forward, smiled at Cecil, and opened her mouth to ask him another question.

Jack turned swiftly to her. 'You need not ask the question,' he said icily.

She glanced at him in mock surprise. 'What *are* you talking about?'

'You know perfectly well. I don't understand what I've done to cause such a drastic change in your attitude towards me in so short a time, but clearly something's come between us. There's no need for you to enlighten me, though. Nor need you strain yourself to drag up another question for Cecil Stanford—I'll direct my future comments elsewhere.'

And he turned his back on her.

AS SHE SAT SWAYING in the rickshaw on the way home, all she could see in her mind's eye was the surprise and hurt on Jack's face, and then the coldness of his expression as he'd turned from her.

But she was the one who'd been hurt, she cried out inside, not him. She had always been honest with him. He was the one who'd been less than honest with her.

If only she hadn't admitted to herself, and in effect to him, that she had feelings for him. More than that—that she'd fallen in love with him. And if only he hadn't implied that he felt the same about her, she might not now be hurting as much.

Everything had seemed so wonderful. It was as if there'd been music in the air, and she'd been so happy and so excited.

But now that she knew the real reason he'd been seeking her company, and that in order to continue doing her father's bidding he'd pretended to have feelings for her, she felt bleak, and forlorn.

She should be showing disdain towards him, not the other way round.

It was only fair, though, that he knew the reason why she had acted that day in the way that she had, and the next time she met him, she would tell him that she now knew the truth about why he was with her.

After that, she'd never speak to him again.

'ARE YOU ALL RIGHT, LILIAN?' Constance asked, pausing in the middle of unpinning her cloche.

She looked anxiously at Lilian, who had followed her into the sitting room. 'You're very quiet, which is most unlike you. After a lively start at the picnic, you hardly said a word. And you do look a little pale. Do you have a headache?'

'I did, but it's gone, thank you. I feel fine now.'

'That's something, anyway. I do hope it didn't spoil the day for you.'

Lilian gave her a wan smile. 'It probably did a bit.'

'What a shame,' Constance said sympathetically. 'I thought it a very pleasant day. We may not have backed any winners, but nor will we have to sell the family silver. I'd quite forgotten the size of the racecourse,' she added, putting her hat on the table and sitting down. 'The horses and riders looked like toys as they galloped around the track.'

Coming into the room, Frederick laughed. 'I've not thought of it like that before, but you're right. And yes, it was a good day. Cecil and Margaret couldn't have been more charming. It was clear to me, though, Lilian, that they would've been happier had it been you getting engaged to Eric, although they did try to put poor Daisy at ease.'

'Poor Stephen more like it!' Lilian exclaimed sitting down on the sofa opposite her parents. 'Did you see his face when Margaret as good as asked if he was thinking of getting engaged? He didn't look at all pleased.'

'I agree.' Frederick settled himself more comfortably in the armchair. 'He did seem annoyed at some of the questions directed at him. That could explain why he was uncharacteristically quiet for the rest of the picnic and during the races.'

'I was amazed at Mrs Stanford talking about something as personal as that,' Lilian said. 'I've heard you say that she's very correct in her ways, Papa, and that everything has to be done according to form. But Stephen's plans are no one's business but his. And as for her organising Daisy's wedding, that was completely wrong. No wonder Uncle Wilfred and Aunt Gladys looked so glum.'

'Lilian's right, Frederick,' Constance said. 'That's something for the bride's parents to do. They're the ones paying, after all.'

'I imagine that Cecil will contribute, too,' Frederick said. 'Like a lot of weddings, there'll be a business side to this. But to be honest, I'm not sure that what Margaret said to Stephen was so very wrong. Just as Daisy's joining Cecil's family, Eric's joining Wilfred's. Margaret will naturally be interested in the members of Eric's new family.'

Lilian shrugged. 'I still think it a bit much.'

'You may be right. But if I was surprised at anything,' Frederick remarked, 'it was that it bothered Stephen as much as it seems to have done. After all, he's not courting— he's working far too hard for that.'

Constance nodded. 'That's true, darling.'

'And if there *was* someone he felt an interest in,' Frederick continued, 'he'd have told Wilfred, and Wilfred would have told me. I know that ladies are meant to be the ones who gossip, but so, too, do men,' he added with a laugh.

'Interesting though this speculation is,' Constance intervened, 'there's still light enough for me to look at the portrait of your father, Lilian. Why don't we go along to your studio and you can show it to me? We can see if there's anything that needs to be done to improve it. Then we'll go to our rooms and dress for dinner.'

Lilian jumped up. 'Good idea. I'm dying to see what you think. Wait here till I call you, though, as I want to uncover it so that you get the full effect as you walk into the room.'

'Off you go, then,' Constance said with a laugh.

Beaming, Lilian half-ran from the sitting room.

HER SCREAM PIERCED THE AIR.

Within minutes, Sunil, Cook, the new housemaid, the *beesti* and the *khitmatgar* were all at her side. Frederick and Constance arrived moments later.

All stood just inside the studio, staring in horrified silence at the portrait of Frederick, which was barely visible beneath the bright red paint that had been thrown over it, some of which had dripped to the floor, resembling a pool of blood.

32

T*he next day*

'I THINK THAT'S ALL,' Frederick finished by saying. 'Lilian already knew the key points. I wanted to spare you any alarm, Constance, but in the light of the destruction to the painting, and the lurid red paint they'd used, so reminiscent of blood, and also the fact that someone obviously broke into the house, you, too, needed to know everything.'

'You should have told me sooner, Frederick,' Constance said in annoyance. 'However, we'll discuss that another time. More important is the fact that the intruder clearly found it a simple matter to break the lock and get into the house, and we need to prevent that from happening again.'

'Sunil's going through the house at this moment, checking the locks and seeing what we can do to improve our security,' Frederick said. 'You can be confident that no one will ever again be able to sneak into the house.'

'That's something, I suppose. But we need to know who did this, Frederick.'

'Can you think of anyone who might dislike you so much, Papa, that they'd do such things?'

He shook his head. 'I'm afraid I can't, Lilian. I've racked my brains, and Wilfred's thought hard, too. We can't think of anyone, though.'

'So you told Wilfred what was happening, but not your wife,' Constance said sharply.

'It's more that he guessed there was something amiss.'

'One thing's certain, we must carry on exactly as we normally would,' Lilian said. 'If we don't, that person will have won.'

'I agree,' Frederick said. 'But for today, I think we should remain indoors, or at least stay close by. Although I hadn't wanted this to go outside the house, given what happened I phoned someone in the police force. He'd been recommended by a colleague in the past for his discretion, and that was his advice.'

'I'm most relieved you've talked to the police, darling,' Constance said. 'That was the right thing to do.'

He nodded. 'I've eventually come round to that way of thinking. The man's assured me that it'll go no further than him and his partner, and they're going to take a look at your studio today, Lilian. And at the garden, just in case there's a clue as to who the person could be.'

'I *do* hope there is,' she said fervently. 'It's all a bit frightening.'

STEPHEN SAT on a pile of cushions, his arm around Asha's shoulders.

'As soon as I wake up each morning, I start counting the

minutes till our next meeting,' he said. 'I'm so lucky that your mother lets me come inside your home.'

She nestled closer to him. 'As *Maan* is near by, she knows we're doing nothing we should be ashamed of. She wants me to be happy, and she sees that I'm happy with you. And she also knows that if she doesn't let you visit me, I'll find a job with another British family, and leave.'

Alarm stabbed him, and he looked at her anxiously. 'You mustn't do that, Asha. If you did, I wouldn't be able to see you, and I couldn't bear that.'

His stomach turned over.

'It won't happen,' she said, a smile in her voice. '*Maan* wants me here, helping her in the shop and the house. She just has to be reminded occasionally that I could get a job somewhere else if I wanted.'

He tightened his hold on her. 'You've no idea how you just scared me, Asha, knowing I might come here one day and find you gone. It's made me think. And so did yesterday's visit to Annandale.'

His voice took on a sudden nervousness, and she glanced up at his face in curiosity.

'At Annandale, everyone was talking about Eric and Daisy getting engaged, so marriage was on people's minds. And it's there even more so now for me at the thought that I could so easily lose you.'

'Oh, Stephen,' she breathed.

'I know I'm not good at saying what I feel,' he went on, trying to steady his voice. 'I've never had any practice as I've never loved anyone in the way I love you. But I adore you, Asha, and even though I can't find the prettiest of words to tell you this, I hope you know that it's true.'

'I do,' she said, her voice low.

'And you know I respect you. I've never urged you to

behave in a way that could cause you regret, even though I'm desperate for the day when I wake up in the morning with you beside me.'

'I know that, Stephen. I love you very much, and I long for the day I can show you this,' she whispered. 'And I'm so happy that you love me.'

She brought her face closer to his, placed a slender hand lightly against his cheek, leaned up and brushed her lips across his.

As she picked up the scent of his skin, felt the warmth of his breath on her face, she kissed him harder.

Then she lay back against the cushions and put both hands in front of her face. 'I mustn't do that,' she scolded herself. 'It makes me want more, and that cannot happen.'

Stephen groaned. He raised himself to look down at her. 'It's no good, Asha. We can't continue like this. I'm desperate for us to live together as husband and wife.' Gently, he moved her hands aside and gazed down into her face. 'Please, will you marry me?'

She lay still.

His stomach lurched.

'Well?' he urged, and he propped himself up on his elbows, staring down at her, fighting a leaden dread that she'd refuse him. 'Put me out of my misery by agreeing to be my wife.'

She looked into his face.

'I love you very much, my Stephen,' she said quietly, 'and I would like to be your wife. Very much. Living with you forever is what I dream of each night. But in my heart, I know it can't be. We can never marry. Our families will never allow it.'

'But we *can* still marry, Asha,' he insisted. 'I agree that it would be impossible if we stayed in Simla or Delhi. But there are places where it would be easier for us to live together, and we could go to one of those.'

Her brow wrinkled. 'Where do you mean?'

'Well, in Bombay, for example. So many people go in and out of the port that the town's a real mixture of races. We could get married there, and live in an area that wasn't dominated by either the British or the Indians. With my education, and with the skills I've learnt while working for the Government, I could easily find work. Possibly in the export trade. I think I'd like that.'

'You'd be unhappy to be away from your family.'

'On the contrary, I think I'd be unhappy if I stayed with them. It's all so conventional here. That's never been clearer than it was yesterday. You must go to the right school, marry the right person, and have a wedding that's more of a business deal than the uniting of two people in love.'

'That's very bad,' she said solemnly.

'You must make the right sort of friends, have the right tea set, give the right dinner parties. And with everyone you meet, you're forced to make the same idiotic small talk. I'd hate that. It wouldn't be living. The only time I feel alive is when I'm with you. So marry me, Asha. Save me from such a life, I beg of you.'

She looked up into his eager face. 'All right,' she said shyly. 'I will.'

'You will?' he echoed, his voice rising in pleasure. 'Oh, Asha. You'll never regret this.'

'I know I won't. Actually,' she said, and she giggled with embarrassment. 'I don't know if I told you but when I last spoke to the man I told you about—the man in the Secretariat who knows you—I mentioned that I thought that you and I might marry. I hope you don't mind, but I love you so much that I couldn't imagine not being with you.'

He smiled happily at her. 'I don't mind at all. I'll bet he was disappointed.'

She shook her head. 'No, I don't think he was,' she said slowly. 'He has only ever tried to be a friend. Not any more than that. From what he's said, I think he must admire British people as he mentions them a lot, especially Mr Hunt. He often asks me about Mr Hunt, and what my day was like when I worked for him. I think Mr Hunt is a hero to him.'

He frowned. 'That sounds very strange. And somewhat unlikely. What does this man look like?'

'He's Anglo-Indian, I think. He's a few years older than you, but not very old. He speaks as a man with some education speaks, but with not a great deal of education. I think he might come from a poor background. He's only a *chaprassi*, after all.'

'What about my father? What does he say about him?'

'Nothing really. He never mentions him. It's always about Mr Hunt.'

'Well, if he's not interested in my father, I'm not interested in him. Not when I'm sitting next to my wife-to-be, and don't have long before I have to get back and make it look as if I've been working all afternoon.'

He gazed down at her. 'You're such a beautiful woman, Asha,' he said, his voice thickening with emotion. 'I can't believe that I'm lucky enough to be going to marry you. You'll never regret saying yes.'

As he walked down the drive to Blue Pine Lodge, swinging his briefcase, his mind on Asha, Stephen heard the sound of men's voices coming from Cedars, and of feet heavy on their verandah.

He paused and glanced towards Cedars, but being unable to make out what they were saying, he carried on into his house. Wilfred was crossing the hall to his office as he went in.

'What's going on next door?' he asked his father as he hung his *topi* on the rack by the door.

Wilfred beckoned to him. 'Come into my office, son, and I'll tell you.' And he went into his office and sat in the chair behind his oak desk.

Stephen followed him in, closed the door behind him and took the chair opposite his father.

'You won't have heard as you've been out for most of the day, and you mustn't say anything to anyone. Frederick doesn't want more people to know than necessary.'

Stephen frowned. 'To know what?'

'While we were at Annandale, someone broke into Cedars and threw red paint all over Lilian's portrait of Frederick. It's completely ruined.'

Stephen straightened up. 'Good gracious, why? And how? How could anyone get into the house? And where were all the servants?'

'The servants can't be blamed. The family was out, and the servants will have been having their afternoon rest. That'll have been when the intruder got in. Lilian's studio was locked, but he broke in from the verandah. At least, we're assuming it was a man.'

'What a nasty, completely pointless thing to do!' Stephen exclaimed.

'You're right, it is.'

'Could Lilian have been rude to someone in Simla?'

Stephen suggested. 'She can be quite spirited at times, and if she doesn't like something, she's never slow to say so.'

'If that were the only such incident, yes, the malice could be directed at Lilian as she was the artist. But I think it more likely expressed the man's feelings about Frederick, who was the subject of the painting. You see, it's not the first unpleasant thing that's been targeted at Frederick since he returned to Simla.'

'At Frederick?' Stephen said in surprise.

Wilfred nodded. 'That's right.' And he told Stephen about the other incidents.

Frowning, Stephen thought for a moment or two. 'I wonder,' he began. Then he stopped and shook his head. 'No, it can't be.'

Wilfred leaned forward. 'What can't be? If you've any idea at all who could have done this, Stephen, you must tell me. Have you seen someone near the house behaving in a suspicious manner? Vera Gillespie saw someone, after all. Or did you hear anyone make a spiteful comment about either Lilian or Frederick?'

Stephen shook his head. 'No, it's nothing like that. I'm sure I'm wrong. It's too far-fetched. But you know I've been taking some of Lilian's paintings to the art shop run by Asha's mother?'

'Yes, I did know.'

'Well, Asha mentioned that a man had been stopping by quite a lot. He appeared to want to be friends, though not in a romantic way. She said the man had actually seemed more interested in Frederick than in her. Apparently, he'd mentioned Frederick on more than one occasion, and he'd asked Asha about her working day when she was with the Hunts.'

Wilfred stared at him intently. 'That's very interesting,

Stephen. I want you to tell me absolutely everything you can about this person.'

'I can't tell you much, I'm afraid.' And he recounted to the best of his memory the description he'd been given by Asha. When he'd finished, Wilfred sat deep in thought.

'And you say he's a little older than you, and works in the Secretariat?' Wilfred said at last.

'That's right. He's a *chaprassi*. And he must come into our part of the building as he knew things about me, like I enjoy a game of billiards. We often shout across the desks about the games we've played at the Club.'

Wilfred stood up. 'Thanks, Stephen. That's been really helpful. You've given me something to think about. I'm going to go across and have a word with Frederick.'

He came round his desk. 'Your mother and Daisy are upstairs, and both are very shaken to think that there was a break in so close to us. Perhaps you'd go up and assure them that our locks are strong enough to withstand any pressure. They don't seem to have listened to me.'

'I'll do that,' Stephen said, standing up and heading for the door.

'Tell them I'll be back in time for dinner,' Wilfred said as he followed Stephen out of the office. 'But what you've said has given me an idea.'

33

C edars
That same day

THE DOOR to the sitting room opened.

'Mr Chatsworth would like to speak with you, *sahib*,' Sunil said.

Frederick rose to his feet. 'We'll go to my office, Sunil.' With a quick nod to Lilian and Constance, he went across to the door and out into the hall.

'Hello, Wilfred,' he said. 'Let's go into my office.' Then he turned to Sunil. 'I imagine that Mr Chatsworth and I will have a whisky. Isn't that so, Wilfred?'

Wilfred nodded. 'Thank you, I will.'

Sunil held the office door open until the two men had gone inside, and then he headed for the kitchen.

'We'll take the comfortable chairs, shall we?' Frederick suggested, and he went across to the chairs in the corner of the room, and sat down.

As Wilfred was taking a seat on the other side of the coffee table, Sunil and the *khitmatgar* entered the room.

Sunil stood by the door while the *khitmatgar* put a bowl of curry puffs and one of shelled walnuts on the low table, poured two glasses of whisky from one of the decanters standing on the cabinet, set a glass next to each of the men, and then both of the servants bowed and left.

Frederick leaned forward and picked up his glass. 'I was ready for this,' he said. 'I take it this is about the break in.'

'It is. I've an idea who the intruder could be.'

Frederick stopped, holding his glass mid-air. 'You have?' he said, and he put the glass back down on the table. 'You've no idea what a relief it would be to know.'

'I can well imagine,' Wilfred said drily. 'No, it's because of something Stephen told me.'

'Something Stephen said!' Frederick exclaimed in surprise.

And Wilfred told Frederick what Stephen had recounted about the man who'd been questioning Asha.

'To sum up,' he said, 'we're talking about an Anglo-Indian working in the Secretariat in a lowly position, about twenty-two or twenty-three, with some education, though perhaps not much. Does that suggest anyone to you?'

Frederick paled. 'Of course, it does. I never really think of him, it was so long ago. But I suppose the boy would be that age by now.'

'Not *the* boy, Freddie, but *your* boy—your son with Binita. We may be a long way from Calcutta, but I'm wondering if it could be Kamesh.'

'Mad as it sounds, I suppose it's possible,' Frederick said slowly. 'I can't think of anyone else it could be. And I suppose I did behave somewhat badly towards him and

Binita.' He shook his head. 'But I don't know. It seems so unlikely that someone would chase me here from Calcutta.'

'They would if they had a strong motive to do so.'

'If it *is* Kamesh—and I'm no way convinced it is—the only reason for coming here would surely be that he wanted to get to know me. But if that were so, he'd have identified himself instead of playing tricks on me.'

Wilfred raised his eyebrows. 'You would have acknowledged him, would you?'

'Of course not! How could I?' He gave a sigh of despair. 'I see what you're saying, but I still think we could be on the wrong path, and it might not be him.'

'Maybe. But now that this possibility has been raised, you need to establish whether or not it *is* Kamesh, don't you?'

Frederick gestured helplessness. 'How would I do that? Even if I saw him, I doubt I'd recognise him—he was two years old when I left.'

'You might see yourself in his features, or maybe you'd see Binita's face, or an expression that reminded you of her. And I could look at him, too. I remember Binita quite clearly. It's worth a try, isn't it?'

'I don't think I've any choice.' He ran his fingers through his hair. 'If it *is* him, Wilfred, what shall I do?'

'That'll be up to you,' Wilfred said quietly. 'No one can tell you how to behave towards your son.'

Frederick sat back and looked around the office. His eyes returned to Wilfred.

'I wonder what Binita's doing now. I wonder if she married again and had more children. D'you know, Wilfred, I'm ashamed to say that I've not given her any thought since I left Calcutta for Delhi and started living as if I'd never got married. Constance and Lilian are my family now, and for years, I'd all but forgotten I'd once had another.'

'D'you have any regrets about what happened?'

'I wish I'd listened to you and never married Binita, for her sake and for mine. I *did* love her, but I was far too young to appreciate what it would be like never to live openly with her, never to be accepted by my family and friends, to live in fear of an exposure that would cost me my job.'

'That's understandable.'

'But I've no regrets about marrying Constance. I'm very glad I did. But to come back to Kamesh, if it *is* him, how will we find him?'

Wilfred thought for a moment. 'Well, the idea of Kamesh resulted from something Asha told Stephen. She's seen him so she could identify him for us. We could ask her to go to the Secretariat in the morning and meet us there. We'd go with her to a position where she could see the *chaprassis* without being seen by them, and then she could point him out.'

Frederick frowned. 'I wouldn't want to put her at any risk.'

'Even if he saw her, I don't think she would be. Looking back at what the man's done, I don't think he intends to cause you physical harm. What he's done has been unsettling, but no one's been hurt. That's another reason for thinking that the perpetrator could be your son. If it *is* Kamesh, he might just want you to notice him.'

Frederick nodded. 'Everything you say, Wilfred, makes good sense. Right, then. I'll go to Asha, shall I?'

'It might be better if we used Stephen as an intermediary. He could tell her when to go to the Secretariat, and what we want her to do. He's used to communicating with her, and we're not. He could visit her tomorrow, and ask her to go to the Secretariat the following morning. He can tell her that she'll be paid for her time.'

'Right,' Frederick said. 'That's what we'll do. And what happens after we've identified him? My mind's a blank, I've been so worried.'

'When Asha's identified the man, Stephen could ask him to come here on Thursday evening.'

'Suppose he refuses?'

'I doubt he will. But it could be made clear that he'd lose his job if he didn't do as he was asked. He wouldn't want that to happen, I'm sure.'

Frederick nodded. 'No, he wouldn't. Thursday will be fine. I don't think the girls are planning on going to the Hut this Thursday, but I can suggest they change their mind. If they do, Constance will go with them.'

'I imagine they'll agree.'

'If they don't, I'll tell them they'll have to retire to their rooms after dinner. The servants will be told to go to their quarters. I need to be able to talk to the man without being overheard. When I do, I'll know very quickly if he's my son.'

'And if he isn't, you can find out why he's been playing tricks on you.'

'Well done, Wilfred. It's a good plan.' Frederick picked up his glass and took a sip of his whisky.

'Whether or not it turns out to be Kamesh, I'm grateful to have some hope that this nightmare might soon come to an end, even if that hope proves to be short-lived. Thank you, Wilfred. I couldn't have had a better friend.'

He raised his glass to Wilfred, and then finished his whisky.

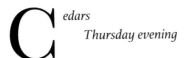

34

C*edars*
  Thursday evening

THE EVENING CHILL had begun to settle on the distant hills and valleys.

Caught in the ivory light of the moon, the pine trees stood proud on the darkened hills, silver silhouettes against a velvet black sky.

Nightjars called in the air above the houses along the ridge road, vying with the plaintive note of a solitary jackal and the barking of the occasional karka deer.

As Lilian crossed the hall to the stairs, she glanced in surprise at the door to her father's office, into which he'd retreated immediately that their dinner was over. It was closed.

It had been very unlike him to go to his office after dinner, and it had been most unusual for him to encourage her to go to the dance in the way that he had.

And then, because she had said that with everything that had been happening, they didn't feel like going to the dances that week, for him to ask her and her mother to go upstairs after the meal, rather than sit in the sitting room, seemed very odd.

He had told them that a colleague would be visiting, who'd requested a degree of secrecy, and that he and the man needed to talk in private.

She hadn't entirely believed him, and from the expression on her mother's face, it was clear that she wasn't convinced, either. But her mother had made it clear that she intended to do as she'd been asked, and that Lilian, too, must go upstairs.

'I'll follow you up,' Lilian had told her, taking as long as she could to pick up her novel.

Who could be visiting her father, she wondered. It was impossible not to feel curious as for the past couple of days he had been acting very strangely.

At times, he'd seemed quite apprehensive. And at other times, there'd been a suppressed excitement about him. At no point, though, had he seemed relaxed.

Her mother had noticed that, too, and she'd asked him on several occasions if all was well at work. He'd assured her that it was, but he wasn't coming across as the confident man he used to be.

While that was not completely surprising, given the number of unpleasant actions that had unsettled him, it suggested that something important was about to happen.

And her every instinct told her that it was something to do with the man who'd be coming that evening.

The rap of the door knocker broke into her thoughts.

Hearing footsteps coming from the kitchen area, she

hastily sped upstairs before Sunil could see her, and ran to the shadowy corner of the landing.

Kneeling on the floor, she peered through the gaps between the wooden banister posts and watched Sunil approach the front door and open it.

Oh, she almost exclaimed out loud at the sight of the Indian who'd come to see her father.

She'd seen him before.

He'd passed her once or twice on the Mall, and she'd seen him near the art stall on several occasions.

The reason he'd stood out was that there was something familiar about his appearance, which had made her glance at his face in a way she wouldn't normally have done, but not so familiar that she'd given him any thought once he'd passed them by.

She watched Sunil lead the man across the hall to her father's office, and she heard him close the office door behind them.

Rising to her feet, she brushed down the skirt of her dress, hurried into her bedroom, closed the door and leaned back against it.

Her every instinct shouted out that this was the man who'd destroyed her painting, and was perhaps responsible for the incidents with the card and horseshoe.

Was her father trying to discover the reason for the attacks? And if he did find out, would he tell her and her mother?

His secrecy that evening suggested not. But she wanted to know. She had a right to know. After all, it was *her* painting that had been destroyed.

She went across to her dressing table, sat down, and picked up the hair brush that had been lying on her sketch-pad. Earlier she'd been outlining the jumble of flowers that trailed over the front verandah, thinking that might be a watercolour for the school, rather than give it to the art stall.

The art stall, she thought in sudden excitement. She'd seen him near the art stall. Asha might know who the man was.

But her excitement rapidly waned.

She'd only glimpsed him a few times in the past, and seen him for a moment or two that evening, when she had been looking down on him, not facing him, so the details she could give Asha about his appearance were few, and would fit any number of Indians.

Or even Anglo-Indians. His skin was on the lighter side, so he could be an Anglo-Indian.

She bit her lip. He was still downstairs. If only she could follow him when he left.

If she could find out where he lived, she could go another day, wait for him to get back home, and then approach him and talk to him.

But she knew she couldn't follow him. Not on her own, and certainly not at such a late hour.

Jack could, though.

Impulsively, she jumped up, went to her door, and opened it. Quietly, she stepped out on to the landing and listened. Apart from the muffled voices coming from her father's office, the house was silent.

Before she thought better of it, her heart beating fast, she crept down the stairs, picked up the telephone, and dialled the Gillespie number. When Vera answered the phone, she asked in low tones for Mr Leighton. If Vera was surprised at her call, she hid it well, and went to find Jack.

Minutes later, Jack came to the phone.

'I can't talk,' Lilian whispered into the telephone. 'There's an Indian man here, talking to Father in his office. I think it's the man who wrecked my painting. Will you follow him when he leaves?'

Without hesitation, Jack said he would, and hung up.

Humbled by Jack's instant support, despite her rudeness to him on the last occasion they'd met, Lilian went quickly back up the stairs, into her room and closed her door.

Please make her father and the man continue talking long enough for Jack to get into a position from which he could follow the man, she mentally pleaded.

35

Frederick and Kamesh stood facing each other in Frederick's office, the desk between them.

Silence hung in the air.

'Who are you?' Frederick said at last, forcing himself to look away from the eyes that were Binita's eyes, from the smile that was his smile, from the strong jawline that was his.

'You know who I am,' Kamesh said quietly.

'And who's that?'

'Your son, Kamesh.'

Frederick forced out a derisory laugh. 'My wife, Constance, and I have a daughter.'

'Your wife, Binita, and you had a son. I am that son.'

Frederick managed a second derisory laugh. 'I don't know what you want, but I can assure you that lies won't get you anywhere.'

Kamesh went up to the desk. He put his hand in his pocket, took something out and placed it on the desk in front of Frederick.

Frederick stared down at it, not touching it.

He didn't need to. He'd have known it anywhere.

It was the gold chain from which a locket hung, the chain he'd given Binita on the day he'd married her.

The years rolled back and he saw himself putting the necklace around her neck, promising her that with it came a love that would never die. And he saw her looking up at him with devotion and complete trust.

And he suddenly wanted to cry.

But he mustn't.

It was the very last thing he should do.

He steeled himself to speak as normally as he could.

'I've never seen that before,' he said with a forced calm.

'Look at the back of the locket, if you wish,' Kamesh replied, a note of scorn creeping into his voice. 'You'll see your name engraved on the back, and that of my mother. Your names are entwined. When you gave it to her in Calcutta on the day you married her, you promised never to leave her.' His tone hardened into accusation. 'But you did. Two years later you were gone, leaving my mother behind with me.'

'That's a lie,' Frederick said, fear sharpening his voice. 'Anyone could have had those names engraved.'

'But they didn't. You did.'

'As for your reference to Calcutta,' Frederick continued. 'Just about everyone knows that Calcutta used to be the capital of India. But that in December 1911, the anti-British situation in Calcutta, and the general political unrest, forced us to shift the capital to Delhi. You've clearly made your accusation fit the known facts.'

'That was my second reference this summer to Calcutta,' Kamesh said, his voice icy. 'The first was the picture of the goddess Kali on the card I sent you. She gave her name to Calcutta. But you wouldn't know that. You British create a little Britain wherever you go, rather than learn about the country that is to be your home.'

'You can say what you like, but you're not my son,' Frederick said tersely.

Kamesh's smile was chill. 'I think anyone who looked closely at my face would see enough of you in me to believe what I say.'

'I think not. I can't see myself in your features. Your father was clearly not an Indian, but he wasn't me. If your mother said she was married to me, then she was lying.'

'She did not lie. And I'm sure you'll want to know what happened to her, and to me, after you left.'

'I don't know her, or you, so why should I?'

Frederick glanced down at the locket, hoping that Kamesh wouldn't see from his eyes that although he'd not thought of Binita for many a year, now that his past had invaded his present, for his peace of mind, he needed to hear that her life had been a good one, despite his cruelty in deserting her.

Yes, it had been an act of cruelty, he could now see, and of cowardice, and even though he'd had no choice, he hated what that said about him.

If only Binita had heeded the warnings of her family and friends, and had refused to marry him! But she hadn't, and their prophesies had all come true.

The movement against British men taking an Indian woman had strengthened, and it had soon become brutally clear that if he admitted to having an Indian wife, he would be socially ostracised and it would be the end of a promising career.

Increasingly, therefore, Binita had become a millstone, and even before the boy had been born, he had deeply regretted his marriage.

When the chance to move to Delhi had come, he'd grabbed it with both hands.

He obviously couldn't take her and the boy with him, so without warning her that he was leaving, he had disappeared to Delhi as a single man, leaving her all the money he could.

Not long after his arrival in Delhi, he'd been introduced to Constance, a banker's daughter who was both well off and from the right background, and he had married her.

He had never really been married to Binita, he'd reasoned with himself at the time.

A sort of religious wedding—her religion, not his—in an upper room of an Indian house, was not a proper marriage, not like his marriage to Constance, which had been in a church, witnessed by their families, friends and work colleagues, and officially registered.

He glanced again at the locket. It looked accusingly back at him.

But his years with Binita were so long ago, and although a part of him, faced with the sudden appearance of Kamesh, felt a definite pang of regret for what circumstances had forced him to do, his past mistakes mustn't be allowed to bring to an end his successful career, and his highly satisfactory life with Constance and his lovely daughter.

At the thought of Lilian, his stomach turned over.

If word got out that he had an Indian son—Lilian's half-brother, in fact—it would end Lilian's chances of making a good marriage.

No one must ever know, he thought in renewed determination.

'My mother died two years ago,' he heard Kamesh say.

A wave of relief swept through Frederick, followed by an intense sadness.

Binita's lovely face filled his mind, and he swallowed hard.

As if from afar, he heard Kamesh tell him that Binita's life had been desperate since Frederick abandoned them.

Discarded by her parents for having brought shame upon the family, which was evidenced by her Anglo-Indian child, she'd been given a home by an unpleasant old Indian, who was a distant relative.

But she was no more than a servant to him, a woman who looked after his house, cooked his meals and had to go to his bed when he commanded.

She'd endured such a life, however, so that he, Kamesh, had a place to live and some sort of education.

It was not a happy life for either of them, living with the disgusting man, but it had been better than it would have been on the streets, where they would have been just two more beggars among the many in Calcutta, and for that he would always love and revere his mother.

Sadly, when his mother had become ill with pains in her stomach, the old Indian had refused to seek medical care for her, and his mother had died.

Before then, encouraged by her, he'd decided to try to take advantage of one of the increasing number of opportunities to work for the British rulers. And to give himself a better chance of succeeding, he had tried to improve on his education.

He had been confident that it would be worth all the hours he put in. The Heaven-born ICS officers couldn't be expected to do the humdrum tasks, he'd told Frederick with a sneer, so they were filling the lower ranks of the administration with an army of subordinate clerks recruited in India.

'I was pretty sure that you'd be coming to Simla for the

summer, and with my mother having died, I came up here as soon as the snows melted, went to the Secretariat and applied to be a *chaprassi*. They had yet to fill all the vacancies, and as I'd had some education, I was given the job.'

Frederick raised his eyes from the locket and stared at Kamesh. 'I don't know you, but it doesn't stop me from being curious as to why you'd want to come up here. Why *did* you?'

Kamesh looked down at the locket, and then looked back at Frederick.

'I vaguely remember seeing you when I was a child, in the days when my mother was happy. Now that I'm no longer a child, I wanted to see again the man whose actions destroyed the happiness in my mother, and replaced it with misery. That man is you.'

'And now you've seen the person you mistakenly believe to be your father,' Frederick said, struggling to hold back tears of remorse, 'what next?'

'My task is not yet finished,' Kamesh said, picking up the locket and returning it to his pocket. 'My mother was your guilty secret for years. And so was I. But for no longer. I intend to identify you as my mother's husband and my father. My mother's marriage to you will be recognised, and she will have died a married woman, not a kept woman.'

'Her family are alive, are they?' Frederick asked.

'No, they are long gone. There are not many people who remember *Maan* these days, or who have an interest in her. But that does not matter. This would please her, so it's for her, to thank her for all she did for me.'

Frederick was silent for a moment.

'I would deny that you're my son,' he said at last. 'And I'd be believed. And even if I wasn't entirely believed by everyone, they'd all pretend to believe me. What it would do, though, is greatly upset and unsettle my wife, Constance, and my daughter, Lilian, and this I cannot allow.'

'You have no choice in the matter,' Kamesh said, his voice icy.

'But *you* do,' Frederick said bluntly. '*You* have a choice. I recognise ambition when I see it, and grudgingly I feel that it should be rewarded. But as things stand, you'll always be hampered by your background and your limited education.'

'Which is *your* fault,' Kamesh countered. 'I got a brain from you, but your desertion made it impossible for me to expand it as I would have liked.'

'However, if you promise never again to make such a ridiculous claim against me,' Frederick continued, ignoring the interruption, 'I'll give you some money and books that will help you to improve your education. I'll also arrange for you to go back to Delhi at once, and be given a job in the Secretariat as a clerk. And I'll see that you have somewhere to live.'

Kamesh gave a sharp exclamation. His hand flew to his mouth, and he stared at Frederick, his dark eyes wide open.

'And when you reach a sufficient standard of education,' Frederick went on, 'I'll discreetly help you with your career. You, yourself, remarked on the greater opportunities today for Indians. Well, the Government's been forced to go even further with the constitutional reforms than it intended as, quite simply, they can't get sufficient Europeans to fill ICS posts. So there'll be a position for you when you're ready, a position with status.'

Breathing heavily, Kamesh stood still, staring at Frederick.

'If you refuse the offer, Kamesh, and persist in accusing me of being your father, no one will believe you, and you'll walk away with nothing.' He paused. 'You talked before about pleasing your mother. What would she advise you to do?'

Tears filled Kamesh's eyes. 'She'd urge me to take the money and take your help,' he said, a sob in his voice, 'so that's what I'll do.' Tears streamed down his cheeks. 'But you *are* my father, though I wish you weren't.'

Frederick nodded dismissal. 'Your transfer to Delhi will be done through official channels. You'd better leave your address and details with the reception in the Secretariat. I'll take it from there. When I return to New Delhi in October with my family, you're not to approach me or them. Is that clear?'

'Yes,' Kamesh whispered.

'I'm doing this as an act of kindness, as a reward for your ambition,' Frederick said. 'But you're not my son. Now you may leave.'

A moment later, the door closed behind Kamesh.

Frederick stood motionless, staring at the place where Kamesh had stood.

Then he sat down heavily, put his head in his hands and wept, grieving for the first time in twenty-one years for the woman and child he used to love.

But not enough.

Unable or unwilling to place them above his own interests, he'd abandoned them as soon as an opportunity had been afforded him. His wife and his little child.

What did that say about him?

Tears flowed again as he faced the fact that he'd been the sort of man who'd been able to deny his family.

And clearly still was.

That evening, had he wanted, he might have been able to open the door and get to know his son. With careful planning, this could probably have been done in secrecy.

But not definitely.

So he hadn't wanted it enough.

Despite the grief he genuinely felt, his ambition was still too strong, and his life with Constance and Lilian much too satisfying for him ever to jeopardise either, not even for his son.

Not even though that evening he'd felt the stirrings of a feeling for his son that had long lain dormant.

But instead of yielding to a resurgence of love, he had again turned his back on his son, and too frightened that the likeness between them might be perceived if Kamesh were to continue much longer in the same building as he, Kamesh was going to be sent to New Delhi as soon as possible.

And when he and Constance returned to the capital, Kamesh would be transferred to a department in a different building from him.

But he would be true to what he'd promised his son, and he'd make sure that he had as good a career as was possible for an Anglo-Indian. And very quietly, and unseen, he'd keep an eye on him.

He owed him that much at the very least.

He wiped his face, stood up, switched off the light on his desk, walked across to the door and opened it. He took one look around his empty office, and then turned to face the hall.

No regrets, he told himself, and he stepped into the hall and firmly closed the door behind him. What's done is done, and it was done because there had been no realistic alternative.

36

L *ater*

UNAWARE THAT HE'D been followed since leaving the Hunts'
house, Kamesh ran through the town to the steps leading up
to the house he shared, his face wet with tears, his mind in
confusion.

Upon reaching the steps, he sank down.

Trembling, he hunched over his knees, trying not to feel
the pain that pierced him; trying not to feel the terrible hurt
that ached deep within him; trying not to feel acute disappointment and despair.

Nothing had turned out as it should have done.

He'd thought that at last, when he'd faced his father and
identified himself, he'd feel a sense of satisfaction that his
campaign had caused well-deserved disquiet, and that it
had ended up with his father noticing him.

He had imagined that the years would roll back for his

father, and he would recognise that his son had the right to be angry at being abandoned, and that he would show some regret for what he'd done.

And that he would also show some affection for the son he'd fathered.

But that didn't happen.

All he'd seen in his father's eyes was fear—fear of an exposure that would end his career and destroy his second marriage. There was no sign of the warmth a father should feel for his son.

It meant that his father didn't care about him.

Any feeling he might have originally had for his child had been lost in the intervening years, and he now had no interest in getting to know his son, and no affection for the boy who'd come back into his life.

And that hurt, really hurt.

He had deserved better.

He wiped his eyes, and stared towards the darkening hills. And then, as if in a moment of sudden revelation, he saw the situation with a startling clarity.

Catching his breath, he straightened up.

He put his hand to his mouth. He'd been blinding himself with a self-pity brought about by not being honest with himself.

Had he truly believed his father would publicly acknowledge him?

Of course, he hadn't!

He was an Anglo-Indian, and he knew what the British thought of Anglo-Indians. If he had been born to a white mother, things would have been very different. His father would never have left them. He and his mother would have gone to Delhi with him. There would have been no second family.

But he had an Indian mother, a mother whom the young Frederick Hunt had loved very much, but whom he'd stopped loving when he'd come to understand the real damage that having an Indian wife would do to his career and to his friendships.

It had been inevitable, and his mother's parents had known that would happen.

They had understood the British people and their values, and they had tried as hard as they could to persuade their daughter not to marry him. But their entreaties had been in vain. His mother, blinded by love, had refused to listen.

If only she had heeded their warnings!

He frowned.

He had spent more than twenty years blaming his father for deserting his mother and him. But in truth, his father wasn't the only person responsible for what had happened.

His mother was partly to blame, too.

He could see now in a way that he'd never been able to see before, that what his father had done was understandable, inevitable even, given the beliefs of the people among whom he lived and worked.

He could see also that the unhappiness in his life and his mother's, and her years of degradation, could have been prevented if his mother had been less stubborn, and had followed the advice she'd been given and not married his father.

A wave of grief swept through him.

Difficult as it was for him even to think it, some of the blame must be placed at the door of his beloved mother.

He shook himself.

He wasn't going to let himself think like that. Not anymore. Not about his father, nor about his mother.

It was time he shed the grievances that had been his companions for years, an ever-present weight on his shoulders, and turned his eyes to the future.

When he'd got up that morning, he didn't have a future. But now, at the end of the day, as a result of the help his father had promised, he did.

He had the chance of a life that would bring him satisfaction, a life suited to his abilities. He'd always believed himself capable of being more than a *chaprassi*, and now that he'd been given the opportunity to prove this, it would be madness to throw it away by dwelling on what had happened years before.

All that mattered now was the career he could have.

He'd work as hard as possible, he resolved, and he'd build on what education he'd had. And while working in the Secretariat in New Delhi, he'd keep his eyes open and learn all he could.

Yes, he was actually going to New Delhi, he thought in mounting excitement. To the capital city of India!

And he'd be given a place to live when he got there!

He'd never been to New Delhi, but he'd heard much about the grandeur of the Secretariat Building, and about the magnificent mansions of the nobles and members of the Royal Court, and about the gilded mosques and beautiful gardens throughout the city.

He'd heard that New Delhi was perfumed by the fragrant blooms that covered the rooftops and walls, and that no matter what street you were on, you could always hear the sound of music.

And now he was going to see it all for himself!

What a life he was going to have!

And there was something else that was going to make it even more perfect for him.

Although no one would ever know that his father was present in his life, he would.

His father would always be there, an invisible hand behind him, helping him to make the most of himself, and that awareness made him suddenly feel very happy.

And when he thought about it, that his father had offered to help him showed that he *did*, indeed, care for him. No matter how many times he'd denied being his father, his actions spoke louder than his words.

And given all the circumstances of their very different lives, that was enough to satisfy him.

With optimism surging through him, he stood up and turned to climb the stairs.

JACK YAWNED.

He might as well get back to the guest house, he decided. He wasn't going to learn anything more that evening.

The Indian was clearly going into his house, and was unlikely to come out again till morning. He now knew where the man lived, and it would be up to Lilian to decide what to do next, if anything.

He started to head for the steps leading up from the Mall to the top road, when from down the hill behind him, he heard the sound of a woman laughing. It seemed to have come from inside the art shop

He stood still, and glanced across at the Indian.

He, too, must have heard the laughter as he'd stopped and was staring down the road to Lower Bazaar.

Then as Jack watched, the Indian swiftly darted towards the stalls on the opposite side of the road from the art shop, slid into a gap between the stalls and crouched down.

If the Indian was interested in the people he could hear, Jack decided, then so was he.

And he inched back down the slope, keeping well in the shadows. Pressing against the wooden wall of the first stall, he waited.

37

I t was Asha talking and laughing with Stephen Chatsworth, Kamesh realised almost at once.

Yet another British man taking advantage of an Indian woman, he thought in a flash of anger. If he could help to make the woman see sense before it was too late, that's what he should do.

And hiding in the shadows as best he could, he listened hard.

As THEY EMERGED from the art shop, Stephen pulled Asha to him and hugged her tightly.

'From now on, every time I go into the Secretariat,' he told her, 'I'll find out what I can about Bombay. It shouldn't be too hard as lots of our officials will have arrived there, and some may even have stayed for a while. I'm sure they'll be willing to share their experiences. Obviously, I won't say why I want to know.'

'I shall do the same, Stephen. If I learn anything—

perhaps from someone who comes in to buy a painting—I shall tell you.'

He hugged her again. 'Between us, we'll find out where to get married when we reach Bombay, and where to live.' He hesitated. 'It's probably better that you don't tell your mother our plans. She might want to stop you from leaving. And if so, we don't know what she might do, or who she might tell. You could write to her when we're settled. Is that all right?' he asked anxiously.

She nodded. 'I won't say anything. I think she won't be happy to lose a shop worker who speaks English, so it's better she doesn't know.'

He kissed her on the top of her head. 'And I certainly won't say anything to my family or friends. My family would do everything in their power to stop us from being together. I can just hear them now. And since nothing will persuade me to change my mind, there's no point in them making the effort.'

'I feel the same,' she said.

'As for my friends,' he went on, 'it's not that I don't trust them, but it would be too easy for something to slip out by mistake, especially when playing billiards or having a drink. No, it's just you and me, Asha,' he said, and he kissed her lightly on the lips.

For a long moment, they stood with their arms around each other, so close that each could feel the beat of the other's heart, until he finally pulled back.

'It's probably better that you go inside now,' he said, his voice heavy with reluctance. 'I'll be with you as soon as possible tomorrow afternoon. Hopefully, I'll be a little earlier than today.'

She kissed the tips of her fingers, rested them lightly against his lips, then glided into the art stall, turned and gave a slight wave. Moments later, she'd been swallowed up by darkness.

His hands in his pockets, he started to make his way back up to Scandal Point.

As he reached the fork, Kamesh stepped out of the shadows and blocked his path.

Stephen's heart missed a beat. He looked at him warily, his momentary alarm giving way to surprise.

'You had me scared for a minute,' he said with a nervous laugh. 'You're one of our *chaprassis*, aren't you? And you're a friend of Asha. You wanted to help us.'

Kamesh inclined his head. 'That's right.'

Stephen nodded, stepped to the side and made as if to continue up the slope.

Kamesh stepped aside with him, again blocking the way. 'I know what you're planning,' he said bluntly.

Stephen glanced at him in disdain. 'I've no idea what you're talking about, and I've no desire to find out.'

He stepped again to the side.

Again, Kamesh moved with him, putting himself in Stephen's path.

A sudden fear gripped Stephen, and he took an involuntary step back.

It was now quite dark, and well past the time when anyone British would be out on the Mall.

He glanced quickly behind him, and the road was, indeed, empty. He suddenly felt very vulnerable and at risk, being completely alone in the part of town inhabited by the poorest of people.

He sized up the *chaprassi*. He was pretty sure he could defend himself against him if he had to, but the man might not be alone.

He peered into the darkness beyond the Indian's shoulder, but the darkness wasn't moving.

He glanced back at Kamesh.

'You're blocking my path,' he said coldly, unable to stop his rising panic from cracking his voice. 'If you value your job, I suggest you get out of my way and go back to wherever you've come from.'

'I intend you no harm,' Kamesh said. 'But of course, to you,' he added, his voice dripping with scorn, 'I've Indian blood in my veins so I must be here to steal from you.'

'Anyone who accosts a person at night, whether or not they're Indian,' Stephen retorted, 'is unlikely to mean well.'

'Accosts. Now that's a harsh word to throw at someone who's trying to do a kindness.'

Stephen took another step back. 'I'm sorry, but you've lost me. What're you talking about?'

'I'm trying to do a kindness to you and to Asha. As you said, I'm Asha's friend.'

'What's Asha got to do with anything?' Stephen exclaimed. Alarmed, he glanced back at the art stall.

'You're planning to run away with Asha and get married,' Kamesh said quietly.

Stephen's stomach lurched. 'No, I'm not.'

'Yes, you are,' Kamesh insisted. 'There's no point in denying it. But you don't need to worry that I might tell the *sahibs* in the Secretariat, as I've no intention of doing so.'

'I'm not admitting anything, but where did you get that strange idea?' Stephen asked, his voice trembling.

'A while ago, Asha told me she hopes to marry you, and I heard you talking to her just now.'

'I see.' Stephen thought for a moment. 'Then you'll have heard me tell her how much I love her, and I do,' he added, a note of defiance creeping into his voice. 'So you might as well get out of my way.'

'I understand you wanting to keep it secret—your friends and family would reason with you that it shouldn't happen, as would Asha's.'

'Well, they wouldn't succeed. Reason doesn't come into it —we love each other. Not that it's any of your business.'

'Reason *should* come into it,' Kamesh snapped. 'No one knows better than I what happens when reason is thrown out of the window and the demands of the heart take over. I know this because my mother was Indian and my father white. I'm what you now call an Anglo-Indian.'

Stephen felt himself relax a little. 'I'm not sure what that's got to do with me,' he said, some of his fear draining away, and curiosity taking its place.

'When they married,' Kamesh told him, 'my father promised to love my mother forever. I believe he meant it when he said it. But in his work every day, he heard the taunts of his colleagues about white men who had an Indian wife or mistress, and he must have grown very afraid of them discovering that he was one of those men.'

Stephen shrugged. 'People say things like that all the time, although I wouldn't. You just ignore them.'

'It's different when those things are about your own situation. When they are, you really hear them, and you can't ignore them. Every time that a man with an Indian woman was shunned by the people with whom my father would have wanted to dine, to whose parties he'd have wanted to be invited, he will have been that bit more anxious.'

'You've got to decide what's important to you,' Stephen said with a touch of impatience.

'He was an ambitious man,' Kamesh continued, ignoring Stephen's comment, 'and he will have feared for his career if his colleagues found out about his wife. So when the opportunity came, he walked away from my mother and me, his son. I was two years old.' He hesitated imperceptibly. 'I believe he's now back in England. I've never seen him since then.'

'I wouldn't do that,' Stephen said firmly. 'I love Asha. I'd never leave her.'

'And my father truly loved my mother at first. My mother was sure of this. But when he came to understand what he was risking losing, he left us. And he made a life somewhere else, from which we were excluded completely.'

'I'd never do such a thing,' Stephen repeated.

His mouth set in a stubborn line.

'And what happens when you've run away with her, Stephen? You'll lose your Government post, of course, and will have to find other work. That part is easy for someone like you. But you'll not be able to mix with the people you work with. All British people, whatever their job, feel the same about men who marry Indians.'

'Then we'd live among the Indian community,' Stephen said defiantly.

'No, you would not,' Kamesh said firmly. 'You would be even less welcomed by Indians than you would by the British.'

He took a step towards Stephen. 'You believe you understand the way Indians think because you know Asha, Stephen, but you don't. The lower classes don't know why you British are here and what your next moves will be. They'd like to laugh in your face, but you're fierce and strong, and they're afraid of angering you, so they resign themselves to silent contempt.'

'I wouldn't be looking to live among such people.'

'That's true. But the class of Indians you'd want to live

among would want nothing at all to do with you. They'd be even more strongly against you than would the British. Politics, religion and caste matter to such Indians. They're a proud people. To them, those of us with mixed blood are not even as good as second-class citizens.'

Discomfort stirred in the pit of Stephen's stomach.

He forced a laugh of derision. 'You want Asha for yourself. That's what this is. Admit it.'

Kamesh smiled. 'I have only feelings of friendship for Asha. That's why I'm trying to help her. Just as my mother was cast out by her people when my father deserted her, Asha will be, too, when you desert her. I don't want her to end up like my mother.'

'Didn't you hear me say I'd never leave her?'

'Oh, you will,' Kamesh said. 'And it may not only be Asha you abandon. If you have children, you'll betray them, too. Children like me, Stephen. What do you think it was like for a child like me'—he struck his chest—'to be brought up in poverty, despite my mother's best efforts, and to see her sink into utter degradation? Is this what you want for Asha?'

'Of course, it isn't,' Stephen said, his voice shaking.

'And your children with Asha, what kind of future would they have, working for white people who shout "chee-chee" after them in the streets? You British are happy to use us when you need help. But when you don't, you look down on us and keep us in lowly positions.'

Stephen shook his head. 'That's just not true.'

Kamesh held out his arms. 'Open your eyes, Stephen. Look around you at the Indians and Anglo-Indians who make your life so comfortable. We're respectable people, and many of us are well educated, but we're seen as inferior, and made to stay that way. You know that's the truth. Is that what you'd want for your children? I think it isn't.'

Seeing the pallor on Stephen's face, he paused.

Stephen gave an awkward laugh. 'You're exaggerating,' he said.

'I'm speaking from my heart, Stephen,' Kamesh went on, a gentleness creeping into his voice, tinged with a note of sympathy. 'If you love Asha, truly love her, you must walk away from her.'

Stephen shook his head in despair. 'I can't.'

'You can, and you will if you really love her. You'll leave her to be married one day to an Indian, perhaps to one of the rich Indians with shops on the Mall. Such a man would welcome a wife with her beauty. This way, Asha has the chance of a good life. Walk away now, and when you've over-come your initial sadness, you, too, will have a happy life.'

A sob escaped Stephen, and he nodded.

NOT UNTIL STEPHEN was out of sight, and Kamesh was back in his house, did Jack step out of the shadows.

As he made his way back to the guest house, his mind was reeling.

38

The following morning

STANDING on the verandah outside her bedroom door, Lilian pulled her shawl more tightly around her shoulders as she watched the pale yellow light of day emerge from the night.

The film of mist that had shrouded the valleys was drifting slowly upwards, uncovering slopes that were forested with dark-green trees.

Their branches sparkling with dew, the trees stood like ghostly apparitions in the eeriness of the breaking day.

But she was too anxious, and too tired, to let herself drink in the beauty around her.

If only she'd been able to get some sleep, she thought as she leant against the wooden balustrade. But sleep had proved impossible, and hour after hour she'd tossed and turned in restlessness, wondering what her father had been talking about with the visitor.

Would Jack find out, she wondered.

She wasn't going to have any peace of mind until she'd spoken to Jack, so she must do so as soon as possible, and she started to think about how to organise a meeting.

It must be done where there was no risk of them being overheard. Given his secretive behaviour the evening before, she wouldn't want her father to suspect that she'd gone against his wishes in any way.

And it must be where she'd feel comfortable enough to talk about her personal feelings. As the night had passed, she'd increasingly come to feel that it was only right she explain to Jack the reason for her change of attitude towards him.

After the kindness he'd shown in agreeing to follow the man, it was the least she owed him.

However, she couldn't think of anywhere to meet that wouldn't necessitate her having her *ayah* with her. But if they weren't alone, it would inhibit what he could tell her and what she could say.

She glanced in despair towards Rose Bank Guest House.

Of course, she thought in excitement.

There *was* a way of speaking to Jack when no one else was there.

The guest house was minutes only from Cedars, and she knew Jack to be an early riser. He liked to take the horse out before the start of his working day, and she could try to catch him before his ride.

It would obviously shock Mrs Gillespie if she went to the door by herself and asked to speak to Jack, so she couldn't do that. But she could throw on some clothes, walk up to the guest house and wait for him to emerge. He hadn't already left or she'd have heard the horse's hooves.

She put her hand to her mouth. Dare she do that?

She'd be alone with him without a chaperone, and if anyone saw them, it would look extremely bad. And if anyone did see her, and told her parents, her parents would be absolutely furious. It wasn't what you were doing, they'd told her on more than one occasion, but what it looked as if you were doing.

She forcibly shrugged off her anxiety.

There was no other way. And it wouldn't be for long. And they'd be outside on the road where anyone could see them, which was hardly placing herself in a compromising situation.

Her heart beating fast, she spun round, ran into her bedroom, threw her shawl on the bed as she sped across to her dressing room, where she pulled a white muslin dress from a rail.

HE REALLY OUGHT to be setting off for his morning ride, Jack thought as he stood in his riding gear on the verandah outside his bedroom, gazing across the empty ridge road to the hills that were hazed in lilac.

The *syce* would have his horse ready by now, and the horse would be pawing the ground in impatience.

But still he stood there, not hearing the dawn chorus of birds—hearing only the beat of his heart as it raced in excitement. He had a genuine reason to speak to Lilian, and to do so soon.

Since the Annandale Races, he'd been asking over and over again in his mind what could have gone wrong between them, and soon he might find out.

When they'd met at the dance in The Hut, Lilian had seemed to feel about him as he'd grown to feel about her. And from the moment they'd parted that evening, he'd been longing to see her again, and he'd been sure that she'd be feeling the same.

And when he'd received his invitation to join the Stanfords for their picnic lunch at Annandale, and Eric had told him that Lilian would be there, too, he had been over the moon at the thought of seeing her again.

Not even his awareness that Frederick might be furious with him that it was Daisy who was to marry Eric, not Lilian, had been able to dampen his longing for the day of the picnic to arrive.

But nothing had gone the way he'd expected. And he didn't know why.

Instead of her greeting him with the same warmth that she'd shown him at the end of the dance, she'd actually ignored him. He'd seen more of her back than he had of her face!

And when she hadn't been able to avoid speaking to him, her words and her manner had been ice-cold.

He'd been desperate ever since then to learn the reason why. But for that to happen, they needed to be somewhere where they wouldn't be overheard by any chaperone or friend, and such an occasion hadn't presented itself.

Until now.

She would expect him to tell her what he'd discovered about the man who'd visited her father, and when he'd done so, he would ask her to explain her behaviour at Annandale.

He'd be very careful how he reported back his findings about the Anglo-Indian, though.

She was already clearly upset with him, although he had no idea why, and the last thing he wanted to do was make matters worse by being blamed for telling her something that wasn't his fault, but which could greatly upset her.

He turned to his left to look in the direction of Cedars,

but it was largely screened by the deodars that separated the two houses.

He'd go for a shorter ride that morning, have breakfast, work at the house for about an hour, and then he'd call on Lilian, he decided.

He'd suggest that they sit on the verandah in sight of her *ayah* or her mother, but far enough from anyone that if they kept their voices low, they wouldn't be overheard.

It wasn't ideal, but it was the only thing he could think of.

Turning, he went back into the house, hurried down the wooden staircase and out through the front door. As he was walking across to the stables, he glanced up at the top of the drive.

A lone figure stood there.

He caught his breath, stopped walking, and turned to stare up the drive at Lilian, ethereal in white.

For a long moment, neither moved. Then each started walking towards the other.

HALFWAY UP THE DRIVE, they met.

They stood facing each other, neither saying a word.

'I was going to wait a little before asking you,' Jack said at last. 'But I find I can't. Before I tell you about last night, I have to know why you turned against me.' He paused. 'Why, Lilian?'

'I found out the truth.'

He frowned. 'What truth?'

'The reason you came out with Daisy and me. It wasn't because you'd fallen in love with me, which you led me to believe. Papa was worried that someone might try to harm us, so he asked you to go out with us to protect us. I was such a fool. You must have been laughing at me,' she added miserably.

He opened his mouth to protest.

'No,' she said quickly. 'There's no need to carry on lying.'

'I wasn't lying at the dance, Lilian. It's true that at first I accompanied you because your father asked me to do so. But I'd already felt drawn towards you, without actually realising it. And the more I got to know you, the more I came to like you. Not just like you, but love you.'

He took a step closer to her. 'That's the truth, Lilian. Surely, you must have felt my love.'

'I admit you made a very good show of it, so much so that I responded,' she said, her voice catching in her throat. 'You *did* make me feel something for you, I confess. And that something was love. I confess that, too.'

He took a step closer to her. She held up her hand to stop him.

'I loved the Jack I thought you were,' she went on. 'But unfortunately for me, the real Jack turned out to be someone who was just making sure that he could carry on coming out with us.'

He gestured helplessness. 'What can I say to make you believe that no matter why I started going out with you, I came to love you very much?'

'Nothing,' she said quietly. 'I'd like to believe you, but I can't. But I still think of you as a friend. You were kind last night, agreeing to follow the man when I asked. You didn't argue, which some people would have done. That's being a friend,' she said. 'So can we talk about last night, please, and nothing else?'

She tried to smile.

'If you wish. But don't think I'm going to settle for being no more than a good friend, Lilian, because I'm not. We're meant for each other, you and me. But yes, I'll tell you what I heard last night.'

She took an audible deep breath. 'I'm ready,' she said.

'Before I do, promise me that anything I say about Stephen remains between us. This is not about Stephen.'

She nodded. 'I promise.'

'Well, to start with, the man's an Anglo-Indian. His name is Kamesh.'

And he told Lilian what he had heard and seen, and then he recounted what he'd overheard Kamesh tell Stephen about his life.

Lilian was very pale when he finished.

'Knowing that he and Papa met in secrecy last night, put alongside what you've told me about the man's conversation with Stephen,' she said eventually, 'it's making me draw conclusions that I don't like.'

She looked up at him, her face distraught. 'Am I wrong, Jack? What do you think?'

'I think you're very tired,' he said gently. 'That's a lot to take in, and you need to give yourself time to digest it all. There's no rush.'

'You know what I'm thinking and you agree with me, don't you?'

He hesitated. 'I don't want to jump to any quick conclusions any more than I want you to do so. So here's a suggestion. You talked about doing a painting of the General Post Office, didn't you?'

'That's right. I haven't yet done one, though.'

'Why don't we try to get back to normality tomorrow by you going off to the post office with your easel? It'll be a settling thing to do, and you'll probably see everything more clearly after that.'

She shrugged. 'I suppose I could do that. I'll need only

paper and pencils at first, as I'll be drawing its outline before applying any colour. I could start on the colour the following day. I'll see if Daisy wants to come.'

'Or you could go with your *ayah* only. I imagine you'll want to think about what I've just told you, and if Daisy's with you, it wouldn't be as easy. With your enterprising mind, I'm sure you can come up with a reason that would satisfy Daisy as to why you wanted to go alone.'

She nodded. 'All right. I'll do that. Thank you, Jack. You're right—I do need time to think.'

'And now I'll go for my ride,' he said briskly. 'You'd better get back to Cedars before the servants are up and about.'

She nodded, turned and went back up the path.

He followed her up the drive and waited until he'd seen her go into Cedars, and then he headed back down to the stables.

39

O utside the General Post Office
The following morning

AFTER WALKING in front of the General Post Office, examining it from both sides, Lilian chose a spot from which she could capture the building at what seemed to be the best angle for an interesting painting, an angle which encompassed the red-painted rickshaws lined up along the side of the building.

It was going to make an interesting picture, she thought, the building being a mixture of a Swiss-chalet-style, and a style that her art teacher had called Victorian Gothic, and there were also elements of a Tudor lodge. This might well be one of the watercolours she gave to the school.

And she wouldn't be surprised if while she was working on the picture, she became the object of some curiosity.

With the post office situated opposite Scandal Point,

where visitors to the Mall left their rickshaws, people might well come across and look over her shoulder at her painting.

If anyone wanted to buy a watercolour, she thought, settling on her chair and positioning her easel, she would tell them that they'd find some of her work in the art stall just below the fork in the road to Lower Bazaar.

Not only would it be good for Asha and her mother to make some sales, but she would feel less bad about the pain that Asha would inevitably feel when she learnt that her friendship with Stephen would have to come to an end.

If Stephen hadn't done her the kindness of helping her in her initial visit to the art stall, and in taking the water-colours to be sold, he was unlikely ever to have drawn so close to Asha. So she was partly responsible for what had happened, and she must do whatever she could to help.

But while having some extra money from the paintings could help Asha though the devastation she was bound to feel, there was obviously a limit to what money could do.

It couldn't completely erase a deep pain.

The sort of pain that her father must surely have felt when he left Calcutta for Delhi, knowing that he was leaving behind him a wife and a little boy of two!

For Kamesh must have been talking about her father. A father they shared. It was the only thing that made sense.

But knowing her father, it was inconceivable that he could have walked away from his first family without feeling deep anguish, and without being aware of the unimaginable pain that would have been suffered by his abandoned Indian wife.

But that's what he must have done, regardless.

What sort of wedding ceremony would they have had, she wondered, leaning back in her chair. It would certainly have been Indian, with lots of red and gold, not British.

But curious as she was, this was something she would never know, as she would never in any way let her father learn that she knew what had happened in the past. She wouldn't tell anyone. Not even Daisy.

It was *his* past and his son's, not hers, and he was entitled to his privacy.

And furthermore, it was better that her mother remain in ignorance.

Her every instinct told her that her mother was completely unaware of what her father had done before she met him. If she had known of his first marriage, he wouldn't have made the effort he had to keep the boy a secret from them.

Not a boy any longer; he was now a man.

A man who must have been desperately hurt at being rejected, first as a child, and then as an adult.

For her father would have again rejected him two nights ago. Of that she was sure. He would have done so for the same reasons that he'd deserted his first family all those years ago.

But she knew him to be essentially kind, and she was confident that he would see that his son had a good life in the future.

In the heat of his youth, her father had obviously fallen in love with an Indian woman, just as many young British men in India had done. However, he had been more rash than some in that he had married her.

But his life shouldn't be ruined because he'd made a well-intentioned mistake.

He had acted properly towards the woman he loved. He hadn't want to use her in the way that a lot of British men did—he had wanted better for her than that.

He obviously hadn't realised at the time quite how

destructive to his career and friendships such a marriage could be. When he eventually came to see that, he did the only thing he felt he could.

So she wasn't going to condemn him for what he'd done, and she hoped very much that Jack wouldn't either. She was going to beg him not to tell anyone about her father's past.

Hopefully, after meeting his father, his son would now understand why his father had behaved in the way he had, and didn't condemn him too much, either.

She arranged her freshly sharpened pencils, eraser and extra paper on the small table next to her, picked up one of the pencils and then glanced to her side to the place where Daisy would have sat had she accompanied her.

She'd told Daisy that she was going painting that morning, but that she'd better go by herself as her mother had threatened to come and whisk her away. There were things her mother wanted to buy her.

She was already missing Daisy, and she was missing Jack, too, she grudgingly admitted to herself as she studied the shape of the building.

She shook herself. He was a friend, and she would only get hurt if she allowed herself to believe that he wanted to be more than that to her.

He'd once told her what he really thought of her. It had been a mistake to let herself forget what he'd said, and she must never do so again. That path ended in pain.

If ever she thought she was weakening, she must think back to that afternoon in the glade, and again hear his words in her head. That had been the true Jack speaking. The Jack who had lied about why he was with them in the first place.

A wave of misery spread through her.

Oh, how could she be so stupid as to still have feelings for him?

But she knew that despite everything she told herself, she did.

As she stared at the blank sheet of paper, her vision misted.

Surreptitiously, she wiped her eyes and began lightly pencilling an outline of the building.

Her skin started to prickle. Her hand slowed. She was certain, absolutely certain, that she was being watched.

She turned to look at the stretch of road next to her.

A young man was standing there, an envelope in his hand. He was facing her, watching her.

A young man who couldn't be more than a few years older than she. Who had dark hair and a light brown skin. Who was more Anglo-Indian than Indian.

It was the man she'd seen at her house the night before.

The man she'd actually seen several times in the street, being struck each time by something familiar about his face. A feature, maybe, that reminded her of someone.

Or more than one feature.

Such as the shape of his jawline, and his nose.

She could see so clearly, now that she knew the truth, that there was such a strong resemblance to her father that were the young man white, anyone who saw them together would automatically assume that the young man was her father's son.

And that he was her brother.

Her pencil slipped from her fingers. Her lips parted in wonder as she stood up, gazing at him, her heart racing.

She hesitated, and then took a step forward.

He held up his hand to stop her.

Then he took a step back, keeping the same distance between them.

Their eyes met. She smiled tentatively.

He smiled back.

'What's your name?' she mouthed.

His lips shaped the name Kamesh.

She nodded.

There was so much she wanted to ask. But at the same time, she didn't need to ask it.

She knew what had happened to him and his mother as Jack had told her. And when she next saw Jack, when they could talk without being overheard, she'd ask him to tell her again what he had learnt, and not to omit any detail, no matter how small.

And the next time, because she had seen him, her half-brother Kamesh, and because he was now very real to her, it would mean so much more.

She took a step forward.

He took another step back.

Both of their smiles widened.

Then he held up the piece of paper, indicated the entrance to the post office, gave her a small wave, went across to the entrance and disappeared.

She stared after him, struggling to breathe.

This was her brother, a brother she'd never known she had.

She desperately longed to run after him and speak to him, but she knew that she mustn't. To do so would destroy her father's reputation and career, and it would bring misery to her mother.

Yet she'd so like to get to know him.

Perhaps just a short word or two might be all right.

Just a quick hello to let him know that although they

couldn't publicly acknowledge each other, he should know that he had a family to which he belonged, and that two members of the family now knew about him.

It wasn't unusual, after all, for a woman to speak to a servant, which is what people would think he was.

She glanced sideways and saw that her *ayah's* attention had been attracted by a rickshaw coolie, and that she had her back to her.

Her gaze swept back to the post office as her brother emerged, his letter sent.

She gave him a hesitant smile, hoping he'd realise that she was inviting him to come over to her, just to talk for a moment or two.

He nodded slightly and stopped, but at a distance.

Then he gave her an almost imperceptible smile—his eyes full of warmth—and with a slight wave, he was gone.

As she stared after him, she put her hand to her cheek and realised to her surprise that her face was wet with tears. She looked down at the sheet of paper on which she'd been drawing. It was damp, and the outline of the building was blurred.

How fortunate she'd been there at the very time that Kamesh came to the post office, she thought.

Then she almost laughed out loud at her blindness. What was she thinking of? It hadn't been a matter of luck. It had been a matter of good planning.

Jack had obviously arranged it. He'd told her the building to paint. He'd told her to go there alone. And he must have gone to the trouble to find the person he'd seen the night before, and had given him a letter to deliver.

He had understood how much she would want to see her half-brother, even if she, herself, hadn't realised how much she wanted that until the moment she saw him.

Jack's understanding of her feelings, and anticipation of her needs, showed that he genuinely cared for her. It was true friendship.

She had to thank him, and as soon as she could.

She couldn't do so in the full glare of the Secretariat, so she'd have to speak to him when he returned to the guest house.

If she sat on the lower front balcony for the latter part of the afternoon, she should see him pass. When he did, she could indicate that she wanted to talk to him and that he should wait, and she could go out and meet him on the drive.

She frowned.

She was assuming that he'd be in the Secretariat all day, and would go straight back to the guest house. But he might have returned to the guest house as soon as he'd given Kamesh the letter to post, or he could have left Simla to work on the task given him by her father. Or he might go straight to the Club after work.

There were too many uncertainties.

The Club, she thought in sudden excitement.

The following day, there was a dance at the Hut to which she and her family, and Daisy's too, had been invited. Jack was almost certain to go. She would be able to speak to him there.

Only as friends, of course. She knew all too well what he thought of her. But even so, she'd make sure that she looked her best. It was a matter of pride to do so.

She bent down, picked up her pencil and stared at it. Having set everything up for a morning of sketching, she really ought to take a fresh sheet of paper and at least complete an outline of the post office.

But she couldn't.

Her mind was in such a turmoil after seeing Kamesh, and on realising the depth of Jack's kindness towards her, that she knew she wouldn't be able to settle. She wanted to be back at Cedars, mulling everything over.

And there were things to do, such as sorting out what to wear the following evening.

She needed to get back now.

Turning, she indicated to her *ayah* and *jampanis* that they should come and help her pack up her equipment and return everything to the rickshaw.

Only one day to wait, she thought, when everything had been loaded and she was leaning back against the padded seat of the rickshaw.

Just one day to get through, and she'd see Jack again.

T*he Club*
       Saturday evening

WHEN THE HUNTS and the Chatsworths arrived at the Hut, the dance was in full swing.

They walked across the grass, past the tables that glittered with fairy lights and candles, past the cluster of chairs and sofas positioned between the tables and the building, and chose a table just inside the entrance to the Hut, which gave them ease of access to the dance floor, while allowing them to enjoy the fresh evening air.

Constance and Gladys sat down, followed by Frederick and Wilfred. The girls went to sit down, too, but Constance stopped them.

'If you and Daisy prefer, you can go and join the other young people,' Constance said. 'After all, you'll want to fill your dance cards, and you're less likely to do so if you're sitting with us.'

'There's only one name I want to see on my dance card,' Daisy said happily, 'and I can see the person who owns that name coming across the lawn.' She beamed at Eric as he came into the Hut.

He held out his hand to her. She took it and he gently squeezed it.

Then she took her dance card from her beaded reticule, and gave it to him. He put it into his pocket, gave a slight bow to the two sets of parents, took Daisy's hand again and led her to the edge of the dance floor.

Watching Daisy and Eric as they stood, their heads close together, waiting for the ongoing dance to end and the next to begin, Gladys and Constance smiled at each other.

'It's Lilian's turn now,' Gladys mouthed to Constance.

Both turned to look at Lilian.

LILIAN WAS MOVING SLIGHTLY FORWARD, surveying the room.

Her dress, which was made of shimmering pale-blue silk, skimmed her body and fell to mid-calf, and she wore matching gloves and shoes. The flower above her right ear was fashioned from layers of pale blue organza.

As she stood there, she felt all eyes turn towards her.

It had been worth the effort she'd made that evening, she thought in satisfaction as she'd glanced around, hoping that among the sea of admiring gazes, she would spy the deep blue eyes of Jack.

But he was nowhere to be seen.

Where was he, she thought, and clutching her dance card, she moved around the room, trying to avoid anyone signing her card before she'd spoken to Jack.

'Are you looking for me?' His voice came from behind her.

She spun round and faced him. A knot tightened in her stomach.

'Of course, I'm not,' she said with an awkward laugh. 'Although actually I am.'

He gave her a smile of exaggerated sweetness. 'I thought I was the one famous for contradictory statements,' he said in amusement. 'But as there's a welcome charm to such statements, I always believe, I'm happy to see that you're taking a leaf out of my book.'

She laughed. 'I'm pleased that you're pleased.'

They smiled at each other.

'I suggest we go outside where we can have some privacy, but still be within sight of any vigilant eyes,' he said. And he turned and headed for the open doorway.

Lilian hesitated a moment, and then followed him out on to the lawn, passing as she went the table where her parents and Daisy's were engrossed in conversation.

'To be honest, I don't really understand the boy,' Wilfred said, shaking his head in bewilderment. 'He seemed to be settling down so well to life in Simla. He appeared to be happy at work, and indeed, worked harder than was necessary. Remember all the siestas he worked through, my dear?' he said, looking to Gladys for confirmation.

'That's true,' she said. 'I must admit, it took me by surprise, too, when Stephen told us he wanted to return to New Delhi as soon as possible.'

'For a young man to ask to leave Simla, with all its entertainments, when he didn't have to, and to choose to go back to the intense heat of a summer on the plains, it really beggars belief. Did he give you any reason?' Frederick asked.

Wilfred shook his head. 'Nothing that made a lot of

sense. He muttered something about the smallness of Simla, and always seeing the same people and doing the same things. I'm sure it's more than that, but I don't think we'll get any more out of him. We'll certainly miss having him here with us.'

'I think he might have felt that there was too much regimentation here,' Gladys volunteered. 'I know he was critical of the way in which Margaret Stanford seemed to be taking over the arrangements for Daisy's wedding.'

'How *are* the wedding plans going?' Constance asked.

'Worry not, you're on the guest list,' Wilfred said with a smile.

They all laughed.

'Lilian's such an attractive girl that I imagine it won't be too long before you, too, have a wedding to plan,' Gladys said, arching her brow at Constance.

Constance laughed dismissively. 'I don't think so. For a time, we wondered if Lilian and Jack Leighton would get together. A mother knows her daughter—better sometimes than the daughter knows herself. But nothing's come of it.'

'She's still young,' Frederick said, 'and more importantly, so is he. He ought to do a few more years with the Service before he thinks about settling down. By then, he'll know his own mind and is unlikely to make a mistake.'

Constance gave a slight exclamation. 'Surely, Frederick, you're not suggesting that an attachment to Lilian would be a mistake?'

'If he were a few years older, then no. At the age he is, yes. He hasn't yet been in India long enough to have proved himself. Don't you agree, Wilfred?'

'Not really, old friend. Not only is he older than Stephen by a few years, but he's mature for his age. He seems thoroughly competent and someone upon whom a person could rely. I'm inclined to think that this is the right time for him to be looking for someone to walk at his side for the rest of his journey through life. Provided that someone is suitable, of course,' he added. 'And Lilian would be eminently suitable.'

'So you think there could be something between them?' Frederick asked.

Wilfred shook his head. 'No, not really. I haven't seen any sign of a romantic attachment between them. On the contrary, I suspect they've clashed on occasions. There's definitely been some antagonism between them at times. At Cecil's picnic, for example, particularly on Lilian's side.'

They all turned to look through the open doorway towards the far table at which Jack and Lilian were sitting close to each other.

'I don't see any signs of antagonism between them this evening,' Gladys said drily. 'On the contrary. And I'm not surprised. She looks truly beautiful, Constance. You must be very proud of her.'

'I'M glad you agreed to come out here with me, Lilian?' Jack said warmly.

'We're still friends, aren't we?' She gave him a tentative smile. 'I wanted to thank you again for doing as I asked and following the young man who came to see Papa.'

Jack inclined his head. 'Since you thanked me when I told you what I'd overheard, I now consider myself well and truly thanked.'

'Prepare yourself, there are even more thanks to come,' she said lightly. 'I wanted to thank you, too, for arranging for me to see Kamesh yesterday.'

Jack's face softened. 'I'm glad that worked out. How did you find him?'

'We didn't talk... We couldn't have done... It would have looked very strange to anyone who saw us... And with the likeness to Father. I *did* try to go up to him, but each time he took a step back. It was as if he didn't want to talk to me, but he wanted to see me and me to see him.'

'That's about right. I spoke to Kamesh earlier yesterday morning. I know what your father's promised to do for him, and it's a lot.'

She beamed. 'Oh, I'm so pleased!'

'He refuses to acknowledge that Kamesh is his son, but by helping him in the way he's offered to, he's showing Kamesh that he knows he is his son. He just can't say so publicly. Kamesh understands why he can't, and accepts the situation.'

'I was sure that Papa would do all he could to help him.'

Jack nodded. 'Me, too. Kamesh has now got the chance of a good life. Everything is conditional, though, on no one ever knowing the truth. But he wants the future your father's made possible for him, so he will always keep his distance from you.'

'I understand.'

'How did you feel when you saw him?' Jack asked. 'It must have been strange. He's your half-brother, after all.'

'I know, and it *did* feel strange. But it felt lovely, too.'

Jack looked at her in surprise.

'I love knowing I've got a brother,' she went on excitedly. 'I know he did things that upset Papa, but I understand why he did them. How else would he have got his attention, attention that I take for granted? I don't think badly of Kamesh because of that.'

'That's very understanding of you,' Jack said, a note of surprise in his voice.

'I think he looks very pleasant,' she went on, 'and I would have loved to have got to know him, and for us to have been friends. But from what you've just said, and with the world being as it is, I realise that's impossible.'

'You *do* amaze me, Lilian,' Jack said, with a slight frown. 'I'd rather thought you'd be hostile towards Kamesh. Not many people would acknowledge an Anglo-Indian member of the family, not even to themselves. and certainly not one as close as a half-brother.'

'Then you don't know me, Jack. Father would never have loved someone unpleasant, and I know him to be a kind man, although he can be firm. With parents like that, Kamesh is sure to have a good heart.'

'But he's had a hard life. That can change people,' Jack suggested.

'That's true. But from what you told me, he's always known that his mother loved him and did the best she could for him, and that will have had a positive effect on him. As for him being Anglo-Indian, that doesn't bother me. It's what you are as a person that matters.'

His face broke out in a broad smile. 'I'm so pleased to hear that! To prove how delighted I am, I intend to refrain from making any further comment—I'm giving you the last word.'

'But I'm so grateful for your help with Kamesh that I want *you* to have the last word,' she said with a laugh. 'You may speak, Jack, and I promise not to say anything when you've finished.'

She clamped her lips together.

Jack grinned. 'Face it, Lilian. You'd be unable to stay

quiet all evening. You're bound to want to answer me back about something.'

Her face dropped. 'Is this about me being overly argumentative, the sort of person no one would ever want to live with?'

Jack smiled. 'You're certainly argumentative, but that doesn't mean that no one would ever want to live with you.'

'Well, *you* wouldn't, so why would anyone else?'

He gave a theatrical sigh. 'I was hoping you would forget my stupid words. I'm sure that you, too, at times have spoken in a way that you later regretted.'

Lilian shrugged. 'Everyone has.'

'Well, then?' Jack gave her a slow lazy smile. 'You can forgive me for being human, can't you?' he asked.

A knot formed low in her stomach as she felt his gaze on her face.

'Why does it matter if I forgive you or not?' she asked, her mouth suddenly dry.

He leaned forward. 'Because you're very special to me.'

At the warmth in his words, the knot in her stomach tightened.

'There's only one Lilian,' he said, his voice filling with emotion. 'And along with being absolutely stunning, as well as highly argumentative and supremely competitive, characteristics I must have in the woman I marry, that Lilian is witty, interesting and lively. She has a good way of thinking and a very kind heart. There are lots of people who would welcome such a person in their life. And I'm one of those.'

'Oh, Jack,' she said with a sigh. 'You may not mean it, but that sounded lovely.'

'I *do* mean it,' he said quietly.

She burst out laughing, and then suddenly stopped.

She put her hand to her mouth. 'Are you proposing to me, Jack Leighton?'

'I'm doing my best, Lilian. But feel free to give me advice as to how to improve my attempt.'

She dropped her hand. 'But what about the docile woman who'd sit all day at your feet and worship you?'

He grinned at her. 'I'd be bored stiff with the docile bit, but I'm quite happy for you to sit at my feet and worship me all day if you wish. I've no objections to that.'

She laughed.

He took her hands in his. 'If you marry me, Lilian, I'll never have a dull moment in my life. Every single day will be filled with colour, laughter and happiness because I'm with you. I love you, and I would do everything in my power to make you as deeply happy as I would be. So please say yes.'

Her eyes sparkled.

'I'm stuck, Jack. I want to answer you with a clever quip, something that would live up to what you've just said about wit and liveliness. But I can't think of anything. All I know is how much I want to spend the rest of my life with you.' Her voice broke. 'I love you so much, and I *will* take the last word, and that word is yes.'

Both rose to their feet, and stood in the beam of golden light that streamed from the building, each staring into the face of the other with an intensity that took their breath away.

'Oh, Jack,' she whispered.

'I think that makes three last words in all,' he murmured.

Each smiled in delight at the other.

He held out his arms, and with a look of sheer bliss on her face, she sank into them.

IF YOU ENJOYED SIMLA MIST...

...it would be very kind if you could take a few minutes to leave a review of the book.

Reviews give welcome feedback to the author, and they help to make the novel visible to other readers.

In addition, reviews help authors to promote their books as a number of promotional platforms today require a minimum number of reviews.

Your words, therefore, really do matter.

Thank you!

LIZ'S NEWSLETTER

You might like to sign up for Liz's newsletter.

Liz sends out a monthly newsletter with updates on her writing life, where she's been travelling, and an interesting fact she's learned. Subscribers also hear of promotions and offers.

Liz would never pass on your email address to anyone else, and if you write to Liz, which you can do through her website, you will always get a reply.

As a thank you for signing up for Liz's newsletter, you'll receive a free full-length novel.

To sign up and get a free book, go to Liz's website:

www.lizharrisauthor.com

ACKNOWLEDGMENTS

Once again, I must start by thanking the brilliant cover designer, Jane Dixon-Smith, for a truly gorgeous cover that reflects the tone of the novel, and my excellent editor, Jane Eastgate. I'm very lucky to have both of them in my writing world.

As ever, I would also like to thank my friend in the north, Stella. Stella is always the first person to see my finished manuscript, and she never fails to be honest about anything with which she disagrees. Such constructive criticism is invaluable.

As with most years, my year has been punctuated by writerly lunches filled with chats about plot lines and characters, and with occasional writing retreats with fellow authors. A huge thank you, therefore, to the many writer friends I've made over the years—too many to mention. You've helped to make the writing process a highly enjoyable one, and I'm very grateful to you all.

In writing *Simla Mist,* I drew upon a variety of sources for my research, including my magical trip to India a few years ago. It would be impossible to list all the articles and books I read, but I should like to highlight S*himla, The Summer Capital of British India,* by Raaja Bhasin, *Plain Tales From The Raj,* by Charles Allen, and *Imperial Simla: the political culture of The Raj*, by Pamela Kanwar.

You may have observed that in the world outside the

novel, the name of the town is spelt in a different way – it's spelt Shimla.

Simla is the spelling that was current at the time of The Raj, 1858 to 1947, and it remained the official spelling until 1972. After that, Simla became Shimla, which reflected the way in which the name of the town had always been pronounced, even during the time of the Raj.

My final thank you is to my husband, Richard, for being the support that he is, and for putting up with me sitting in front of my laptop, lost in my fictional world, hour after hour, day after day, week after week. I'm extremely grateful to him.

INTRODUCING 'HANOI SPRING'

If you enjoyed reading *Simla Mist* – and I hope you did – and you haven't yet read *Hanoi Spring*, which is another novel in the series The Colonials, you might be interested in doing so.

Although part of a series, each novel is a standalone novel and is complete in itself.

To give you a taste of the book, in the next few pages you'll read the first chapter of *Hanoi Spring*.

HANOI SPRING: CHAPTER ONE

The French Territory of Hanoi
  March 1932

'Would you stop here for a moment before turning into the drive?' Lucette Delon called from her seat behind the chauffeur.

The chauffeur nodded. 'Of course, Madame.'

The sleek Peugeot 301 drew gently to a halt at the kerb.

Lucette stared through the car window in delight at the three storey house with fern-green wooden shutters, which she could see through the gap between the tamarind trees that lined Boulevard Henri Rivière. Wrought-iron railings surrounded the house and the front garden, which was filled with magenta bougainvillea, hydrangea bushes and an abundance of lush tropical flowers whose names she had yet to learn.

Her gaze travelled up the honey-coloured walls of the house to the exquisite metal grillwork that fronted the upper balconies, and thence to the sloping tiled roof that glowed rich red in the sunlight, and she found herself smiling with pleasure at the welcome thrown out by her new home.

'We can go now,' she said happily, and she sat back in her seat.

The chauffeur put his hand on the gearstick.

Thud!

Immediately behind her, metal met metal with a loud, resounding clang.

The Peugeot shuddered, and she was thrown forward.

Wide-eyed with shock and surprise, she grasped the seat in front of her, and clung to it tightly as the car settled.

The chauffeur started to open the driver's door.

But before he could do so, a current of air rushed in as the door next to her opened.

A hand, light beneath her elbow, encouraged her to get out, and trembling, she allowed herself to be guided on to the pavement.

'I'm so sorry,' she heard a man say, his voice full of apology. She was vaguely aware of a tall man in a lightweight white suit standing beside her. 'It was my fault, Madame. Entirely my fault. My concentration lapsed for a moment and I let my car slide into yours.'

'It was a shock, Monsieur,' she said, trying to steady her voice. 'But no more than that. I'm not hurt, as you see. And nor is my chauffeur. Or are you hurt, Tuan?' she asked the chauffeur in sudden anxiety.

'No, Madame.'

Her hand flew to her mouth. 'What about the car! Is it damaged?' she asked in sudden alarm. 'I don't want my husband to be angry. The car's new, you see,' she told the stranger.

'I'm confident that no one will blame you for what was my fault,' he said.

'But we stopped so that I could look at my house. We've been stopping like that every day for the past two weeks, not thinking how dangerous it must be. If we'd driven straight on to the drive—'

'No one will blame you for an accident I caused,' he repeated firmly. 'I should have been paying attention to what was happening on the road, and I wasn't.'

The chauffeur moved to the back of the car, and bent down to look at the bumper.

'There are a few scratches on the back bumper, but nothing serious, Madame,' he told Lucette, straightening up. He glanced at the bumper touching hers.

'Your front bumper is scratched, Monsieur,' he said. 'But neither car has any dents in the bodywork.'

'You must allow me to have your bumper replaced,' the man told Lucette, his hand still lightly under her elbow. 'If you'll permit me to see you into your house, I can explain to your husband what happened, and we can talk about how best to arrange for the work to be done. I know a place not far from here that'll do it.'

Feeling a little steadier, she looked properly at the stranger for the first time.

He was a handsome man, well built, with dark brown hair. She guessed he was about ten years older than she was —about thirty or thirty-one, which was a couple of years older than Philippe. The eyes that were looking at her with genuine concern were a piercing grey in his lightly tanned face.

She shook her head. 'He won't be home, I'm afraid. He's one of the administrative staff of the Résident Supérieur so he'll probably be at the Résidence.'

'Then perhaps you'll allow me to see you into the house, Madame? You're somewhat pale, and I wouldn't feel comfortable leaving you to go in alone, especially as all this was my fault.' With his free hand, he indicated the two cars standing bumper to bumper.

He turned back to her. 'I'd better introduce myself. My name is Gaston Laroche. I'm one of the many diplomatic attachés you'll find in Hanoi. I suggest I take you inside, and leave my card with you. Your husband will then know how to contact me about the bumper.'

She gave him a wan smile. 'I do feel a little shaken, I must admit, and I wouldn't mind something reviving. Perhaps you would care to join me for some refreshment? This is bound to have been a shock for you, too.'

He gave a slight bow. 'It's very kind of you, Madame. You're right, it was. And, yes, a short break before I continue on my way would be the sensible thing to do.'

And angling himself towards the gate in the iron railings, he started gently propelling her towards the short drive that led up to her house.

'So, Gaston?'

The police chief supervising Gaston leaned back in his chair in the small, undistinguished building on the southern edge of the Old Quarter that was a branch of the French Sûreté Générale, and folded his hands across his ample stomach. 'From the expression on your face when you came in, I imagine this morning went according to plan.'

Gaston laughed. 'It's that obvious, is it, Emile? Yes, I can truly say it did. Watching her routine throughout the past week certainly paid off. A tap that was just sufficient for her to feel a little shaky and in need of support, and a few scratches on the bumper, but not enough to bankrupt the Sûreté.'

'I take it you were invited into the house?'

'Indeed, I was. We had brandy for our nerves, followed by sweetened tea.'

'What's the wife like?'

'It's too soon to be able to answer that. But Lucette, as she asked me to call her, seems like any young woman of about twenty-one or twenty-two, who's had a somewhat sheltered upbringing. She's looking forward to getting to know Hanoi's range of restaurants, and the many cafés with live music. From the short amount of time I spent with her, I'd say she's a typical newlywed, who clearly adores her husband, and who doesn't have a single political bone in her body.'

'I assume you didn't get to meet the husband?'

Gaston shook his head. 'No, I didn't. It worked out as I'd planned. I was certain he'd be at work, and he was. I wouldn't have wanted him taking over from me before I'd achieved my goal. As it is, I've made her acquaintance, and got her trust, if that's the right word.'

'That's a start, anyway.'

Gaston grinned at him. 'Oh, I went somewhat further than that. The brandy settled Lucette sufficiently for us to talk a little about Hanoi, and for her to mention that her husband was one of those who were supervising the smooth-running of the Hoa Lo Prison. I was naturally greatly impressed to learn that her husband held so important a post.'

The police chief chuckled. 'I'm sure you were.'

'I insisted that she and her husband permit me to show my regret for the accident by taking them to dinner at the Hôtel Métropole on Saturday. They'd be delighted to go, she told me. She knew they weren't doing anything—they hadn't been there long enough yet to build up a circle of friends. She'd seen the advertisements for the hotel and café on the trams, and had heard it was excellent from Monsieur Bouvier, the man her husband assists, so she'd been very keen to go. And she knew her husband would be, too. It means that I'll be meeting Philippe Delon in a couple of days.'

'You *have* done well,' the chief said in satisfaction.

'And there's one more thing,' Gaston added with a smile. 'The Bouviers will be joining us on Saturday.'

The chief sat up sharply and stared at Gaston in amazement. 'I don't believe it! Just how did you organise that?'

'By assuring Lucette before I left that she was still very pale—fortunately, she didn't have a mirror to hand or she would have seen that her colour was fully restored and that she was looking remarkably pretty, in fact—and by saying that she should have someone with her other than the servants. I asked if she'd a friend nearby. She said that the Bouviers lived in the house next to theirs, and I suggested that her maid go across for Madame Bouvier.'

The chief burst out laughing, and shook his head.

'Minutes later, Simonne Bouvier was rushing into the house, the picture of concern. As I got up, I made a great thing of saying that I'd be in touch before Saturday about our dinner at the Métropole. Madame Bouvier visibly pricked up her ears, expressed great envy of Lucette, and before you could say successful ploy, I'd invited her and her husband to join us. It was my way of thanking her, I explained, for coming to the support of Madame Delon in her hour of need, a need for which I'd been responsible.'

The chief laughed again. 'Well done, Gaston. To get all that out of a scratch on the bumper was, indeed, a triumph! I don't know how you did it.'

Gaston gave him a dry smile. 'You can do anything when

you've mastered the inanity of the small talk favoured by your peers.'

'All I can say is, France did well to send you to us. Via Africa, of course,' he added, and laughed again. He paused. 'You're sound on the Côte d'Ivoire, I take it?'

Gaston smiled. 'I've done my homework so well that I'm actually beginning to believe I've been there.'

'Good. This could work. By worming your way into Marc Bouvier's circle of friends, you'll have a strong chance of finding out whether or not Bouvier's smuggling papers out of the prison and generally supporting terrorist activity. And if he *is* guilty, you'll be well placed to discover the person helping him in the prison, and to whom he passes the information. We need to find out the delivery chain.'

'That's the idea. First of all, I intend to get an invitation to take a look at the prison from the inside.'

'From what I've seen of you, I'm sure you'll succeed. I'd like you to come here tomorrow morning and meet the operatives you can call on for help. You'll be told how to get hold of them. I know you prefer working alone, but there're bound to be occasions when you need help.'

'If that's what you want, fine.'

Emile nodded. 'It is. Whoever's responsible must be stopped, and once and for all. Take the time you need, but get it right. The prison has become a school for terrorists, thanks to the newspapers circulating among the inmates. And the papers they're smuggling out of the prison are encouraging anti-French feeling among the local population. We've uncovered one or two arms' dumps, and rumour has it that the garrison troops have been infiltrated. They're obviously planning an uprising at some point, but all our intelligence can tell us is that the terrorists are organised in cells of fifteen to twenty people. It's just not good enough.'

Gaston leaned forward. 'Believe me. I'll find out for certain if Bouvier *is* responsible, and if he isn't, I'll discover who is. Whoever it is, they're going to learn that France won't tolerate any betrayal of the colonial administration. If Bouvier's guilty, he'll pay the highest price. And so will anyone else involved.'

ABOUT THE AUTHOR

Born in London, Liz Harris graduated from university with a Law degree, and then moved to California, where she led a varied life, from waitressing on Sunset Strip to working as secretary to the CEO of a large Japanese trading company.

Six years later, she returned to London and completed a degree in English, after which she taught secondary school pupils, first in Berkshire, then in Cheshire and finally in Oxfordshire, before becoming a full-time author.

In addition to the sixteen novels she's had published, she's had several short stories in anthologies and magazines.

Liz now lives in Berkshire. An active member of the Romantic Novelists' Association and the Historical Novel Society, her interests are travel, the theatre, reading and cryptic crosswords. To find out more about Liz, visit her website at: www.lizharrisauthor.com

ALSO BY LIZ HARRIS

Historical novels

The Colonials

Darjeeling Inheritance

Cochin Fall

Hanoi Spring

Simla Mist

The Linford Series

The Dark Horizon

The Flame Within

The Lengthening Shadow

Distant Places

The Road Back

In a Far Place

The Heart of the West

A Bargain Struck

(A 2nd edition will be published in July 2023)

The Lost Girl

(A 2nd edition, under the title 'Golden Tiger', will be published in November 2023)

A Western Heart

Contemporary novels

The Best Friend

Evie Undercover

The Art of Deception

Word Perfect

Printed in Great Britain
by Amazon